KT-459-594

Vocabulary	Pronunciation	Writing
Leisure activities; Adjectives and verbs of likes and dislikes	Word stress; Intonation in questions; Weak form of *do* in questions	Personal information
Clothes	Present Simple endings; Linking in connected speech	Punctuation
Nationality words	Past Simple endings; Weak forms of *was/were* in Past Continous; *Used to*	Linking expressions; Narrative (from sounds)
Deducing meanings	Intonation in question tags; Contracted forms of Present Perfect	Spelling
Weather	Contracted form of *will* Weak form of *to* in *going to*	Telephone dialogue
Adjectives ending in *-ed* and *-ing*; Word building with suffixes	Syllable stress: schwa (/ə/)	Semi-formal letter Clauses of reason and result
Describing personality and appearance	–	Personal letter
Making opposites	Word stress	Linking expressions Description of place
Illness; Antonyms and synonyms	–	Connecting sentences to make a narrative
Phrasal verbs with *up* and *down*	Vowels	Styles of writing
Hotels; Changing verbs into nouns; Food	Intonation of requests	Notes and messages
Money; Theft	–	Letter of advice
Colloquial English: slang; idiomatic expressions	Sentence stress	Summary
Leisure; Words often confused	*Have to, must*	Opening and closing a letter Letter of application
Deducing words in context; Phrasal verbs	Consonants (voiced/unvoiced)	Report
Animals; Idiomatic expressions (animals)	–	Descriptive writing (poem)
Fear; Changing adjectives into verbs	Diphthongs	Linking words and expressions
Make or *do*?	–	Comparing narrative styles
Collocation	Contrastive stress	Story

My favourite things

SPEAKING 1

Things people like

1   Look at the pictures. They suggest six different activities which people like (doing). Match each of the activities with the categories in the box. Example:
sport: picture 1 (horse-riding)

sport	hobbies	books	clothes	music	animals

2   What do *you* like and dislike (doing)? Copy the table below and write down at least one example of your likes and dislikes, using each of the categories from the box in Exercise 1.

	LIKES	DISLIKES
sport	*badminton*	*football*
hobbies		

3   Go round the class and tell other students what you like and dislike (doing). Examples:
'I really love playing badminton.'
'I don't like opera.'

When you find someone who shares any of your likes and dislikes, note down their names on the table you made for Exercise 2.

	LIKES	DISLIKES
sport	*badminton (Javier)*	*football (Paola)*
hobbies		

4   Report back to the class. Example:
'Both Javier and I love badminton. Neither Paola nor I like football.'

Intermediate

Matters

JAN BELL
ROGER GOWER

LONGMAN

with Extra
Communicative
Activities

Contents chart

READING

Lenny Henry is one of Britain's most popular comedians and has his own television programme – *The Lenny Henry Show*. As well as that, he is frequently on the radio and has sold many records. One of seven children, Lenny grew up near Birmingham but now lives in London with his wife.

1 Read the first three paragraphs of the text quickly and write down six things that Lenny Henry likes. Example: *food . . .*

Lenny Henry's **favourite things** ◀◀◀

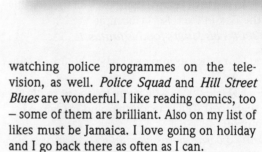

1 'Good food is a very high priority with me, especially as I'm nearly always on a diet, so there are times when I break the rules and go absolutely crazy and eat the entire contents of the fridge in one go, or I go to a restaurant and order the whole of the left-hand side of the menu. I really enjoy eating Indian and Mexican food (especially chilli), and my Mum's food is fantastic, too (of course!).

2 I've got a superb record collection – over 3,000 albums as well as various CDs – so you can guess that I just adore listening to music. I really like Stevie Wonder, whose early music is terrific, and Prince and Hip Hop. Ever since I was young I've loved looking round record shops.

3 I am very fond of cats – I've got two of them, Aretna and Flossie. I like actors who are also good comedians like Peter Sellers, who was great in the good Pink Panther films, and Richard Pryor for his stand-up comedy. I love watching police programmes on the television, as well. *Police Squad* and *Hill Street Blues* are wonderful. I like reading comics, too – some of them are brilliant. Also on my list of likes must be Jamaica. I love going on holiday and I go back there as often as I can.

4 I tend to wear good clothes – maybe because I couldn't afford them when I was young. I like wearing baggy suits and shiny shoes, but I can't stand shirts when the arms aren't long enough! One of my other pet hates is when expensive shoe shops don't have shoes in my size. I think that's really awful.

5 There are lots of other things I don't like. I detest violence, and the idea of nuclear war is very frightening indeed. I don't mind being interviewed, but I get annoyed when I'm misquoted in newspapers. I absolutely hate racist jokes because they promote ignorance. I'm also not too keen on rude people and Australian soap operas – they're really dreadful.'

2 Read the final two paragraphs of the text and write down several things that Lenny Henry dislikes. Example:
Shirts, when the arms aren't long enough.

3 Discuss the following questions in pairs.

a) Which of Lenny Henry's likes and dislikes do you share with him?
b) What things would you want to ask Lenny Henry if you were interviewing him?
c) Which famous person would you like to interview? Give reasons for your choice.

VOCABULARY

Likes and dislikes: adjectives

1   Which adjectives in the box mean *very good* and which mean *very bad*?

fantastic	brilliant	terrific	awful
great	dreadful	wonderful	superb

2   Mark the stress on each of the words in the box in Exercise 1, putting the stress mark (') as used in many dictionaries before the strongest syllable (e.g. *fan'tastic*). Note that *great* has only one syllable, and the stress for one-syllable words is not normally marked in dictionaries.

3   In the text, Lenny Henry uses all the adjectives in the box in Exercise 1. Example:
*He thinks his Mum's food is **fantastic**.*

Find four other examples of when he uses them.

4   List five things which you think are really good or really bad. Tell your partner and explain why. Example:
'I think the transport system in this country is awful because it's too expensive.'

Likes and dislikes: verbs

The verbs in the box refer to likes and dislikes. Draw a line and write *most positive* above one end of the line and *most negative* above the other end (see the example below). Position the verbs along the line according to how positive or how negative they are.

adore	don't mind	can't stand	enjoy
detest	be keen on	hate	be fond of

most positive   **most negative**
| adore

LANGUAGE POINT 1

Verbs + -ing

Verbs of liking and disliking are often followed by verbs in the -*ing* form. Examples:
*He **loves watching** police programmes on TV.*
*He **doesn't like being** misquoted.*

List five things you love doing and five things you can't stand doing. Tell your partner and explain why. Example:
'I love gardening because I enjoy being outdoors.'

Similarities and differences

1   Read the three example exchanges. (The words in **bold** are stressed.)
'I hate cold weather.'   'So do I.'
'He doesn't like fruit.'   'Neither do we.'
'I love this weather.'   'Do you? I don't.'

Match the sentences in column A with the appropriate replies in column B. One has been done for you. Then practise saying the dialogues in pairs. (Look at Section 4 in the *Language reference* for notes on the stress and intonation patterns used in the reply sentences.)

A	**B**
a) 'I can't swim.'	'So do I.'
b) 'She is keen on jazz.'	'Neither do we.'
c) 'He lives in Paris.'	'Neither can I.'
d) 'They don't like it here.'	'Do you? I don't.'
e) 'I love English food.'	'Is she? I'm not.'

2   Work with a partner.

STUDENT A
Choose five of the words or phrases in the box and tell your partner how you feel about them. Example:
'I hate travelling by coach because it makes me feel sick.'

spiders	horror films	football	discos
travel by coach	babies	romantic stories	
go on holiday with your parents		do exams	

STUDENT B
Respond to your partner. Example:
A: *I hate travelling by coach because it makes me feel sick.*
B: *So do I. And it's really boring too.* **OR**
   Do you? I quite like it.

PRONUNCIATION

1 [🔊 1.1]   Listen to these questions and divide them into Group A (questions which sound interested and friendly) and Group B (questions which sound bored or even rude).

a) 'How old are you?'
b) 'Are you married?'
c) 'Have you got any children?'
d) 'Why do you listen to classical music?'
e) 'Where do you work?'
f) 'Can I ask you some questions?'

What makes some of the questions sound more interested or friendly?

Check with Section 8 in the *Language reference* for notes on intonation in questions. Then practise all the questions above, trying to make them sound friendly.

2 [🔊 1.2]   Listen to the following dialogues and practise them in pairs. Pay special attention to the weak pronunciation of *do* after a question word (*'Where do they live?'* /də/). After question words *do* often combines with *you* to sound like /djə/ or /djʊ/ (*'Do you ever play tennis?'*). In a short reply, *do* is pronounced in its strong form (*'Yes, I do.'* /duː/).

a) 'Do you like travelling to other countries?' 'Yes, I do. I go abroad at least twice a year.'
b) 'What do we want to drink?' 'Let's have a bottle of wine, shall we?'
c) 'Do you ever play tennis?' 'Yes, I do, but only in the summer.'
d) 'Where do they live?' 'In Brazil. They really love it there.'

LANGUAGE POINT 2

Question forms and short answers

1   Roleplay the following dialogue between an interviewer (Student A) and Lenny Henry (Student B).

STUDENT A
Ask questions about the subjects listed in the box. In each case, first ask general questions which require a *Yes/No* answer (e.g. *'Are you interested in food?'*). Then ask more specific questions (e.g. *'What is your favourite kind of food?'*).

| clothes   music   food   giving interviews television programmes |

2   Change roles, so that Student B asks the questions and Student A answers.

STUDENT B
Answer Student A using information from the text. Give short answers first. Example:
STUDENT A: *Are you interested in food?*
STUDENT B: *Yes, I am.*
STUDENT A: *What kind of food do you like?*
STUDENT B: *I love Indian and Mexican food.*

> See **Use your grammar**, page 40, for further practice of question forms, short answers and similarities and differences.

LISTENING

Before listening

1   You are going to listen to an interview with Judi Dench. What can you guess about her from the pictures?

2   Write down some questions asking about her family, hobbies and interests. Some of these questions may be answered when you listen to the interview.

Listening

1 [1.3]   Listen to the first part of the interview and say whether the following statements are *True* or *False* according to the text.

a) Judi's husband is an actor.   *True.*
b) She's got two sons.
c) She pays somebody to help her with the housework.
d) She doesn't stay in London at the weekend.
e) None of her pets go to London with her.

2 [1.4]   Listen to the second part of the interview in which Judi is talking about her hobbies. Put a tick next to the things she likes in the list below. One has been done for you.

a) painting ✓   g) swimming
b) drawing   h) football
c) horror films   i) gardening
d) jewellery   j) dolls' houses
e) cooking   k) pop music
f) travelling abroad   l) opera

3   Listen to the second part of the interview again and answer these questions.

a) What are Michael and Finty good at?
b) What do you think a *meat and two veg man* is?
c) Do you think they are a close family? Give your reasons.

4   Would you like to be an actor? Give your reasons.

LANGUAGE POINTS 3

The definite article (*the*)

1   Look at the following extracts from the interview with Judi Dench. Decide whether *the* should go in each space, and give reasons.

a) 'He loves _____ bread and butter pudding I make.'
b) 'I was in _____ Yugoslavia last year.'
c) 'I've got a passion for _____ doll's house I have at home.'
d) 'I like _____ classical music very much.'

Check with Section 3 in the *Language reference* for notes on when to use the definite article.

2   Put a line through *the* when it is used incorrectly in each of the following sentences. The first sentence has been done for you.

a) My hobbies are reading ~~the~~ books and studying ~~the~~ languages. I like the Spanish lessons I'm having at the moment very much, but I'm finding the pronunciation and the grammar in Spanish really difficult.
b) The English food you get in the restaurants is often boring but in the private homes the cooking can be excellent. I usually like drinking the dry German wine with the meals, although I sometimes have the beer.
c) The animals are very important to English people, and they like the pets very much. However, some of the pets they keep are very strange.
d) My brother is very keen on the cars. He has to drive the models he sells, but according to him the Italian cars are the best.

Direct and less direct questions

Judi Dench's interviewer asked some questions which were direct and others which were less direct. Examples:
'Do you prefer the cinema or the theatre?' (direct)
'Could you tell me if you prefer the cinema or the theatre?' (less direct)

1   Look at some of the other questions which the interviewer asked. Say whether each question is direct or less direct, and why you think the interviewer decides to ask some less direct ones.

a) 'I wonder if you'd mind answering one or two more personal questions?'
b) 'Have you got any pets?'
c) 'Could I ask you how old you are?'
d) 'Do you like travelling abroad?'

2   Ask your partner questions about his/her life. Use some of the cues in the box below. Make some of the questions less direct if you think it is a more personal or difficult question. Examples:
'Which subjects do you study at University?'
'Could you tell me what your father's job is?'

Check with Section 6 in the *Language reference* for notes on how less direct questions are formed.

> Do you . . . ?   Could you tell me . . . ?
> Have you got . . . ?   Which . . . ?   What . . . ?
> Would you mind telling me . . . ?
> How many . . . ?   Are . . . ?   Where . . . ?
> I wonder if you'd tell me . . . ?

SPEAKING 2

Asking and answering questions

1   Choose someone in the class who you don't know very well and who you would like to know more about. Interview them, remembering to mix direct and less direct questions and trying to keep your intonation polite.

a) Ask them at least five questions about their life (e.g. about where they live, their job, their studies, their family, and the languages they speak).

b) Find out about their 'favourite things' – their hobbies and interests.

2   Make notes on what your partner says. This will be important for the writing task below.

WRITING

Personal information

1   Write up the notes you made in the last *Speaking* section in the form of a short text. Use the Lenny Henry text as a model for your piece of writing. Don't give the name of the person in the text. The rest of the class will have to guess who you have written about.

a) In the first paragraph include information about the person's family, place of birth, etc.

b) In the second paragraph write about their likes and dislikes.

2   Check your writing for the correct use of:
– verbs ending with *-ing* (e.g. *enjoys dancing*).
– articles (include or leave out *the*?).
– Present Simple endings (e.g. *she likes* . . .).

Language reference

1 Likes and dislikes

The verbs *enjoy, adore, don't mind, can't stand, don't like* are usually followed either by nouns, or by verbs in the *-ing* form.

> *I enjoy Chinese food.   I enjoy eating Chinese food.*

2 Word stress

In words of two or more syllables one syllable is pronounced more strongly than the others: we say it is stressed.

> **'ter**rible   su**'perb**   fan**'tas**tic   **'won**derful

A good dictionary usually tells you the correct syllable to stress, and uses a symbol called a stress mark ('). This means that the syllable that follows the mark is stressed.

3 The definite article (*the*)

The definite article (*the*) is used to refer to:
a) Specific things:
> *I don't like **the** man over there in the leather jacket.*

b) Things which the speaker and the hearer both know about:
> *Where's **the** sugar?*

c) Some geographical locations:
> **the** *United States*, **the** *Alps*

The definite article is NOT used to refer to:
a) Things in general:
> *I like cats.* (i.e. cats in general) (NOT *I like the cats.*)

b) Languages and most countries:
> *I speak Italian.* (NOT *I speak the Italian.*)
> *She lives in Turkey.*

4 Similarities and differences

Similarities

So
> *'I like having a sleep after lunch.' '**So** do I.'*

So can be used instead of *too* and *as well*.
> *'I like having a sleep after lunch.' 'I like having a sleep after lunch, **too** / **as well**.'*

If there is no auxiliary verb (*be / have / can / will*, etc.) in the first sentence, *do* or *does* is used in the answer.
> *'I hate getting up early.' 'So do I.'*

If an auxiliary verb is used in the first sentence, this is repeated in the answer.
> *'She**'s** Japanese.' 'So **is** he.'*
> *'I**'ll** help him.' 'So **will** I.'*

Neither
> *'I haven't got any brothers'. '**Neither** have I.'*

Neither is used like *So*. It means *not either*.
> *'I haven't got any brothers.' 'I have**n't** got any brothers **either**.'*

Note that the repeated subject is usually stressed.
> *So do **I**. Neither do **we**.*

Differences

If you are surprised by or interested in a statement, you can respond with a reply question. This is formed by using the same auxiliary verb as in the statement followed by a personal pronoun.
> *'I can't swim.' '**Can't** you? I can.'*

If there is no auxiliary verb in the statement we use *do / does / did*.
> *'I love English food.' '**Do** you? I don't.'*

Note that you stress the auxiliary ('**Do** you?') and your voice normally goes up at the end of the reply question. Note also how in the examples above *I* is stressed to indicate a difference of opinion between the two speakers.

5 Present Simple questions

See page 157.

6 Less direct questions

QUESTION PHRASES	
Would you mind telling me *I wonder if you'd mind telling me* *Could you tell me*	*which you prefer?*

Less direct forms are often more formal and polite. Compare the word order in the following two questions.
> ***When** does the shop open?* = direct

(question word + auxiliary verb + subject + base form of verb)
> ***Can you tell me when** the shop opens?* = less direct

(question phrase + subject + verb)
Notice that the question word (*when / what / how*, etc.) is still used in less direct questions, but it is followed by the subject (*the shop / it / he*) rather than a verb form.

7 Short form answers

> *'Do you speak English?' 'Yes, I **do**.' / 'No, I **don't**.'*

In *Yes / No* questions the auxiliary verb in the question (*do / be / have*) is often repeated in the answer. This helps to make the answer more polite.
> *'**Does** she like cats?' 'Yes, she **does**.' / 'No, she **doesn't**.'*
> *'**Are** you tired?' 'Yes, I **am**.' / 'No, I**'m not**.'*
> *'**Has** he got enough money?' 'Yes, he **has**.' / 'No, he **hasn't**.'*

8 Intonation in question forms

When a question starts with the voice high in pitch, this often helps to make the question sound more polite ('*Excuse me. What's your name?*'). If your voice is flat, low and has little expression in it, your question can sometimes sound bored and unfriendly.

How do I look?

READING

Before reading

Look at the photograph below of Rachel Lewis.

a) What kind of person do you think she is?
b) What kind of job do you think she does?

Reading

1   Read the text quickly. In the list below put a cross next to the things Rachel does *not* talk about.

a) where she lives   d) how she relaxes
b) her family   e) her favourite clothes
c) her childhood   f) her work

24
HOURS WITH
RACHEL LEWIS

1   **M**y first waking thought is usually along the lines of, oh God, is it really morning already? He knows I'm not naturally a morning person, so I have three alarm clocks set for about 6.30 a.m.

2   It's at this time of the day when I often think it would be nice to have a mum or man around the place to help me. By the time I've got ready, stuck the washing into the machine, had a gallon of black coffee and 200 cigarettes, I find myself flying out of the door late.

3   Home is a small, modern house, owned by the Church.

4   I don't really pray formally, I just have a running conversation with God. Too many people don't pray because they think you have to use formal language and they feel silly.

5   Wearing black every day means deciding what to put on doesn't occupy much time. The badge on my handbag says: 'The best man for the job is a woman.' It's a bit naughty, but a friend pinned it there, and that's my excuse.

6   Most mornings I wash my hair, which is driving me mad at the moment because I'm growing out a colour, and put on a little make-up, but I'm not very good at it.

7   I've just bought a small Volvo so I drive to church for a morning service between 7.30 a.m. and 8 a.m. From church, it's only five minutes to college.

8   My work involves seeing individual students who want to discuss problems, like exams, religious doubts, emotional difficulties, their futures – the usual things. I know there are people who don't approve of women in the church. I just keep out of their way and respect their views. It's important to keep your sense of humour and not take yourself too seriously.

9   Lunch, low-fat yoghurt and fruit, tends to be eaten on the move, usually on my way to talk to a group, which may include staff or students, or a luncheon club.

10   I usually get home around 5 p.m. and do some work on a sermon. To unwind I play the piano very loudly, go for a walk, or lie on the floor and practise very elementary yoga. Sometimes I have a bath and read. Getting dinner involves taking something out of the freezer and popping it into the microwave. I have a reasonably active social life, mostly with friends I grew up with in Hale, in Manchester. The evenings I spend alone. I occasionally just slump into a chair and watch some telly. I don't get lonely, although I do sometimes miss my black cat, Satan, who died last year.

11   I have had lots of boyfriends, and the idea of marriage does appeal, when the right one comes along. But I'm not at all maternal and I haven't yet had the urge to steal babies in supermarkets.

12   My parents live in Swansea. I'm one of four children and the only one who has gone into the church. The others are more interested in money. Well, I am, too, but ministers earn £7,500 a year so I'll just have to find myself a wealthy man.

13   Bedtime tends to be about midnight. But before that I always write a Dear Diary, except it's Dear God, a kind of prayer.

a gallon: 4.55 litres   *sermon*: religious speech   *Satan*: another word for the Devil

(from *Riva*)

2 Decide whether the following statements are *True* or *False* according to the text. If they are false, give the correct answer.

a) Rachel finds it easy to get up in the morning.
b) She lives alone.
c) She spends a lot of time cooking.
d) She's got brothers and sisters.
e) She wants to have children.
f) She has a pet.

3 Read the text more carefully and answer the following questions.

a) Who do you think *He* might be?
b) Does Rachel really drink a gallon of coffee in the morning?
c) Where is she working at the moment?
d) How does she relax?
e) Find examples in the text of Rachel's sense of humour.
f) Does she earn a lot? How do you know?
g) Does being a woman cause her any problems in her job?

4 When we are talking about how often we do or do not do things we frequently use words such as *always* or *never* (adverbs of frequency).

a) Find four examples from the text of adverbs of frequency. Example:
I always write a Dear Diary. (paragraph 13)
b) What is their position in the sentence?

5 This is what people often imagine a typical minister of the church will be like. In what ways is Rachel different?

LEARNING FOCUS

Guessing meaning

You can often make a guess at what an unfamiliar word means by using one or both of the following strategies.

Looking at grammatical function
Examples from the text about Rachel Lewis:
– *pinned* (paragraph 5): Because it ends in *-ed*, it is probably the regular Past Simple form of a word that describes an action or a state (i.e. a verb).
– *Volvo* (paragraph 7): It must be the name of something (i.e. a noun) because it is described by an article (*a*) and an adjective (*small*).
– *wealthy* (paragraph 12): It is probably a word which describes a noun (i.e. an adjective) because it comes after an article (*a*) and before a noun (*man*).
– *formally* (paragraph 4): It is probably a word which adds information to a verb or an adjective (i.e. an adverb) because it ends in *-ly* and comes after a verb (*pray*).

Looking at context
Examples:
– *pinned* (paragraph 5): *a friend **pinned** it there*
The badge is on the handbag. We know that badges are normally *attached* to something, so *pinned* must mean *attached* in some way.
– *Volvo* (paragraph 7): *I've just bought a small **Volvo** so I drive to work.*
If Rachel *drives* a Volvo then a *Volvo* is probably a car.
– *slump* (paragraph 10): *I just **slump** into a chair.*
She is tired so she probably feels *heavy* and *drops* into the chair.

(Another important strategy for guessing meaning is to analyse parts of the word. Prefixes and suffixes are examined in Units 6 and 8.)

1 Say whether each of the following words is a noun, verb, adjective or adverb. Use the passage to help you.

a) *thought* (paragraph 1)
b) *naughty* (paragraph 5)
c) *approve* (paragraph 8)
d) *unwind* (paragraph 10)
e) *reasonably* (paragraph 10)
f) *maternal* (paragraph 11)

2   Look back at the text and try to work out what these words mean in context.

a) *naughty* (paragraph 5)
b) *approve* (paragraph 8)
c) *unwind* (paragraph 10)
d) *maternal* (paragraph 11)
e) *wealthy* (paragraph 12)

What was there in the context to help you?

3   The two words below are used colloquially (they are typical of informal spoken language), and in context they both mean the same thing.

a) *stuck* (base form: *stick*) (paragraph 2)
b) *popping* (base form: *pop*) (paragraph 10)

Do they mean *see*, *put* or *give*?

4   Look back at the text again and try to work out the meaning of some other words you do not know.

LANGUAGE POINTS

Present habits and routines

1   Read these sentences about Rachel's morning routine.
*Rachel **always** sets three alarm clocks for 6.30 a.m.*
***Most mornings** she washes her hair.* OR *She washes her hair **most mornings**.*

Think about your own morning routine and write five sentences, using the words in the box or similar expressions.

always   never   occasionally   every day
hardly ever   once/twice a week/month
most mornings   every couple of weeks

2   Work in pairs. Use the picture cues below (and your own ideas) to ask and answer as in the examples.
A: *Do you have a bath in the morning?*
B: *No, hardly ever. (I hardly ever have a bath in the morning.)*
A: *How often do you travel to work by bus?*
B: *Once a week. (I travel to work by bus once a week.)*

STUDENT A
Find out about Student B's morning routine. Use the weak form of *do* where appropriate and try to make your questions sound polite. Use the pictures to help you and ask any other questions you want to ask.

STUDENT B
Reply to Student A's questions. Give information about your morning routine, using expressions from the box in Exercise 1.

3   In groups, report back on any interesting things which you have found out about your partner's morning routine. Example:
'Anna and I both get up at the same time, but she eats a cooked breakfast . . .'

Talking about present events

1   Read the example sentence below. What is the name of the verb form printed in **bold**? When is it used? (Check with Section 4 in the *Language reference* to find how it is used.) Example:
*At the moment Rachel **is living** in Bolton and **working** at a college.*

2   Choose verbs from the box below to complete the numbered gaps in the text. In some cases there may be more than one possible answer. Be careful to use the correct form of the verb. The first one has been done for you.

have	eat	forget	clean	ask	water
keep	cook	wear	do		

'Hi. Yes, it's Clare ... We're OK ... Yes, of course we're (1) *watering* the plants ... They're fine ... No, the house isn't a mess – one of us is ___(2)___ it every day ... Yes, I loved the dress ... No, really! I'm ___(3)___ it at the moment, actually. Are you ___(4)___ a good time? ... Great! ... David? Er, I expect he's ___(5)___ his homework in his room ... Yes, the dog's fine, too ... Of course, we're not ___(6)___ to feed him. What do you think we are?! ... Yes, I know he's not allowed in the sitting room – we're ___(7)___ him in his basket in the hall ... No, we're not ___(8)___ junk food. Pauline is ___(9)___ at this very moment ... Er, I can't remember. Chicken, I think. OK, give Dad our love. See you soon ... What? ... Tomorrow! Well, why are you ___(10)___ me all these questions then?!'

3 [🔲 2.1]   Listen and find out what Clare actually says. Check your answers.

4   Make guesses about:

a) who Clare is talking to.
b) what the situation is.
c) what the other person's questions are.

5   Look at the picture on page 160 to find out what was really happening. Find five things that are not true in what Clare is saying.

> See **Use your grammar**, page 40, for further practice of the Present Continuous.

Simple or Continuous?

In four of the following sentences the Present Continuous is used incorrectly. Mark the four incorrect sentences with a cross.

a) Can you answer the phone? I'm having a bath.
b) I'm not understanding this exercise.
c) He's thinking about Helen. That's why he's sad.
d) She is liking the film.
e) They are watching television.
f) I am thinking English is a difficult language.
g) The seasons are changing four times a year.

If necessary, check the rules in Section 5 in the *Language reference*.

PRONUNCIATION

Present Simple and Continuous

1   There are three different ways of pronouncing the *-s* ending in the Present Simple tense: /s/ (as in *speaks*); /z/ (as in *comes*); and /ɪz/ (as in *finishes*).

a)   Tick the correct column for each of the following Present Simple verbs according to their endings. One has been done for you.

	speaks /s/	*comes* /z/	*finishes* /ɪz/
a) works	✓		
b) loses			
c) goes			
d) drives			
e) gets			
f) watches			
g) knows			
h) starts			
i) dances			

b) [🔲 2.2]   Listen and check your answers.
c) Practise saying each word.

2 [🔲 2.3]   Listen to the recording.

a) Count the words in each of the questions.
b) Listen again and write each question down.
c) When we speak there is no pause between *What* and *are* in the following question: *What are you doing?* The two words are pronounced as if they are one (/ˈwɒtə/). Find a similar example in the questions you have written down and practise saying it.

SPEAKING 1

Social situations

Work in groups to decide what you might say in the following situations. There are many possibilities. Remember to choose your language carefully, according to who you are speaking to and the situation itself. For example, if the person is a friend you will probably be more informal than if you are speaking to someone you don't know very well. Example:

Someone offers you a ticket to a concert. Refuse politely.

'Thanks very much. That's very kind of you. Unfortunately, I can't go. I'm going to the cinema tonight.'

a) You don't understand the meaning of the word *pray*. Ask your teacher.

b) You want your friend to help you spell the word *photograph*, but at the moment she's reading. Interrupt her.

c) You are late for class. Apologise to your teacher when you come in.

d) You are not sure how to pronounce the word *naughty*. Interrupt your teacher, who is talking to another student.

e) Ask your teacher for permission to leave the lesson early.

f) Introduce your friend to another friend.

g) Somebody thanks you for helping them. What do you say?

h) Your friend tells you she has won a lot of money. What do you say?

i) Your brother tells you he's failed his exam. What do you say?

WRITING

Punctuation

1 Match the punctuation shown in red in column A with the terms in column B. One has been done for you.

A	B
1 **I** like hats.	a) comma
2 I have to wear it.	b) speech marks / inverted commas
3 How much is it?	c) dash
4 What a lovely coat!	d) capital letter
5 Yes, I think so.	e) full stop
6 It's fun.	f) exclamation mark
7 'They're too big,' he said.	g) question mark
8 Magazines – except for one or two – are really boring.	h) apostrophe

2 Punctuate the following text.

how do the rich and famous spend their lives the answers are sometimes surprising at princess dianas private parties for example there are no cooks or servants the food provided is simple pasta and salad and the conversation is relaxed and lively she and her friends like to laugh at the latest pictures of her in the newspaper talk about her latest dresses or examine her new shoes they also like to gossip about friends and tell plenty of jokes typical diana expressions on these occasions are i just dont believe it and that sounds like fun

LISTENING

Vocabulary: clothes

Use the words from the box to describe what each of the people in the picture at the foot of the page is wearing.

jacket	tights	leather skirt	suit	waistcoat	dress	boots
shirt	blouse	high heels	training shoes	jumper	T-shirt	tie

Before listening

1   What can you guess about the people in the picture (for example, their job, their personality, the kind of place they live in)? What adjectives would you use to describe them?

2   In your opinion, which of the words in the box best describe the people in the picture? What other words could you use?

fashionable	stylish	conventional	formal	powerful	fun
different	attractive	casual			

3   When you choose clothes to wear, what is important to you?

4   What are you wearing at the moment? Is this different from what you wear at other times?

Listening

1 [🔊 2.4]   Listen to these people talking about the clothes they like wearing and answer the questions.

Annie
a) Does she like changing the colour of her hair?
b) Does she spend a lot of money on clothes?

Liz
a) Does she feel comfortable in smart clothes?
b) Does she have to wear a suit to work?

Sara
a) Is it necessary for her to wear a skirt for her job?
b) Is she a business woman?

Mike
a) Does he have to wear formal clothes?
b) Does he like wearing formal clothes?

2   Listen to the recording again and look back at the picture.

a) Which of the people in the picture do you think the speakers most look like? What differences are there?
b) Write down words which describe the image each of the speakers is trying to create through his/her appearance. Example: *Annie: unconventional, fun, young . . .*

3   Which of the clothes shown in the pictures on the right are *not* mentioned by any of the four speakers?

SPEAKING 2

Group report

1   Work in groups. Which clothes would you recommend for the following people?

a) An older man who wants to show everyone he is young and fashionable.
b) A young woman attending an interview for the job of managing director.
c) A young fashion designer who intends to visit an aunt and uncle on their farm.
d) A man or a woman who wants to make a good impression on someone of the opposite sex on a first date.

2   Are the following true (never/sometimes/usually/always)? Give reasons and examples.

a) Young people wear the same clothes as old people.
b) We don't wear the same clothes to a funeral as we do to a wedding.
c) We can tell what social background people come from by looking at them.
d) We dress according to our personality.
e) We dress according to the image we want to create.
f) People judge each other too much on appearances.

3   Report your conclusions to the class.

Language reference

1 Adverbs of frequency

Adverbs of frequency (e.g. *always, usually, hardly ever, occasionally*) answer the question *How often . . . ?* They are often used with the Present Simple and usually come between the subject and the main verb.
> I **usually** get home around 5 p.m.

With the verb *be* the adverb of frequency comes after the verb.
> I am **rarely** late.

The following adverbs of frequency can also come at the beginning or the end of a sentence: *usually, occasionally, sometimes.*
> **Sometimes** I feel lonely. OR I feel lonely **sometimes**.

2 Frequency phrases

Frequency phrases like *every day, every couple of weeks, once / twice a week / month, most mornings* normally come at the beginning or the end of a sentence.
> **Once a year** I try to get to the dentist.
> I wash my hair **twice a week**.

3 Present Simple

USE

The Present Simple is usually used to talk about:
a) Actions in the present which happen again and again:
> I often **wash** my hair in the morning.
b) Situations in the present which remain the same for a long time:
> Her mother **lives** in Swansea.

FORM See page 157.

SPELLING

-es is added to the base form in the third person singular (*he, she, it*) if the verb ends with *-ss, -sh, -ch, -x,* or *-o*:
> miss → miss**es**; push → push**es**; go → go**es**

A consonant + *y* in the base form (*marry*) changes to consonant + *-ies* in the third person singular:
> marry → marr**ies**; fly → fl**ies**

PRONUNCIATION

There are three different ways of pronouncing the *-s* ending in the Present Simple.
/s/ after most unvoiced consonants (sounds like /p/, /t/, /k/, /f/, /θ/): stop**s**, put**s**, like**s**
/z/ after vowels (e.g. /iː/) and most voiced consonants (sounds like /b/, /d/, /g/, /v/, /ð/, /l/, /m/, /n/, /ŋ/): see**s**, need**s**, give**s**
/ɪz/ after /s/, /z/, /ʃ/, /ʒ/, /tʃ/ or /dʒ/: danc**es**, los**es**, push**es**

4 Present Continuous

USE

The Present Continuous (sometimes called the Present Progressive) is usually used to talk about an activity, temporary action or situation in progress in the present.
> 'Look! Somebody**'s getting out** of the car.'

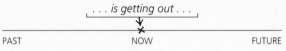

PAST	NOW	FUTURE

FORM See page 157.

SPELLING

The base form is usually followed by *-ing* unless:
– it ends in *e*, in which case the *e* disappears:
> come → coming.
– the verb ends with a stressed syllable containing one vowel followed by a consonant (except for *y* and *w*). In this case we double the consonant: stop → stopping.

PRONUNCIATION

In connected speech, we usually do not pause between each word:
> What **are** you reading? (In this case *What* and *are* are closely linked: /ˈwɒtə/.)

Also, notice that the verb *be* is often contracted (made shorter) in speech and in informal writing: *I am → I'm; She is → She's; We are leaving now. → We're leaving now.* It is not contracted when it begins a question or ends a sentence:
> 'Are you happy?' 'Yes, I am.'

5 States and actions

Some verbs are not usually used in the continuous form. They are called *state* verbs because they normally describe states rather than actions. These states usually continue over a period of time. Examples:
a) emotion: *dislike, hate, love, want, wish, prefer, like*
b) the mind: *believe, doubt, feel, know, mean, remember, think, understand*
c) the senses: *hear, see, smell, taste, sound*
d) possession: *belong, need, owe, own, have*

However, these verbs can be used in the continuous form when they describe an action or a process.
> Look! He**'s thinking** about Helen again! (= mental action)
> He **thinks** about Helen all the time. (= mental state)

Foreign adventures

LISTENING

Before listening

1 In recent years, there have been kidnappings in a lot of countries. What reasons can you think of for kidnapping someone? Look at the headlines below and say what you think the reasons were in each case.

£2 million ransom demanded for champion racehorse

Kidnapped oil heir set free

Hostages to be freed by rebel forces

2 What other kidnappings have you read about? What happened and why?

3 You are going to listen to Sue talking about the time she was involved in a kidnapping incident while teaching abroad. These pictures refer to things that she talks about in her story. In groups, try to predict what happened in Sue's story.

Listening

1 [3.1] Listen and check your predictions.

2 Answer the following questions.

a) What nationality were the kidnap victims?
b) Why were they kidnapped?
c) Where did the kidnappers take them?
d) What happened in the end?

3 The following report contains eight factual errors. In pairs, find and correct the errors.

JAFFNA KIDNAP SCARE

1 An Australian couple were kidnapped and kept for one month while their captors demanded large sums of money for their release.

2 Stanley and Penny Walters were having breakfast on a holiday weekend, just before setting off on a trip to Kandy to meet a friend, when two masked men broke into their home, tied them up and blindfolded them.

3 They then searched the house for money and jewellery before pushing them into a car and taking them to an isolated part of the island. The couple finally managed to escape after suffering badly at the hands of their captors and have now returned to their own country.

4 In pairs, retell the story using the cues below. Change the verbs to the Past Simple (e.g. *went*), the Past Continuous (e.g. *was going*), or *used to* and add prepositions, articles, etc. Example:
Sue / live / Sri Lanka / when / kidnapping / happen
*Sue **was living** in Sri Lanka **when the** kidnapping happened*.

a) American couple / watch video / when / knock on door
b) Stanley / send boys away / close door / go back / bedroom
c) men / wear masks / carry guns
d) men / put blindfolds on / push into van / take them away
e) while / this happen / Sue / wait / hotel in Kandy
f) after kidnapping / friends / check doors and windows every night
g) they also / have / nightmares for some time afterwards

19

LEARNING FOCUS 1

Using a monolingual dictionary

1   This is part of a sentence from Sue's story:
. . . *masked men rushed into the room* . . .

a) Underline two nouns.
b) Circle an adjective.
c) Put a box round a preposition.

2   According to this dictionary entry *masked men* means men who are hiding their face with a covering.

> into a so.   . after cooking
> **mask¹** /mɑːsk/ /mæsk/ *n* a covering for the face to
>   hide or protect it – **masked** *adj*
> **mask²** *v* to cover with a mask; hide
>   . .   . . olid lump or pile, usu.

a) What symbol tells you which part of speech (e.g. noun, verb, adjective) *masked* is?
b) How do you pronounce *mask*? (Use the pronunciation chart on page 160 to help you).

3   Look at the dictionary entry for *rush*. Which of the meanings of *rush* goes best with . . . *masked men* **rushed** *into the room*?

> **ruse** /ruːz/ *n* a trick to c
> **rush¹** /rʌʃ/ *v* to (make someone or something) hurry
>   or act quickly: *There's plenty of time; we needn't
>   rush*
> **rush²** *n* **1** a sudden rapid hasty movement   **2** too
>   much haste: *We needn't leave yet, what's all the
>   rush?*   **3** a period of great and hurried activity: *I
>   hate shopping during the Christmas rush when
>   everyone's buying presents*
> **rush³** *n* a grasslike water plant
> **rushes** /rʌʃɪz/ *n* (in fil   first prints of

4   Use a dictionary to do the following:

a) Look up the noun *captor* (paragraph 3 in the newspaper article). How many other words can you make from it (e.g. *capture*)? What parts of speech are they (adjective, noun, etc.)?
b) Find out which meaning of *manage* (paragraph 3) goes best with *The couple finally managed to escape* . . . What other meanings of *manage* can you think of?

VOCABULARY

Guessing meaning

Guess which of the definitions of the word(s) printed in **bold** is correct. Then check your answers with a dictionary.

a) . . . *some* **remote** *part of the island*
    i) boring   ii) quiet and lonely
b) . . . *were trying to* **get autonomy**
    i) have their own separate government
    ii) buy machine guns
c) . . . *eventually they* **were released**.
    i) became conscious   ii) set free
d) . . . *suffer from terrible* **nightmares**.
    i) visitors at night   ii) bad dreams
e) . . . *difficult experience to* **get over**.
    i) recover from   ii) explain

Nationality words

1   See how well you know the words which refer to a country (including the people who live there, and the language). Complete the word puzzle by reading the clues below. What is the country in the box?

1					E		K			
2	P			T			E		E	
3					W		D		N	
4						I	L			K
5			E					S		
6					R		B			

1 Crete is a _____ island.
2 The language spoken in Brazil.
3 A country in northern Europe.
4 The capital city is Colombo.
5 They live in the United States.
6 This language is spoken in the Middle East.

2   In teams of four, work out five similar clues using nationality words and make five gapped sentences. Example:
Warsaw is the capital of: _ _ l _ _ d

Make sure you check the spelling of the nationality words in a dictionary. Then give another team the questions and ask them to fill in the gaps.

LANGUAGE POINTS

Past Simple

1   Read the newspaper report quickly to find answers to the following questions. (Ignore the gaps for the moment.)

a) Where did the family's ordeal take place?
b) What were they doing?
c) Why did it happen?
d) What happened in the end?

2   Are the following statements *True* or *False* according to the text?

a) The family had never been to the island before that day.
b) They had hired the boat.
c) They didn't have enough to drink.
d) The weather was calm all the time.
e) Raymond works in a pub.

3   Divide the verbs in the box into two groups according to whether their Past Simple tense is *regular* or *irregular*. (There are five verbs in each group.) Then write down the Past Simple of each verb.

appear	eat	become	be	taste	say
carry	drift	try	drink		

BASE FORM	REGULAR PAST	BASE FORM	IRREGULAR PAST
appear	*appeared*	*eat*	*ate*

4   Complete the newspaper report by putting the Past Simple form of the correct verb in each space. Use verbs from the box in Exercise 3.

5   Raymond was interviewed about his ordeal for the newspaper report. Work in pairs and roleplay the interview between Raymond and the journalist. Student A should take the part of Raymond, and Student B the part of the journalist interviewing him. Student B can use some of the cues in the box below the report opposite. Start like this:

STUDENT B: *Mr Kearne, I'm from the 'Daily Mirror' and I'd like to ask you a few questions about your terrible ordeal.*
STUDENT A: *OK. What kind of questions?*
STUDENT B: *Well, firstly how long . . .*

BOAT ORDEAL BRITONS SURVIVE ON SEAWEED!

Family at sea for three days

A British family .....(1)..... **seaweed to stay alive as their boat** .....(2)..... **helplessly for three days on stormy seas.**

A two hour pleasure trip .....(3)..... a nightmare for Raymond Kearne, 48, his wife Jacqueline, 39, and seven-year-old son Jimmy, when their motorboat ran out of petrol. And all the time they .....(4)..... only 11 miles away from the crowded holiday beaches of Majorca. Raymond .....(5)..... yesterday at his villa on the island: 'We now know what it's like to face death – a horrible death at that.'

The family, who come from Lichfield, Staffs, ran out of fuel on their way back from a round-the-bay trip on Saturday.

Raymond said, 'The winds got very violent and .....(6)..... us out to sea.'

All that the family had taken with them was one bottle of orange juice.

Raymond said: 'On Monday, we were dying of thirst. We .....(7)..... filtering seawater so that we could drink it but it didn't work. So we .....(8)..... our own urine to save our lives. Then we ate seaweed. It .....(9)..... bloody awful.'

Just as they had given up hope, a Spanish fishing boat .....(10)..... and picked them up. The family were all suffering from sunburn, thirst and hunger.

Raymond used to have a pub on the holiday island but has now retired. He has put his boat up for sale.

'I didn't use to be afraid of the water, but I think I'll stay on dry land for a while,' he said.

(from the *Daily Mirror*)

How long / at sea?	What / eat?
What / weather like?	How far / from shore?
How / feel then?	How feel / now?

Past Simple or *used to*?

1   Which of the following sentences are not correct?

a) I used to get up very late yesterday.
b) When I was a child I used to live in Spain.
c) I use to speak Spanish.
d) She used to work here.
e) Did he use to play tennis?
f) He didn't use to like what I said to him that day.

Discuss when *used to* is used in preference to the Past Simple, and how it is formed. Check with Section 3 in the *Language reference* as well as with page 157.

2   Use *used to* or the Past Simple to complete the following sentences about your own life.

a) Last year . . .
b) Four years ago . . .
c) When I was a child . . .
d) . . . but I don't any more.
e) . . . but there isn't any more.
f) . . . but now I can.

Past Simple or Past Continuous?

1   Circle the correct verb forms in each of the following sentences.

a) Someone *stole / was stealing* his clothes while he *swam / was swimming* in the river.
b) When she *met / was meeting* Stephen for the first time she *went out / was going out* with somebody else.
c) While I *drove / was driving* along the motorway my car *made / was making* a funny noise so I stopped at once.
d) They *lived / were living* abroad when the disaster *happened / was happening*.
e) Three men *attacked / were attacking* my brother as he *walked / was walking* home from work last night.
f) When I *left / was leaving* home at 8 o'clock this morning the sun *shone / was shining* brightly. However, by 9 o'clock it *rained / was raining* heavily again.

2   Match the sentences in column A with the appropriate ones in column B. Then join each pair of sentences using *while* for sentences b) to d) and *when* for sentences e) to g). Examples:
***While** I was waiting at the bus stop I found a purse full of money.*
*I was waiting at the bus stop **when** I found a purse full of money.*

A	**B**
a) I was waiting at the bus stop.	I saw the left wing was on fire.
b) We were flying over the sea.	I found a purse full of money.
c) I was doing aerobics.	She heard a noise downstairs.
d) They were walking through the jungle.	I twisted my ankle.
e) He was having lunch with his boss.	He broke her favourite vase.
f) She was reading in bed.	He spilt red wine over her white suit.
g) He was washing up.	Sue nearly stood on a snake.

3   Say what happened after each of the events above. Example:
'When I found the purse, I took it to the police station.'

See **Use your grammar,** pages 40 and 41, for further practice of the Past Simple, Past Continuous and *used to.*

Time expressions

1   Which of the words in the box can you use with the expressions below?

ago   last   this   in   at   on   during

a) Friday   *last/this/on*
b) Christmas
c) January
d) the afternoon
e) ages
f) winter
g) the weekend
h) the 19th century

2   Write down five dates or time expressions that have some significance to you. Examples:
5th May 1972   last Monday

Then tell other people in the class why your dates are important to you and what happened. Example:
'On the 5th of May 1972 my son was born.'

PRONUNCIATION

Past Simple

1 [🔊 3.2]   The Past Simple endings of regular verbs have three different pronunciations. Listen to the pronunciation of these examples:
asked /t/   *arrived* /d/   *started* /ɪd/

Listen to the pronunciation of the following Past Simple verbs. Tick the appropriate column according to the sound of their endings. One has been done for you.

	/t/	/d/	/ɪd/
a) asked	✓		
b) tasted			
c) retired			
d) drifted			
e) appeared			
f) talked			
g) tried			
h) waited			

2   What is the rule for the pronunciation of the Past Simple endings of regular verbs? Check your ideas with Section 1 in the *Language reference*.

Past Continuous

1 [🔊 3.3]   Listen to the following exchange. There is a circle round the weak form of *was* (/wəz/) and the strong form (/wɒz/) is underlined.
'He ⟨was⟩ driving too fast.' 'Was he?'

2 [🔊 3.4]   Check with Section 2 in the *Language reference* for when *was* and *were* are strong and when they are weak. Then listen to the following sentences and circle the weak forms and underline the strong forms. Finally, practise reading the sentences.

a) I was eating my lunch when he arrived.
b) Was it an accident, or did he do it on purpose?
c) While they were playing football they broke a
   window.
d) I'm not sure, but I think they were.
e) It wasn't possible to fly there direct.
f) She was having a drink when he arrived.

LEARNING FOCUS 2

Keeping vocabulary records

Remembering what words mean
Here is an example of an entry from a Spanish learner's vocabulary book.

> *mask* (n) = máscara - a covering for the face, used as a disguise.
> e.g. They were wearing a mask and we couldn't see their faces.
> *masked* (adj) = encapuchado - wearing a mask (like a kidnapper). e.g. He was kidnapped by masked men.

1   What do *n* and *adj* mean?

2   What are the abbreviations for the following?

a) verb b) adverb c) preposition d) example

3   What three methods has the Spanish learner used to record the meaning of the words she wanted to remember? Which of these methods do you prefer?

Organising a vocabulary notebook
1   Discuss how you keep vocabulary records. Make a note of an item of new vocabulary that you want to remember from this unit. Compare with a partner.

2   Read these suggestions for how to record vocabulary.

– Keep two vocabulary notebooks for recording new vocabulary: a small one, that you carry around with you (so that whenever you meet a new word or expression you can write it down); and a larger notebook in which at the end of the day you can write down the words you want to remember.
– Keep a few pages for each 'theme' (e.g. *Clothes*). This helps you find vocabulary quickly.
– Divide each page into different parts of speech, e.g.
   Verbs: *try on* (Past Simple: *tried on*)
   Nouns: *blouse*   **Adjectives:** *stylish*
– Have a few pages at the back of your vocabulary book for words that do not fit in your 'themes'. Try to organise them alphabetically, or into parts of speech.

3   Write down some of the words you want to remember from the first three units. For example, for Unit 1 start a section on *Interests*.

SPEAKING

You are going on a three-week 'adventure' walking holiday in Northern Thailand. You will be walking through jungle and across high hills in a remote part of the country where there are very few people and a lot of wild animals. You hope to stay with families in small villages. You can carry only a rucksack and it must not be too heavy. You have already packed the basic clothes and food supplies you will need, and you will have your money in your pocket. You have only got room left for *ten* more items. You are going to meet your travelling companion in Thailand and you will not be in contact before you set off on the trip.

1   Look at the items in the box and decide which ones you will definitely *not* take. Then put the rest of the items in order of priority.

soap and toothpaste   mosquito cream   tent compass   swimming costume   water bottle map   binoculars   water-purifying tablets Thai phrasebook   matches   sunglasses cassette recorder   knife and fork   towel camera   radio   torch   notepad and pen

2   Discuss your list in groups, justifying your choices. Agree on the ten things you want to take, in order of importance. You might want to use expressions like these:

Making suggestions
Let's take . . .
Shall we . . . ?
Why don't we . . . ?

Giving opinions
I think we should
  take . . . because . . .

Agreeing/disagreeing
Great idea!
Rubbish!
I think that's a good/
  silly idea.
Yes, but . . .

WRITING

Linking expressions

1   Read the newspaper report and then, in pairs, decide on the main facts of the story.

Into the mouth of the volcano

In 1986 Shell Sanders, a young American, arrived in Sumatra, an island in Indonesia, to climb one of the active volcanoes. (As soon as) he got there he tried to find a guide (but,) unfortunately, the only guide was out of town. Although it was a dangerous climb, Shell decided to go up alone. Before he left, Shell said goodbye to Esther, the manager of his hotel.

When he got to the top of the 9,000 foot volcano there was fog everywhere. While he was looking down 120 feet into the mouth of the volcano, he fell in and nearly killed himself.

Four days later, when her guest didn't return, Esther realised she must do something. However, she didn't know who to ask. Finally, she asked a local man to help. The man communicated with spirits, who told her where Shell was. He said that, as well as broken bones, he had bad spirits inside him, too.

Eventually, the police found the injured man and took him to hospital.

2   *As soon as* and *but* are linking expressions. Circle eleven other linking expressions in the text. List them in the columns below according to whether they add extra information (*addition*), indicate when something happened (*time*), or contrast facts (*contrast*).

ADDITION	TIME	CONTRAST
	as soon as	*but*

3 [📼 3.5]   Work in groups. Last year, Francesca went to Australia.

a) Listen to the sounds on the recording and guess:
  – why she made the trip.
  – what happened to her.

b) Write a story based on the sounds, using linking expressions. Begin: *Last year . . .* Add two or three sentences to give the story either a happy or a sad ending.

Language reference

1 Past Simple

USE

We use the Past Simple to talk about something that:
– took place at a specific time in the past.
– is finished.
It does not matter if the events are short, long or repeated, or if they are in the near past or the distant past. We always think of them as complete events.

Sue **went** to Sri Lanka last week. She **stayed** in Jaffna.
She **went** abroad four times the year before, too.

The Past Simple is often used with time expressions such as: *ago, last Sunday, on Tuesday, when I was young.*

FORM *See page 157.*

PRONUNCIATION

There are three different ways of pronouncing the endings of regular verbs in the Past Simple.

/d/ after a vowel (e.g. /i:/) or a voiced consonant (e.g. /b/, /g/, /v/, /ð/, /l/, /z/, /dʒ/, /ʒ/, /m/, /n/, /ŋ/): e.g. arriv**ed**, climb**ed**

/t/ when the previous sound is not voiced (e.g. /p/, /k/, /f/, /θ/, /s/, /ʃ/, /tʃ/): e.g. talk**ed**, ask**ed**

/ɪd/ when the previous sound is /t/ or /d/: e.g. tast**ed**, drift**ed**

SPELLING OF REGULAR VERBS IN THE PAST SIMPLE

With verbs of one syllable, one vowel and one consonant; double the consonant: e.g. *stop → stopped*
In two-syllable verbs, double the consonant if the stress is on the second syllable: e.g. *pre'fer → preferred*
If the verb ends in a consonant + *y*, change to *ied*: e.g. *try → tried*

2 Past Continuous

USE

For activities in progress at some time in the past:
It **was raining** at 8 o'clock yesterday morning.
To describe a longer background activity during which a shorter completed action (Past Simple) takes place.
When the kidnappers **broke** into the house, we **were watching** a video.

```
                ... the kidnappers broke into the house ...
                                    ✗
 ─────────────────────────────────────────────────────────
 PAST            (... were watching a video)          NOW
```

Unlike the Past Simple, the Past Continuous gives no indication if the action is finished or not.
I **was painting** the house yesterday afternoon. (We don't know if the painting is finished.)
I **painted** the living room. (It's finished.)
The Past Continuous is frequently used in descriptions.
Shell was very happy. He **was wearing** a new pair of shoes and **carrying** his favourite rucksack.

FORM *See page 157.*

PRONUNCIATION

In connected speech *was* and *were* are usually pronounced /wəz/ and /wə/.
He was right and they were wrong.
Was and *were* are pronounced /wɒz/ and /wɜ:/ when they are emphasised or when they come at the beginning or end of a sentence.
'**Was** he right?' 'Yes, he **was**.' /wɒz/
Note the pronunciation of the negative forms.
'I wasn't late.' /wɒznt/ 'We weren't happy.' /wɜ:nt/

3 Past Simple or *used to*?

USE

Used to is important when we want to contrast habitual events and states which existed in the past but which have been discontinued.
She **used to** visit us (but she doesn't any more).
Unlike the Past Simple, *used to* does not refer to single past events.
I **got up** very late yesterday. (NOT ... *used to get up* ...)
Used to can stand alone without a time expression, as it already means 'at an indefinite time in the past'.
I **used to** speak Spanish means I **spoke** Spanish at some time in the past (but I don't now).

FORM *See page 157.*

PRONUNCIATION

Used to is usually pronounced in its weak form: /'ju:stə/.
We **used to** play a lot of football.
In short answers, it is pronounced in its strong form: /'ju:stu:/.
'Do you play football?' 'No, but I **used to**.'

4 Time prepositions

at: refers to exact time (I'll see you **at** five past six.)
on: refers to days of the week and dates (**on** Monday, **on** May 1st)
in: refers to some time during a period (**in** the evening, **in** May, **in** spring)
during: refers to a whole period (I'll be away **during** July.) or some point within a period (He left **during** the film.)

5 Linking expressions

Some linking expressions come under the categories of addition, time and contrast. Some of the expressions found in this unit are:
addition: *and, as well as, too*
time: *before, when, while, finally, later, as soon as, eventually*
contrast: *but, although, however*
Some of these expressions can connect parts of a sentence.
Although it was dangerous, he decided to do it.
Others can connect ideas across sentences.
I'd love to come. **However**, I'm busy at the moment.

Home thoughts from abroad

READING 1

Before reading

1   With a partner, discuss the advantages and disadvantages of living in your country.

2   You are going to read two short extracts by non-British people living in Britain. Write down three positive things and three negative things you think they might mention about living in Britain.

Reading

1   Read the first text quickly and answer the following questions.

a) What nationality is the person?
b) Is his impression of Britain generally good or bad?

2   Make notes on Richard Shortway's opinions of:

a) the people.   *He loves them . . .*
b) the public services.
c) the weather.
d) the countryside/towns.
e) the cost of living.

What would he think of your country?

3   What does Richard Shortway *really* think of estate agents?

4   Richard Shortway says he likes the social atmosphere. What type of people does he seem to like?

5   Notice that he says *'I've met Prince Edward'* but *'at a polo match I had a long talk . . .'* (paragraph 2). Why does he use two different verb forms? Check your answer with Section 1 in the *Language reference*.

6   Read the text again quickly.

a) What other things does he say he has done in England? Example:
He's been to shooting parties.
b) Find one example of where he talks about doing something at a specific time.

1   I've always loved London – it's a passion of mine. I think it's one of the great cities of the world.

2   I love the people here. I've been invited to everything – shooting parties, polo, Wimbledon, Royal Ascot. I've met Prince Edward, and at a polo match I had a long talk with Prince Charles. He's absolutely charming. It's a super social atmosphere here. I can't believe, though, how much people eat and drink.

Richard Shortway, publishing director

3   One thing I've learned is never to call British Gas. All they do is turn off your gas – and then send you a bill for doing it. I couldn't believe that. I think British Telecom is impossible. In New York you get a phone in three days – here I was told three months. You call directory enquiries and you get a busy signal – that's *unheard* of in the States. I call America – and I get cut off. Why?

4   I've had dealings too with the wonderful estate agents of London. You can be – what is it? – gazumped. Nowhere else in the world could you agree to buy a flat, put your money down – and then have the guy sell it to somebody else.

5   I like tennis, but I have hardly played here because of the weather. Last summer seemed to last about a week and that was it. I went to the Cotswolds and to Devon, both beautiful. I've always loved the British ambience, and British clothes. I really wonder, though, how you manage to live on the salaries that are paid here. London is every bit as expensive as New York.

ambience (paragraph 5): the character, quality and atmosphere of a place

(from *YOU*)

VOCABULARY

Deducing meaning

1   The following words from the text are connected to life in Britain. Use the context to work out what they refer to.

a) *British Telecom* (paragraph 3)
b) *estate agents* (paragraph 4)
c) *gazumped* (paragraph 4)

2   The expressions below are called *phrasal verbs* (a group of words containing a verb that acts like a single verb). Choose the correct definitions.

a) *turn off* (paragraph 3)
   i) start   ii) stop (the flow of . . .)
b) *cut off* (paragraph 3)
   i) disconnect   ii) connect
c) *put down* (paragraph 4)
   i) pay (a deposit)   ii) collect

3   The following expressions in **bold** type are 'Americanisms'. (Note that the first expression is now often also used in British English.) Find out the British English equivalents.

a) *I call America* (paragraph 3)
b) *you get a busy signal* (paragraph 3)
c) *have the guy sell it to somebody else* (paragraph 4)

Ask other people in the class if they know any more Americanisms and their British English equivalents.

4   Decide on how to group any new words you want to remember and put them into your vocabulary notebook. (See page 23 in Unit 3.)

READING 2

1   Read the article by Chantal Cüer and make notes on the topics discussed. Compare your notes with a partner.

Chantal Cüer, TV presenter

I fell in love with England because it was so quaint – all those little houses, looking terrible old-fashioned but nice, like dolls' houses. I loved the countryside and the pubs, and I loved London. I've slightly changed my mind after seventeen years because I think it's a filthy town now.

Things have changed. For everybody, England represented gentlemen, fair play, good manners. The fair play is going, unfortunately, and so are the gentlemanly attitudes and good manners – people slam doors in your face and courtesy is vanishing.

I regret that there are so few comfortable meeting places. You're forced to live indoors. In Paris I go out much more, to restaurants and nightclubs. To meet friends here it usually has to be in a pub, and it can be difficult to go there alone as a woman. The cafés are not terribly nice.

As a woman, I feel more threatened here. I spend a bomb on taxis because I will not take public transport after 10 p.m. I *used* to use it, but now I'm afraid.

The concept of the family seems to be more or less non-existent in England. My family is very closely knit and that's typically French. In Middlesex I had a neighbour who is 82 now. His family only lived two miles away, but I took him to France for Christmas once because he was always alone.

(from *YOU*)

closely knit: tightly connected, doing lots of things together

2   If you have visited or know about Britain, give your opinions about life there. Do you agree with the opinions expressed in the two texts you have read?

LANGUAGE POINTS

Past experiences and events

1   Work in pairs. Using the cues below, take it in turns to ask about what your partner has done. Ask for more details using words like *when, how, what* and *why*. Example:
be / to Disneyland?
A: *Have you ever been to Disneyland?*
B: *Yes, I have.*
A: *Really? When did you go?*
B: *Two years ago. (I went there two years ago.)*

STUDENT A
a) win / competition
b) have / nightmare
c) meet / somebody famous
d) be / on safari
e) be / to hospital
f) ride / horse
g) see / lion
h) lose / anything important

STUDENT B
a) give / big party
b) be / to Hungary
c) hold / snake
d) have / car accident
e) work / in factory
f) feel / embarrassed
g) eat / caviar
h) steal / anything

2   Work with a partner and take it in turns to pretend you have done the things in the pictures. Your partner does not believe you and asks more questions. (Example. *'Rubbish! I don't believe you. When did you do that?'*)

3   Talk about past events and experiences in your own life, using the cues below and any appropriate past verb forms (e.g. the Present Perfect, the Past Simple, the Past Continuous).

a) I remember a very cold day when . . .
b) On my last birthday . . .
c) I have never . . .
d) I have just . . .
e) Ten years ago . . .
f) . . . in my life

Time expressions

Complete the sentences, using the time expressions in the box. Try to use a different expression for each sentence.

| already | just | in November | recently |
| yet | before | always | two seconds ago |

a) 'Would you like an expresso coffee?' 'Thanks, but I've _____ had one.'
b) 'Have you seen Liz _____?' 'No, not for a few weeks.'
c) It was grandfather's eightieth birthday _____ .
d) 'Can I have the newspaper?' 'I haven't finished with it _____ . You can have it later.'
e) What an amazing computer! I haven't seen one like that _____ .
f) 'Have you been to the shops _____? That was quick!'
g) I saw Francisco _____ .
h) I have _____ hated swimming.

> See **Use your grammar,** page 41, for further practice of the Present Perfect and the Past Simple.

Question tags

Check the rules for question tags with Section 2 in the *Language reference* and match the statements in column A with the question tags in column B. One has been done for you.

A
a) You know Stephen,
b) They'll check the flight,
c) She took the dog for a walk,
d) You've been here already,
e) We don't need to book,
f) She can swim,
g) You couldn't lend me some money,

B
do we?
can't she?
could you?
don't you?
won't they?
didn't she?
haven't you?

PRONUNCIATION

Intonation in question tags

[📼 4.1]   Listen to the sentences from the last exercise. Decide whether you think the speaker is certain or uncertain (waiting for confirmation) and tick the appropriate column. Example:
You know Stephen, don't you? (certain)
You know Stephen, don't you? (uncertain)

	CERTAIN	UNCERTAIN
a)	✓	
b)		
c)		
d)		
e)		
f)		
g)		

In pairs, practise the questions, with one person asking the questions and the other person giving a reply. Pay particular attention to the intonation in the questions. Example:
'You know Stephen, don't you?' 'Yes, I do.' OR *'No, I don't, actually.'*

Contracted forms

[📼 4.2]   Listen to the recording and count the words in each of the five sentences. Example:
Where's she been? (= *Where has she been?* – 4 words)

Listen again and write down each sentence, using the contracted form (e.g. *Where's* for *Where has*) where possible.

LEARNING FOCUS

Keeping a grammar book

You may find it helpful to write down in a notebook or in another part of your vocabulary book areas of grammar which you find difficult. You might like to make a record of the rules given by your teacher or from the *Language reference*, or you might prefer to express the rules in your own way.

Read what a student from Germany has written about the Present Perfect.

Work in pairs. Try to write the rules for how to use the Present Simple. Then check what you have written with the *Language reference* pages in Units 1 and 2.

> *Present Perfect*
> *I have seen the Statue of Liberty. (important past experience – when it happened not important)*
>
> *Past Simple*
> *I saw the Tower of London last year. (definite time)*
>
> *In spoken German we can use the Present Perfect for definite time.*
>
> *Expressions often used with the Present Perfect: ever, never, already, not yet, before.*

Ways of learning English

1 [4.3]   Listen to Dany, a nineteen-year-old Brazilian who has reached a good intermediate level in English. She is talking about the strategies she finds useful when she is learning English.

a) Which of these opinions would Dany agree with?
    i) You do not need vocabulary to be fluent in a language.
    ii) You can learn vocabulary from watching TV.
    iii) You always have to make a lot of effort to learn any new word.
    iv) Trying to correct yourself is not important.
    v) It is important to be corrected.
b) Which do you agree with?

2   Which of these opinions are true for yourself?

> I can understand people and talk fluently but I do make a lot of mistakes.

> I am good at grammar but I'm not very good at communicating with people.

3   When Dany remembers a word she has heard on TV she tries to check its meaning in the dictionary. How do *you* try to improve your vocabulary? Explain why you find your methods useful.

4   Is good pronunciation important? Give your reasons. If you feel good pronunciation is important, how do you try to improve it?

5   Which of these activities do you find most useful in your English classes?

a) Practising speaking in pairs or groups.
b) Doing written work on your own.
c) Listening to the teacher. / Listening to a cassette recorder.
d) Using a dictionary or a grammar book.

e) Reading texts.
f) Doing written grammar exercises.
g) Oral grammar practice.

Which other activities do you find useful?

Learner diaries

Some students like to keep a diary where they write about their progress in learning English and describe how they feel about it.

Look at the extracts from four learner diaries on the page opposite.

a) What do you agree or disagree with in the diaries?
b) What do you think of the method the teacher has used to correct the students' work? What do the different symbols stand for?

You asked us about correction. I prefer if you wrote on the pages what was wrong because after I will read all the compositions again and for me it's all right if she just writes on the paper what was wrong I will read it and I will study it. If you just underline then I have to ask what was wrong and then this is boring because I feel I am losing my time.

I like writing and one of the lessons which I liked most was when my teacher asked us to close the eyes and started telling us about some place. It was very nice and I began imagineing exciting new expereince and I could write things I hadn't written before.

Today we listened to a tape of two people speaking together. It made me feel depresed. I didn't like it. My listening is not very good – for me if I am speaking or listening face to face I can understand everything but if I listen to a tape I can't understand it very good – I don't know why, maybe because I can't see the mouth and lips.

I think grammar is neccesary – if it wasn't I wouldn't stay here I would just go and work somewhere in England. Here we can mix all the things like reading and speaking. I don't like the traditional class. But I think it is good when the teacher gives us exercises to do at home that we have practiced in the class.

I love to have a vocabulary book. I've had it since I first started learning English – since I was 12. I still have my books and it's very interest to come back to them.

WRITING

Spelling

Correct spelling is very important, particularly in pieces of formal writing. To train yourself to correct your own spelling, do a *draft* of your text and then go through it quickly and underline the words that look wrong. Then try to write out the words you are not sure about in different ways to see which one looks right.

Here are some other techniques.
– Leave a gap for the bit of the word you are unsure of and try to complete the word with different spellings. Which looks right?
  rec ___ ve: receeve, receave, recieve, receive (= *receive*)
– Think of words with a similar pattern. Is the rule the same?
  hurry → hurries is like *fly → flies* and *try → tries*.
– Break the word into bits and look at each bit (e.g. *mech/an/ic/al*).

Finally:
– Check the spelling in a dictionary.
– Record the word in your vocabulary notebook together with some other words with similar spelling.
– If possible, think of a memory trick to help you remember the spelling, e.g. *receive: 'i before e, except after c'*. (This is a rhyme taught to children in Britain.)

1　The words in *italics* below are spelt incorrectly. If necessary, use some of the techniques above to correct them.

a) When you pay, ask the taxi driver for a *reciet*.
b) I was very *mizerable* on *Thersday*.
c) Why are you *smilling*?
d) I want to cut my nails. Pass the *sissers*.
e) How did you get on in your *examinashon*?
f) I'm glad you're *happyer* now.

2　Look at the learner diaries again.

a) Underline the spelling mistakes and write *sp* in the margin.
b) Write out the words with their correct spelling.

3　Over the next few lessons, keep a diary of what you do in your English lessons. Note your impressions of the lessons.

Language reference

1 Present Perfect

USE

In general, the Present Perfect (*has / have walked*) connects the present and the past and refers to the past from the point of view of the present. The Present Perfect is used for:

a) Talking about recent past experience important at the time of speaking.
   *'Look! The taxi **has arrived**.'* *'Yes, I know. Let's go.'*

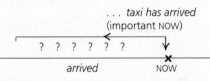

... taxi has arrived
(important NOW)

PAST   arrived   NOW

The results of the recent action are still there in the present.
*Here is the news. A Boeing 707 **has crashed** on the outskirts of Rome.*
*I**'ve poured** you a drink. Here it is.*
*I**'ve** just **finished** this book. You can have it back now.*

b) Talking about general past experience – indefinite time. At the moment of speaking it doesn't matter when the experience happened. The important thing is the experience itself.
   *'**Have** you **been** to New York?'* *'No, but I**'ve been** to Washington.'* (It doesn't matter when.)

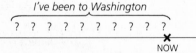

I've been to Washington

PAST   NOW

When we refer to a specific occasion in the past and to the details of what happened we use the Past Simple. With the Past Simple the past is separated from the present.
   *'I **went** to Disneyland last year. I **met** Mickey Mouse.'*
   *'Really! What **did** you **say** to him?'*

... went to Disneyland
last year

PAST   NOW

The Present Perfect Simple is often used with indefinite time adverbials: *ever, never, already, yet, before, just, recently, always*.
   *I have never ridden a horse **before**.*
   *'Have you seen Bob **yet**?'*
(For the Present Perfect with *for* and *since* see Unit 13.)

FORM

Have / has + past participle (regular verbs: add *(e)d* to the base form of the verb; irregular verbs: see list on page 159).

AFFIRMATIVE
*I / You / We / They**'ve** (**have**) lived abroad.* *She**'s** (**has**) lived abroad.*

NEGATIVE
*We **haven't** (**have not**) been there.* *He **hasn't** (**has not**) seen me.*

QUESTION
*Where **have** they **been**?* *What**'s** she **done**? (What has . . .)*

SHORT ANSWER

'Have you found it yet?' *'Yes, I **have**.'* / *'No, I **haven't**.'*
   (NOT *~~Yes, I've.~~*)
'Has he finished?' *'Yes, he **has**.'* / *'No, he **hasn't**.'*
   (NOT *~~Yes, he's.~~*)

Note that *go* has two past participles: *been* and *gone*. Compare their meanings:
– *They**'ve been** to Rome.* (... and they have come back again.) *They hope to go again next year.*
– *They**'ve gone** to Rome.* (... and they are still there.) *They intend to stay there for two years.*

PRONUNCIATION

The verb *have* is usually contracted in speech and informal writing (*I have → I**'ve**; he has → he**'s***).

It is sometimes difficult to tell the difference between the contracted *is* and the contracted *has* (*It**'s** finished = It **has** finished; It**'s** finished = It **is** finished*).

Forms of *have* are not contracted when they are stressed (*'**Has** she finished?'* *'Yes, she **has**.'*).

2 Question tags

USE

In many languages, when we ask someone to agree with or confirm what we have said, there is a single fixed expression to convey the idea of 'don't you agree?'. In English, question tags vary in form and can convey different meanings depending on the intonation used.

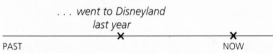

   *'You**'ve** been to Russia, **haven't** you?'* (certain)
   'Yes, I have.'
   *'You **haven't** got any matches, **have** you?'* (uncertain)
   'I'm not sure. I'll have a look.'

FORM

If the main verb in the statement has an auxiliary (like *has / have*), a modal auxiliary (like *will, can, must*) or a form of the verb *be* (*is / are*), the tag consists of the same auxiliary.
   *You**'ve** been here already, **haven't** you?*
   *He**'ll** think we're out, **won't** he?*
   *She**'s** right, **isn't** she?*
The verb *do / does* is used in the tag when there is no auxiliary or modal auxiliary (e.g. *has, will,* etc.) or verb *be* in the main clause.
   *Paul **plays** chess, **doesn't** he?*
   *Carl and Lizzie **got** married, **didn't** they?*
If the statement is positive (*It's raining outside . . .*) the tag is usually negative (*It's raining outside, **isn't it**?*). With a negative statement (*The English aren't unfriendly*) the tag is usually positive (*The English **aren't** friendly, **are they**?*).

A bit windy

LISTENING

Before listening

1 Match the headlines with the photographs.

a **Coastal towns hit by flooding**

b **EARLY SNOW CATCHES LONDON BY SURPRISE**

c **Hurricane winds batter Caribbean island**

d **Second year of drought for South of France**

2 Look at the photographs and say what you think has happened in each of them. Have you ever experienced any extreme weather conditions like these?

3 Opinions about the weather.

a) What kind of weather do you like best?
b) How would you describe the weather in your country?
c) What effect do you think weather has on a nation's character?

Listening

1 [5.1]   Listen to the recording and decide which of these is the best summary of the weather report.

a) There will be a hurricane, but only in Spain and France.
b) There won't be a hurricane, and it will only be windy in Spain and France.
c) There won't be a hurricane, but it will be very windy, especially in Spain and France.

2 [5.2]   Listen to a second weather report. This was broadcast the day after the report in Exercise 1.

a) Why do you think the weather forecaster in the first report became famous?
b) Read the summary below. Then listen to the recording again and complete the gaps.

'Hurricane-force winds battered much of ____(1)____ England in the small hours. At least ____(2)____ people have died and many more were ____(3)____ , hit by falling ____(4)____ and masonry toppled in the ____(5)____ . Power ____(6)____ have been disrupted and large sections of the ____(7)____ network were left out of action. Our reporters have been assessing the scale of the ____(8)____ and the ____(9)____ . We begin with the ____(10)____ from the south coast.'

3 [5.3]   Listen to the reports from Southampton and London.

a) How do the reporters introduce themselves?
b) What tense do they use when they first talk about the situation – Past Simple or Present Perfect?
c) Which tense do they continue in?

4   Listen to the two reports again.

a) What have been torn off in Southampton?
b) What have partially collapsed?
c) What happened overnight in the emergency centres?
d) How many people were killed in London?
e) How fast were the winds?
f) How did the man in Croydon die?

VOCABULARY 1

Weather

1   Match the adjectives in box A with the nouns they often go with in box B. There may be more than one possibility.

A

| heavy | thick |
| strong | dense |

B

| fog | wind |
| rain | cloud |

2   Choose the most appropriate word in the box to complete the gaps.

| dull   drizzling   showers   overcast   pouring |

a) Scattered _____ are expected so take your umbrella!
b) The match was abandoned because of the _____ rain.
c) What _____ weather! I hate it when the sky is _____ .
d) It was only _____ so we didn't put our umbrellas up.

3   Put the nouns in the box in order, with the strongest first.

| gale   breeze   strong wind   hurricane |

4   In which of the following sentences is the weather the hottest? Put them in order beginning with the hottest.

a) It's a bit chilly out there. You'd better take a coat.
b) Stephen said they didn't stay on the beach very long – it was absolutely boiling!
c) It's very mild for November, isn't it?
d) This weather gives me a headache – it's too heavy and close.
e) It's freezing outside. I'm staying indoors.

5   Describe what the weather is like at the moment.

6 [5.4]   Listen to the four sounds on the recording and say what the weather is like in each case.

LANGUAGE POINT 1

Predictions and decisions

Look at the pictures.

Which of the four speakers:

a) makes a sudden decision at the time of speaking?
b) has made a decision or plan before speaking?
c) makes a prediction based on something that is already in the process of happening?
d) gives a personal opinion which he/she seems very sure about?

Check with Sections 1 and 2 in the *Language reference* and make sure that you know how *will* and *going to* are used.

PRACTICE

1 Use *going to* to discuss your plans for:

a) your next holiday.
b) this evening.
c) the weekend.
d) a month's time.

Example:
'I'm going to stay with my parents.' (/'gəʊɪŋ tə/)

Note that the *to* in *going to* is usually pronounced weakly in continuous speech (/tə/). The strong form is used in short answers:
'No, I'm not going to.' (/tuː/).
If you have made no plans, say what you will probably do:
'I think we'll probably stay at home.'
Remember that in continuous speech *will* is usually contracted (e.g. *we'll* /wiːəl/) unless it is in a short answer:
'Yes, we will.' (/wɪl/).

2 Which of the things below will happen sometime in the future? Tick the sentences you agree with. Put a cross next to the sentences you think will never happen. Put a question mark next to those you are not sure about. Compare your answers in pairs.

a) Robots will do our housework.
b) There will be a cure for the common cold.
c) Cigarette smoking will be illegal.
d) Nobody will use cash to buy things.
e) There will be no more famine in the world.
f) Most people will live for at least a hundred years.
g) We will eat pills instead of food.
h) We will be able to control the weather more than we do now.
i) Holidays in space will be normal.
j) We will be able to replace most parts of our bodies.

3 Look at boxes A and B and write down at least one more expression for each.

A Opinions

I think	I'm sure	There definitely won't be

B Time expressions

by the year 2500	in a hundred years' time

4 In groups, discuss your answers to Exercise 2 using some of the expressions in Exercise 3.
Example:
'I'm sure there won't be any more famine in the world by the year 2500 because . . .'

What other things do you think will happen in the future?

5 Use *will* or *going to* in these sentences.

a) 'Have you got any aspirins?' 'Yes, I think I've got some upstairs. I (*go*) and get you one.'
b) 'I hear Brian's giving up work.' 'Yes, apparently he's got a place at college. He (*study*) law.'
c) 'Have you been invited to dinner, too?' 'Yes. Belinda's cooking. I expect it (*be*) awful!'
d) 'Do you like this present I've got for Margaret?' 'Yes, I'm sure she (*love*) it.'
e) 'Have you made plans for this evening?' 'Yes. I (*finish*) this work and then I probably (*watch*) the film on BBC2 at 10 o'clock. Why?'
f) 'Your mother phoned earlier while you were out.' 'Oh really? OK, I (*phone*) her after dinner.'
g) 'Have you decided what you (*order*) for the main course?' 'I can't make up my mind. Yes, I think I (*have*) the duck, please.'

6 Work in pairs. What do you think would be said in these situations? Use *will* or *going to*.
Example:
The phone rings. Your friend offers to answer it.
You say, *'It's OK. I'll answer it.'*

a) Gillian is discussing her plans for decorating the house. *'I . . . '*
b) Pam tells Adam what she has decided to buy her parents for Christmas. *'I . . . '*
c) The sky has gone very dark. *'Look, it . . . '*
d) Sara is very worried about her exam. Her friend says: *'Don't worry. I'm sure . . . '*
e) Mr Cartland tries to lift a box that is too heavy for him. Gary warns him: *'Be careful or . . . '*

> See **Use your grammar**, page 41, for further practice of *will* and *going to* for predictions, offers and decisions.

LANGUAGE POINT 2

Verbs and prepositions

Notice in the following exercise that after the preposition there is either a noun or the *-ing* form of the verb.

In pairs, choose a preposition from the box to fit the gaps in the sentences below.

about	in	for	of	for	on	in	on
with	about						

a) They apologised _____ arriving late.
b) She agrees _____ you.
c) I've decided _____ Bali for my next holiday.
d) What were you talking _____?
e) Don't worry _____ me! I'm OK.
f) Do you believe _____ fairies?
g) I can't concentrate _____ my work today.
h) I succeeded _____ changing his mind.
i) Good idea, but think _____ the cost.
j) Our course prepares you _____ the exam.

LISTENING AND SPEAKING

1 [🔊 5.5] When British people want to start up a conversation with someone they don't know, they often begin by talking about the weather. Listen to the recording and write down the weather expressions used.

2 In pairs, compare your notes and practise saying the weather expressions.

3 Use similar expressions to start up conversations with your partner. Imagine you are in the following situations.

a) You are sitting next to an attractive stranger on a railway station.
b) You are in the dentist's waiting room and very nervous. You try to start a conversation with the receptionist.

READING AND SPEAKING

A news broadcast

1   Look at the newspaper report below. You are going to prepare a story for a television news broadcast based on the report.

Write down:

a) the names of the people involved.
b) exactly what happened.
c) what the weather conditions were like.

'Second time unlucky' tree-car drama

A delivery man, Mr Philip Shaw, found himself involved in a rescue drama during the gale last Thursday.

He and a colleague were driving along towards Cambridge when 'about six trees came down just seconds before we got there'.

Said Mr Shaw: 'It all happened as we approached. The roof of a car was all crushed in and there were two old men trapped inside.'

The two delivery men tried to pull the tree off, but it was too heavy. In the end they had to break the windscreen and pull the old men out through there. 'It was lucky we were around. It took the fire brigade about thirty minutes to get there,' said Mr Shaw.

The rescued men were Mr George Kidd, aged 80, and his 78-year-old brother-in-law, Mr William Ollington. Both escaped with shock and minor injuries.

It was the second time a tree had crushed their car, and in the same place.

Two years ago, during the October hurricane,

they had had their first lucky escape when another falling tree crushed their car in the same road!

'It's a very funny thing to happen twice,' said Mr Kidd. 'We are very fortunate. On both occasions I was driving a yellow car so I don't think I'll get another one.'

(from the *Cambridge Weekly News*)

2   Think back to the radio news broadcast (*Recording 2*) at the beginning of the unit. Remember how the newsreader began by announcing the news using the Present Perfect and then reported the events in the Past Simple.

Work in three groups.

GROUP A	GROUP B	GROUP C
You are the television newsreader. Plan a short report using the newspaper text for your facts.	You are the television reporter sent to Cambridge to interview Mr Shaw. What questions will you ask him?	You are Mr Shaw. What will you say about the rescue? Remember to report what Mr Kidd said about the yellow car.

3   Act out the broadcast in groups of three.

a) One of you is the television newsreader. Briefly tell the story of what happened and introduce the reporter from Cambridge.
b) The reporter should interview Mr Shaw about his experiences.

VOCABULARY 2

Telephoning

1 Put the lines in the following two telephone conversations into the correct order.

A

a) Do you want him to phone you back?
b) Hello, is that Ann? This is Penny.
c) I'm afraid he's just gone out.
d) Is Steve in, please?
e) Norwich 21523.
f) No, I'll phone back later, thanks.
g) Hi, Penny.
h) Oh dear. I needed to speak to him urgently.

B

a) James Wilson.
b) Could you put me through to extension 631, please?
c) Good morning. MacArthur and Company.
d) Yes, certainly. What name is it, please?
e) Actually, I'll just leave a message, if I may.
f) I'm sorry, the line is engaged. Would you like to hold?

2 Practise reading the conversations in pairs.

3 In what ways is the 'telephone procedure' different in your own country? For example, what do you say when you pick up the phone? How do you ask to speak to somebody?

CREATIVE WRITING

This photograph shows an example of the damage caused by the storm which you heard about at the beginning of the unit.

1 You are going to write the telephone conversation the man is having in the telephone box. Use your imagination and decide:

a) who the man is speaking to.
b) what has happened. Give details.
c) what he has decided to do.

2 Quickly make a draft version of the telephone dialogue. Remember to use contracted forms (e.g. *'I've got a problem.'* NOT *'I have got a problem.'*). (You may want to use some of the 'telephone vocabulary' practised in the section above.)

3 Show your draft to another student. How can it be improved? Are the spelling and punctuation correct? Ask for suggestions.

4 Rewrite the dialogue as carefully as you can.

5 Act out the dialogues.

Language reference

In English there is no formal future tense as there is in many other languages. In this unit, *going to* + base form is contrasted with *will*. Which form you choose depends on the situation and how you see the future at the moment of speaking.

1 Predictions and sudden decisions (*will*)

USE

Will expresses the speaker's opinion at the moment of speaking. It is often used in reaction to something in the present to make a confident prediction or a sudden decision.

> '*Is Tom cooking? In that case I'm sure the meal* **will be** *awful.*' (confident prediction)
> '*Oh, no! It's raining! I'll bring the washing in.*' (sudden decision)

Will is often used to make requests (**Will** *you close the door, please?*), promises (*I* **won't** *tell anyone.*), refusals (*I* **won't** *do it.*), warnings (*Be careful! You'll hurt yourself.*), and offers (*I'll help you.*).
In predictions, the speaker often assumes that an event is sure to happen.

> *The weather* **will be** *cold with some fog until midday.*

Note that *shall* is usually only used for suggestions and offers.

> **Shall** *we meet tomorrow?*
> **Shall** *I collect you?*

FORM See page 158.
Will + base form of the verb.

AFFIRMATIVE
*I / You / We / He / They***'ll** (**will**) **be** *all right.*

NEGATIVE
I **won't** (**will not**) **say** *it to you again.*

QUESTION
When **will** *they* **telephone** *you?*

SHORT ANSWER
'*Will she do it?*' '*Yes, she* **will**.' / '*No, she* **won't**.'

Will is often contracted to *'ll* in continuous speech. The full form is used in question forms that begin with *will*, question tags and short form answers.

> *What***'ll** *they do with it?*
> *They***'ll** *sell it.*
> **Will** *you take this for me?*
> *She won't tell him,* **will** *she?*
> *Yes, she* **will**.

Will not contracts to *won't.*
> *There* **won't** *be a hurricane today.*

PRONUNCIATION

It is very important to practise the sound of the *'ll* (/əl/) contraction (*I'll* /aɪəl/; *we'll* /wiːəl/) as it is very common in spoken English. Also, be careful not to confuse the two words *won't* (/wəʊnt/) and *want* (/wɒnt/).

2 Predictions and decisions (*going to*)

USE

When we have evidence for a future event, such as something in the present situation which has already begun or a decision that has already been made, we use *going to*.

> *Look at those clouds. It***'s going** *to pour down!* (The first statement is evidence of the second.)
> *I've already decided. I***'m going** *to watch television tonight.* (The event has been pre-planned.)

When using this verb form the speaker is not expressing a completely personal opinion or decision at the moment of speaking. Compare:

- *I'll do it for you!* (This is an immediate offer by the speaker based on a personal desire to help in a present situation.)
- *He***'s going** *to do it for you.* (He has taken the decision before now.)

With *going to*, the future event referred to is often, but not always, close to the present.

FORM See page 158.

PRONUNCIATION

The *to* in *going to* is usually weakened except when it comes at the end of a sentence.

> '*I don't think she's going* **to** *come tonight.*' /tə/
> '*Really? Her husband says she's going* **to**.' /tuː/

3 Verb + preposition

The prepositions below frequently follow the verbs listed beneath them.

in	on	of	for	with	about
believe	concentrate	think	apologise	agree	talk
succeed	decide		prepare		worry
					decide
					think

The preposition is followed by a noun, pronoun (e.g. *him / her / us / them*) or a verb in the *-ing* form.

> *I don't believe in ghosts.*
> *I'm very worried about him.*
> *Cathy's thinking of writing a book.*

Use your grammar

UNIT 1

Present Simple

Go around the class and ask questions to complete the Bingo board. Examples:
Do you like pizza / chips?
Are you a Leo / a Scorpio?

a) If someone says *Yes*, write their name in the square.
b) When three squares are completed – down, across or diagonally – shout *Bingo!*
c) Report back to the class. Who is similar to you? Who is very different? Examples:
Juan likes ... and so do I / but I don't.
Katerina is a ... and so am I / but I'm not.

.... likes my favourite food.	.... is the same star sign as me.	.... speaks more than three languages.
.... prefers tea to coffee.	.... can play the piano.	.... isn't interested in sport
.... believes in ghosts.	.... never wears jeans.	.... doesn't like hot weather.

UNIT 2

Present Continuous

Work in pairs. STUDENT A: look at page 153. STUDENT B: look at page 156.

UNIT 3

Present and Past Simple: short answers

Work in groups.

a) Do the quiz. If the sentences are false, rewrite them correctly.
b) Listen while your teacher reads each sentence to you. Give the correct short answer.
Example:
A: *Spiders have ten legs.*
B: *No, they don't.*
c) If the statement is false, give the correct answer.

TRUE OR FALSE?

1 Spiders have ten legs.
2 Shakespeare wrote *War and Peace*.
3 Istanbul is the capital of Turkey.
4 Beethoven was deaf.
5 Tigers live in Africa.
6 Jimmy Carter used to be President of the United States.
7 Bears don't eat meat.
8 Italy won the 1994 World Cup.
9 Alexander Graham Bell invented the television.

(Answers on page 153.)

Past Simple and Past Continuous

Work in groups of three.

STUDENTS A AND B
Look at page 153.

> STUDENT C
> You are a security guard at an airport. Yesterday there was a robbery at the Duty Free Shop.
>
> **a)** Look at the picture on the right. This was the scene a quarter of an hour after the robbery. The photographs above are of the two people you suspect. You are going to interview the two people in the circle who were there at the time of the robbery. Write down questions to find out who was there and what they were doing. Examples: *Was there an old man wearting a blue jacket? What was he doing?*
> **b)** Ask your questions. Who was there at the time of the robbery? Who is not in your picture? Who do you think committed the robbery?

UNIT 4

Present Perfect and Past Simple

Work in pairs.

STUDENT A
Look at page 153.

STUDENT B
a) Read the first newspaper article on the right. Then ask Student A questions to complete it. Use the Present Perfect or the Past Simple and the words in brackets to help you. Example: *Who has escaped from Pentonville Prison?*
b) Now read the second newspaper article on the right and answer your partner's questions about it.

> _____(Who?) has escaped from Pentonville Prison. He made _____ (What?) in order to get out. He has now kidnapped _____ (Who?) and taken him _____ (Where?). He flew there _____ (When?). _____ (Who?) have promised a reward for information leading to Wilson's arrest.

> An airbus has crashed in the United States. But, by a miracle, no one was seriously hurt. At the time the weather was foggy, and the pilot landed on a motorway. Fortunately there was no traffic because the crash happened at two o'clock in the morning. The pilot announced his retirement last night. The police have just reopened the motorway.

UNIT 5

Will and *going to* for predictions

a) Write four predictions about the future on different pieces of paper. Write two about the future of the world and two about your own life. Use *will* or *going to*. Examples:
I think someone will find a cure for AIDS.
I'm going to leave university next year.
b) Work with three other students. Mix up your predictions and guess who wrote each one. Talk about them.

Will and *going to* for offers and decisions

Work in groups of four. You have been staying at your sister's house with three friends while she was on holiday. Your sister has just phoned to say that she will be home in two hours. The house is in a mess and the fridge is empty.

a) Make a list of things you need to do. Everyone must offer to do something. (Example: *I'll wash up.*) Write the person's name next to each job on the list. Example:
Wash up.   Sue
b) Report back to the class on your plans. Example:
Sue's going to wash up.

Are you 'green'?

READING

Before reading

1 Work in pairs. Make brief notes on two environmental problems the world is facing at the moment (e.g. *The world is getting warmer.*).

2 In some countries there is a political party called the 'Green Party' or 'The Greens'. What is its purpose? Discuss with your partner.

Reading

1 Read the text. Match each of the paragraphs with one of the items in the pictures (e.g. *paragraph 1* refers to *f*). You should be able to work out most of the more difficult words from the context.

Are these people criminals?

1 For a start, Julia Moore's not just killing flies with that spray. By using it, she is helping to create a hole in the ozone layer - the 'gas screen' which helps protect us from the dangerous rays of the sun. The spray is full of chemicals called chlorofluorocarbons (CFCs) that eat up the ozone gas. There are now huge holes in the ozone layer, which is why CFCs should be banned.

2 The cooking pots are boiling over and wasting power. This means that more and more oil and coal has to be burned and this causes pollution and 'acid rain'. 'Acid rain' has already killed more than half of Germany's trees.

3 The vegetables you can see have probably been treated with pesticides - chemicals which kill the small animals and insects that live on them. They have also been fed with fertilisers which can exhaust the soil and kill wild animals. The pesticides and fertilisers end up in our water which is then polluted by them. In many shops you can now buy organic fruit and vegetables which are not treated with chemicals.

4 The eggs Emma is eating come from battery farms which cause great cruelty to millions of hens kept in confined spaces. Free-range eggs are more expensive but are healthier and are not as cruel to hens.

5 The hardwood which the kitchen furniture is made of comes from the tropical rain forests, which are disappearing as they are cut down to provide hardwood for the western world. Fewer trees means more carbon dioxide in the air and this traps the sun's heat and leads to the 'greenhouse effect' - a hotter climate which melts ice, causes floods and drought and changes our climate.

6 The fridge is full of meat. Tropical rain forests are often cut down to provide space to breed cattle to provide our hamburgers.

7 Julia doesn't always save her plastic shopping bags. Yet it is impossible to recycle them and plastic can harm animals.

8 The Moores throw a lot of rubbish out but glass and aluminium cans can be recycled and used again.

9 Julia's cupboard near the sink is full of washing powders and cleaners, many of which are packed with things which pollute water.

10 Out in the garden Derek Moore is spraying his plants with insecticides, which not only kill animals and birds but can also harm human eyes and skin and are also related to birth defects and cancer.

(from *Bella*)

2 Look back at the text and find these words and phrases which are often associated with the environment. Try to work out their meanings from the context. If necessary, check your answers with a dictionary.

a) *ozone layer* (paragraph 1)
b) *acid rain* (paragraph 2)
c) *battery farms* (paragraph 4)
d) *greenhouse effect* (paragraph 5)
e) *recycle* (paragraphs 7 and 8)

3 What do the words in *italics* refer to?

a) By using *it* . . . (paragraph 1)
b) *which* helps protect us . . . (paragraph 1)
c) *that* eat up the ozone gas . . . (paragraph 1)
d) *This* means that . . . (paragraph 2)
e) *which* are not treated with . . . (paragraph 3)
f) *this* traps the sun's heat (paragraph 5)
g) to recycle *them* . . . (paragraph 7)
h) many of *which* are packed . . . (paragraph 9)

4 List the things which, according to the article, are bad for the environment.

LISTENING AND SPEAKING

1 [6.1] Listen to the extract from an interview with Mrs Moore. Make notes on why she finds it hard to be 'green'. Organise your notes under these headings: *Shopping, Food, Recycling, Transport*.

2 Work in pairs to see how 'green' you are. Fill in the questionnaire yourself and then compare your answers and final score with your partner.

	YES	NO	SOMETIMES
1 Do you re-use plastic carrier bags?			
2 Do you buy organically-grown vegetables?			
3 Do you buy glass (not plastic) bottles?			
4 Do you take empty bottles to a 'bottle bank'?			
5 Do you buy CFC-free sprays?			
6 Do you buy vegetables and fruit loose rather than in plastic packets?			
7 Do you buy white tissues rather than coloured ones?			
8 Do you buy free-range eggs?			

	YES	NO	SOMETIMES
9 Do you buy rechargeable batteries?			
10 Do you buy soap and cosmetics not tested on animals?			
11 Do you try to save energy in the home?			
12 If you have a car, do you use unleaded petrol?			
13 Do you try to use public transport or ride a bicycle as much as possible?			
14 Do you try to avoid using chemicals to kill garden pests?			
15 Do you keep paper or aluminium cans for recycling?			
TOTAL			

SCORE

Score 1 point for every YES.

More than 10 points: You obviously care about the environment and try to preserve it.
5–10 points: You are beginning to show more interest in the environment.
Less than 5 points: You don't seem very interested in being 'green'.

3 Discuss which of the ways of being 'green' listed in the questionnaire you think are the most important and which are the most difficult. Give your reasons.

4 Are the Moores really 'criminals'? Discuss and vote.

LANGUAGE POINT 1

Defining relative clauses

Relative clauses, like adjectives, add extra information to a noun. Defining relative clauses give essential information and tell us more precisely what something or someone is.

1   Look at the following examples and then complete the sentences below with one of these words: *that, which, who, where, whose.*
Examples:
*The ozone layer is something **that/which** helps protect us from the sun.*
*An ecologist is a person **who/that** studies the environment.*
*That's the shop **where** you can buy CFC-free sprays.*
*Is that the man **whose** dog bit you?*

a) If you are talking about *possession* you use the relative pronoun _____ .
b) If you are defining *people* you use the relative pronouns _____ or _____ .
c) If you are defining *things* you use the relative pronouns _____ or _____ .
d) If you are talking about *places* you can use the relative adverb _____ .

2   In the following sentences the relative pronoun can be left out.
The money (which/that) he lost is in my wallet.
The woman (who/that) you were speaking to is my neighbour.

In this sentence the relative pronoun cannot be left out.
The person who wrote 'Strange Encounter' has just written another novel.

Check with Section 1 in the *Language reference* to find out when the relative pronoun or adverb can be left out. Then, where possible, cross out the relative pronoun or adverb in the following sentences.

a) The place where we met was very romantic.
b) I'm the person that you spoke to on the phone.
c) Malcolm is an English teacher who works in Spain.
d) These are the vegetables that were grown organically.
e) The house which Caroline has bought is in my street.

PRACTICE

1   Work in pairs and complete the following sentences orally. In each case, give a reason.

a) I don't like people who . . .
b) I'm really keen on films that . . .
c) Eating food that . . . is disgusting!
d) Going on holiday to places where . . . is great.
e) I get very angry with people whose . . .

2   Work in pairs. Make one sentence from the two given, using a relative pronoun. You may have to add or delete words. Example:
I have a dog. It barks a lot.
*I have a dog **that** barks a lot.*

a) I saw a film yesterday. It really terrified me.
b) That was my mother. You met her last week.
c) Let's go to that nice restaurant. We ate there on my birthday.
d) Margaret is an energetic person. She hardly ever sleeps.
e) I have contact lenses. You can wear them all the time.
f) She's the woman. We bought her car.
g) I bought you a new pair of shoes. Have you worn them yet? (*Have you worn . . .*)
h) A microwave is a machine. It cooks food.
i) Look, that's the house. You were born there.

> See **Use your grammar,** page 78, for further practice of defining relative clauses.

LANGUAGE POINT 2

Clauses of purpose

Notice that after *so (that)* we need a subject (*we, you,* etc.) and a verb. Clauses of purpose answer the questions *Why?* Examples.
Wear gloves so (that) you keep your hands warm.

In groups, discuss the answers to the following questions using *to* and *so (that).*

a) Why do people cut down trees?
b) Why do farmers use insecticides?
c) Why do people kill elephants?
d) Why do people go on diets?
e) Why do we go on holiday?

PRONUNCIATION

In order to stress a syllable in a word we make the syllable(s) next to it weak. Example: *vegetables* /'vedʒtəbəlz/: /vedʒ/ is the stressed first syllable; the syllables /tə/ and /bəlz/ are weak.

The vowel most commonly used in unstressed syllables is called a *schwa* (/ə/).

1 [🔊 6.2]   Copy the words below. Listen to the recording and mark the stressed syllables using stress marks ('), then underline the syllables pronounced with a schwa. Example: *'paper*

a) machine   e) chemicals
b) animals   f) suggestion
c) banana   g) tropical
d) environment   h) Parliament

2 [🔊 6.3]   Listen to the recording. Circle the syllables containing schwas in the words in *italics*.

a) I don't like the *colour*.
b) Robert's a very good *actor*.
c) The *pollution* here is dreadful.
d) That armchair's very *comfortable*.
e) What an intelligent *elephant*!

3   Practise saying the sentences in Exercise 2.

VOCABULARY

Adjectives

Adjectives formed with *-ed* describe our reaction to someone or something. Example:
*I was **terrified** when I saw that film.*

Adjectives formed with *-ing* describe the person or thing that causes the reaction. Example:
*The film was **terrifying**.*

1   Match the adjectives in the box with the pictures below, and then make a sentence using each of the adjectives.

> amused   annoyed   bored   tired   disappointed
> interested

1

2

3

4

5

6

2   Complete the sentences below using the verbs in the box to make adjectives with *-ing* or *-ed*.

> amuse   annoy   bore   tire   disappoint
> interest

a) The film was very _____ and I fell asleep.
b) His jokes weren't very _____ and nobody laughed.
c) Andy said he was very _____ in hearing about your trip abroad.
d) My sister was very _____ with her exam results. She had expected better.
e) I fell asleep early. It had been a _____ day.
f) He was _____ with me for not telling him about Jasper's birthday.

3   Adjectives can also be formed from verbs and nouns by using suffixes. Recognising a suffix often helps when you are trying to work out the meaning of a new word in context. Use the suffixes to form adjectives from the nouns and verbs. Example:
attract → *attractive*

SUFFIXES

> -y   -ous   -ic   -ful   -able   -al   -ive

NOUNS/VERBS

> attract   colour   religion   sympathy
> romance   crime   dirt   hope   imagine

45

WRITING

Semi-formal letters

1 Read the letter and decide who is writing to who and the purpose of the letter.

3 Mr Adam Crew MP,
4 Conservative Club,
South Road,
SALISBURY.

1 25 Green Avenue
Salisbury

2 19th March 1995

5 Dear Mr Crew,

6 I am writing to express my concern that our country still continues to give money to organisations that are helping to destroy tropical rain forests.

7   For various reasons these rain forests have an ideal climate for plants and animals, so it is essential that we help preserve them. Firstly, they house over half the world's wildlife, such as tigers, mountain gorillas and birds of paradise. Secondly, one in every four products obtained from the chemist contains compounds from these rain forests and more are being discovered every year. Thirdly, and perhaps most importantly, these forests play an important role in the world's climate.

8   Rain forests are usually only found in the Third World, countries with weak economies which often owe large sums of money to the more developed countries. In some places, areas of forest are cut down to provide farmers with space to breed cattle. This earns valuable currency and gives us cheap beef for our hamburgers.

9   The only answer is for Britain to cancel the debts that these countries owe us. We need to try to influence those policies which result in forest destruction. If we do not act soon, we will destroy millions of years of evolution. This catastrophe must be stopped!

10 Yours sincerely,

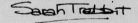

11 Sarah Trebbit (Mrs)

2 Match the parts of the letter (1 to 11) with the following. Example: a) –7

a) Background information: saying why the rain forests are useful to us.
b) The date of the letter.
c) Concluding the letter by suggesting a solution and requesting action.
d) The name of the Member of Parliament (MP).
e) The formal close of the letter.

f) Saying what the reason for writing is.
g) The address of the person writing the letter.
h) Explaining why rain forests are destroyed.
i) The name of the person writing the letter.
j) The address of the Member of Parliament.
k) The formal start of the letter.

3   Sarah Trebbit is not a personal friend of her MP, Mr Crew, and so she has written to him using a fairly formal (*semi-formal*) style.

a) Say whether the following statements are *True* or *False* about writing semi-formal letters. One has been done for you.
  i) We use contractions (e.g. *it's, I've*).   *False.*
  ii) The letter begins with an introduction and ends with a conclusion.
  iii) The close of the letter is something like *Best wishes.*
  iv) Each paragraph usually contains a different topic.
  v) When we start the letter with the person's name (*Dear Mr/Mrs/Ms,* etc.) we close with *Yours sincerely.*

b) How do we start and close a semi-formal letter to a person whose name we don't know?

4   The phrase *I am writing to express my concern* . . . is appropriate in a semi-formal letter. In a more personal, informal letter we might say, *The reason I'm writing is to tell you I'm worried about* . . . The phrases in list A come from semi-formal letters.

Match the words in *italics* in list A with their informal equivalents in list B.

A
1 *As requested* . . .
2 Please send it *at your earliest convenience* . . .
3 How can I *obtain* . . .
4 When can I *make an appointment* . . .
5 I am very *dissatisfied* with . . .
6 I need to see you *concerning* . . .
7 *I apologise* for . . .

B
a) get hold of
b) about
c) as you asked
d) I'm sorry
e) as soon as possible
f) arrange to come and see you
g) unhappy

5   Clauses of result and reason.

In the following sentence the second clause is a clause of result.
*These rain forests have an ideal climate for plants and animals, **so** it is essential that we help to preserve them.*

The two clauses above are joined by *so* to make one sentence. How is the example below different?
*These rain forests have an ideal climate for plants and animals. **Therefore / As a result / That's why** it is essential that we help to preserve them.*

In the following sentence the second clause is a clause of reason.
*It is essential that we help to preserve these forests **because/as/since** they have an ideal climate for plants and animals.*

A clause of reason can also come at the beginning of a sentence.
***Because/As/Since** these forests have an ideal climate for plants and animals, it is essential that we help to preserve them.*

a) Decide whether each of the four clauses below express a reason or a result.
  i) There are many droughts. The world's temperatures are rising.
  ii) I didn't vote for the 'Green Party'. I didn't think they would win.

b) Join each pair of sentences, using reason or result linking expressions.

6   Writing to the Prime Minister.

a) You are a Member of Parliament and you are going to write to the Prime Minister to give your views about what the Government should do to protect the environment. The letter will be semi-formal and consist of four or five short paragraphs. Make notes for each paragraph.

b) Write the letter (of no more than 150 words in total) to include at least one sentence which describes a result or a reason. Make sure you use the correct layout for a semi-formal letter.

Language reference

A clause (e.g. *An ecologist studies the environment*) is a group of words containing a subject (e.g. *An ecologist*) and a finite verb (a verb which changes according to subject and tense: e.g. *studies*). The verb will often be followed by an object (e.g. *the environment*).

1 Defining relative clauses

Relative clauses are like adjectives because they describe (or 'relate' to) a noun. Unlike most adjectives they come after the noun.

Defining relative clauses (sometimes called 'identifying' clauses) contain essential information about a person, thing or place to help us identify who or what we are talking about. They are linked to the main clause by the relative pronoun *who* or *that* (for people), *which* or *that* (for things), and *whose* (for possession).

> *An ecologist is someone **who** / **that studies the environment***.
> *The ozone layer is something **which** /**that helps protect us from the sun***.
> *Is that the man **whose dog bit you**?*

For places you can use the relative adverb *where*:

> *This is the house **where I was born***.

You can also use *which* or *that*:

> *This is the house **which I was born in** / **in which I was born***.
> *This is the house **that I was born in***. (NOT ~~in that . . .~~)

When defining people, *that* is often used in place of *who*, especially in conversation.

> *She's the woman **that** used to live next door to us.*

When *who* or *that* is the object of the relative clause (i.e. when it describes a person or thing that the action is done to) it is usually left out.

> *There's the woman (**who** /**that**) I met yesterday.* (the woman is the object of *I met*)

Who or *that* cannot be left out when it is the subject of the relative clause.

> *The person **who** /**that wrote** 'Strange Encounter' has just written another novel.*

2 Clauses of purpose

To describe the purpose of an action (and answer the question *Why?*) we use *to* or *so (that)*.

> *We left early **to** get there on time.*
> *We left early **so (that)** we could get there on time.*

Note that after *so (that)* a subject (e.g. *we*) and a verb are necessary.

3 Clauses of result and reason

Clauses of result are linked to other clauses by such words as: *so, Therefore, As a result, That's why*.

So

> *They have an ideal climate for plants **so** it is essential we preserve them.*

(The clause of result *it is essential we preserve them* is linked to *They have an ideal climate* by *so* and made into one sentence.)

Therefore, as a result, that's why

> *Temperatures are rising. **Therefore** / **As a result** / **That's why** there are many droughts.*

(With the expressions *Therefore*, *As a result* and *That's why* a separate sentence is usually necessary.)

When a reason is given in a sentence, there are usually two clauses joined by such words as *because*, *as* or *since*.

> *I stayed at home **because** /**as** /**since** it was too dangerous to go out.*
> ***Because** / **As** / **Since** it was too dangerous to go out, I stayed at home.*

Usually the reason clause (*it was too dangerous to go out*) comes last.

4 Pronunciation: the *schwa*

The *schwa* /ə/ is the most common vowel sound in English and can be represented by any vowel letter. It is the vowel sound that is most commonly used in unstressed syllables. Examples:

paper /'peɪpə/	*banana* /bə'nɑːnə/
vegetables /'vedʒtəbəlz/	*suggestion* /sə'dʒestʃən /
under /'ʌndə/	

5 Adjectives with *-ed* or *-ing*

We can use a past participle to describe our reaction to someone or something.

> *I'm very **interested** in your ideas. I think you're very intelligent.*

We can use the *-ing* form of verbs to talk about the person (or thing) that causes the reaction.

> *He's a very **interesting** man. He's very intelligent.*

It is very important not to confuse the two forms as there is a big difference in meaning between them. Compare:

– *I'm very **bored**.* (I want to go home. This film has no interest.)
– *I'm very **boring**.* (My personality has no interest for you.)

These are some common past participles used to describe reactions. Note the prepositions which usually follow them.

amused by / at	*terrified of / by*
tired of	*bored with / by*
interested in	*disappointed with / at / by / in*
annoyed with	

Choosing a partner

VOCABULARY

1   In pairs, describe the people in the photographs. If you wish, use some of the words in the boxes below.

PERSONALITY
confident   generous   patient   ambitious a sense of humour   shy   boring   easy-going extrovert   lively   supportive

APPEARANCE
pretty   overweight   elderly   well-built balding   smart   scruffy   plump in his/her mid-thirties   curly   suntanned double chin   freckles   glasses   shortish moustache

2   Work in pairs and agree on your descriptions for each picture.

LISTENING

Before listening

There are two couples in the five photographs. Which people do you think are partners? Give your reasons. Example:
'I think the man with the glasses and the beard is with the woman with the dark, curly hair, because they both look as if they have a sense of humour.'

Listening

1 [🔲 7.1]   Listen to the two couples talking about their partners. From their descriptions try to guess the names of each of the people in the photographs. Example:
'I think the person in the second photograph is Françoise.'

2   Copy the table below and write the names of the people being described down the left-hand side.

NAME	APPEARANCE	PERSONALITY
Françoise	*big, black eyes*	*sense of humour*

Listen to the recording again. Make notes under *Appearance* and *Personality* about the qualities of each of the people.

3   Which of the people interviewed sounds most attractive to you? Why?

4 [🔲 7.2]   Listen to an extract from what Emma said, and then fill in the gaps in the following sentences.

He's young: he's in his ___(1)___ . He's very ___(2)___ and ___(3)___ . He's got lovely ___(4)___ eyes. He's got ___(5)___ hair. He's ___(6)___, although he does like to wear his jeans. He's quite ___(7)___ in that manner, although he's very ___(8)___ when we go out.

5   In pairs, make a list of as many other words as you can to describe someone's *eyes*, *hair*, *age* and *build*.

SPEAKING 1

1 Work in pairs.

STUDENT A
Write down five sentences which describe the kind of person you are attracted to. Example:
I am attracted to a man with a sense of humour.
OR *I like women with curly hair.*

STUDENT B
Write down five sentences which describe the kind of person you are not attracted to. Example:
I can't stand mean people.

Try to guess what qualities your partner likes/dislikes. Then explain why you wrote what you did.

2 Take it in turns to imagine you are someone else in the class. The others must ask *Yes/No* questions to guess who you are. Example:
STUDENT A: *Have you got dark hair?*
YOU: *No, I haven't.*
STUDENT B: *Are you middle-aged?*
YOU: *Yes, I am.*
STUDENT C: *Are you Carlos?*
YOU: *No, I'm not.*

If the other students make a wrong guess, you win. They can only ask ten questions.

LANGUAGE POINT 1

Asking for descriptions

A: *What does Lucy look like?*
B: *You'd recognise her easily. She's tall and dark.*

A: *What's Chris like?*
B: *Great! He's got a wonderful sense of humour.*

A: *What do Lucy and Chris like doing?*
B: *Lots of things. Skiing, going to the theatre, collecting modern art.*

Read the example sentences above carefully. Then read the three questions in column A and match them with their meanings in column B.

A	**B**
1 What do they look like?	a) what they enjoy
	b) their appearance
2 What are they like?	c) the type of people they are
3 What do they like?	

PRACTICE

1 Complete the gaps in the following conversation about Beth's grandfather.

ANDY: _____?
BETH: He's tallish, with grey hair and twinkling eyes.
ANDY: _____?
BETH: Quite serious but very kind and he's got a nice personality.
ANDY: _____?
BETH: Well, mainly indoor things such as reading and watching videos.

2 Answer the following questions about yourself.

a) What are you like?
b) What do you look like?
c) What do you like doing?

3 Using the questions above, ask another student to describe a relative or a friend. Draw a picture of the person as they are describing him/her. Discuss the result.

> See **Use your grammar,** page 78, for further practice of describing people.

LANGUAGE POINT 2

Putting adjectives in the right order

There are no strict rules about the order in which adjectives come before a noun but general qualities usually go before particular ones. Example:

a	*large*	*plastic*	*bag*
	general	particular	

Personal opinions go before more objective words. Example:

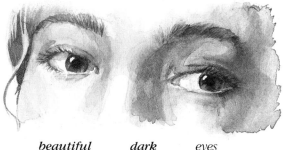

beautiful	*dark*	*eyes*
personal	objective	
opinion		

We usually use no more than two or three adjectives before the noun. Extra details are added afterwards, connected by a word like *with* or another linking word. Example:
*He was an **attractive brown-haired** man with a beard and glasses.*

Decide on the correct adjective order for each of the items below. Check with Section 2 in the *Language reference* for more help on adjective order.

a) lawyer / Italian / clever / a / middle-aged
b) nice / cats / grey / two / Siamese
c) leg / a / round / a / broken / large / with / table / wooden
d) woman / Polish / smile / an / lovely / with / elderly / green / a / eyes / and

LANGUAGE POINT 3

Possessive -s

1   Look at these examples and answer the questions below.
*Nick and Hilary**'s** friend is here.*
*The cat**'s** name is Charlotte.*
*The name **of** the cat is Charlotte.*
*The boy**s'** mother is nice but I don't like their father.*
*Are these the children**'s** clothes?*
*What is the Government**'s** policy on this?*
*Look at the bird on the roof **of** that house!*

How do we form the possessive:

a) when two names are joined by *and*?
b) for parts of non-living things?
c) for regular plural nouns?

2   Join the noun on the left with the noun on the right to make possessive phrases in the singular and the plural. One has been done for you.

a) girl   eyes   *the girl's eyes*
                               the girls' eyes

b) table   legs
c) a person   rights
d) my sister   friends
e) drawers   key

3 [🎞 7.3]   Pronouncing the possessive -s.

a) Listen to the recording. Copy the table below and write the phrases in the correct column according to how the possessive -s is pronounced. The first three have been done for you. (Only write *s'* where necessary.)

/s/	/z/	/ɪz/
the cat's name	both boys' sisters	my boss's brother

b) Practise saying each phrase in a sentence. Example: *'The cat's name is Charlotte.'*

LANGUAGE POINT 4

Adverbs of manner

In the phrase *She speaks quietly* the adverb *quietly* describes the verb *speaks*. The adverb describes how the action was performed. An adjective, on the other hand, describes a noun (e.g. *a quiet person*).

Adverbs are normally (but not always) formed by adding *-ly* to an adjective.

ADJECTIVE	ADVERB
polite	*politely*
bad	*badly*
happy	*happily*
good	*well*

However, some adjectives end in *-ly* (e.g. *silly*) and some words can be used both as an adjective and an adverb (e.g. *fast: a fast car* – adjective; *he drove fast* – adverb).

Divide the following words into adjectives and adverbs. Which can be used as both? If necessary, use your dictionary to help you.

loudly	rude	straight	carefully
angry	quiet	badly	friendly	quickly
slow	cleverly	serious	lively	hard
softly	perfect	nervously	

PRACTICE

1 Write down how you think you do the following actions. Example:
I think I speak quite slowly.

a) speak
b) walk
c) behave in class
d) treat your friends
e) dress
f) drive a car
g) work
h) behave at parties

2 Tell your partner how you think they do the same actions. Example:
'I think you speak very quickly.'

3 Compare opinions. Example:
'I don't agree with you. I think I speak quite slowly.'
OR *'You're right. I do speak quickly.'*

LANGUAGE POINT 5

Adverbs of degree

1 Which of the expressions in the box make the adjective or adverb less strong? Example:
He's a bit tired.

a bit	rather	quite	extremely	a little
incredibly	fairly	pretty	really	very
on the . . . side	terribly	remarkably		

2 Which of the expressions make the adjective or adverb stronger? Example:
She drives very fast.

3 Which expressions suggest the highest degree (e.g. *extremely*) and which suggest the smallest degree (e.g. *a bit*)?

PRACTICE

Make sentences using the expressions above
(+ means make the adjective or adverb stronger;
− means make the adjective or adverb weaker.)
Example: I'm late. (+)
I'm sorry I can't stop. I'm extremely late already.

a) I'm bored. (+)
b) This car is fast. (−)
c) It's a violent film. (−)
d) She's lazy. (−)
e) They speak English badly. (+)

READING

Before reading

1 Read what five people said when asked about the qualities they looked for when choosing a partner. Write the letter *M* next to those you think were said by men and *W* next to those you think were said by women.

2 Compare your answers (if possible, with someone from the opposite sex) and give reasons for your opinions.

> *I like my partner to look good. Who cares about their brains?*

> *Being able to talk to the person is more important than sex.*

> *Kindness is the most important quality I look for.*

> *I always insist on my partner being faithful.*

> *I always like my partner to be the dominant one in the relationship.*

Reading

1 The texts opposite are extracts from two surveys on relationships between men and women in Britain. One survey asked men their opinions, the other asked women. How would you respond to two of the questions they were asked?

a) Would you prefer your partner to be similar to or different from yourself?

b) How important are 'good looks' in a partner?

2 Read the texts using one of the following words in the gaps:
man/men, woman/women, husband(s), wife/wives.

3 Compare your answers. Give reasons for your guesses.

4 What would you think of your present sex if you were a member of the opposite sex?

5 Imagine these surveys were conducted in your country. How similar or different would the results be?

A The survey discovered that only two per cent thought it important to have a .....(1)..... who looked good. On the other hand 79 per cent thought that being able to talk to each other was an important ingredient in a good marriage. The younger .....(2)..... – 86 per cent of them – rated good communication most highly, while older .....(3)..... placed greater emphasis on kindness and humour.

Less than half the .....(4)..... believed that a good sex life was important. Moreover, even sexual fidelity came well down the list with only a third of the .....(5)..... saying it was of major importance.

Married partners tend to be alike when it comes to age, racial and social background and religion. They share attitudes and values, and are similar in intelligence and sociability. And they are similar when it comes to physical attractiveness. When it comes to these qualities, it's true that like marries like.

(Information from *I Do – Your Guide to a Happy Marriage* by Hans J. Eysenck)

B To our surprise, 57 per cent preferred brains over good looks and 83 per cent preferred a pleasant personality over good looks.

Even the younger .....(1)..... in the survey were not looking for someone who just looked good. Though 19 per cent hadn't a clue what they liked, only 11 per cent wanted their ideal .....(2)..... to be conventionally attractive. It seems that .....(3)..... prefer their .....(4)..... to look interesting.

But what puts .....(5)..... off? An aggressive, domineering .....(6)..... proved unpopular. This turn-off was closely followed by .....(7)..... smoking; more than one in five .....(8)..... hate to see .....(9)..... with a cigarette in their mouths.

By far the most important attribute these .....(10)..... asked for was kindness. Only two .....(11)..... in a hundred said this wasn't important, and in the older group kindness received 100 per cent of the vote.

Also, more than three-quarters of the younger .....(12)..... wanted an independent .....(13)..... and two-thirds of the older ones preferred .....(14)..... to have lives of their own.

(Information from survey conducted by *Audience Selection*)

SPEAKING 2

1 Read the three points of view given below. Which of them do you most agree with? Why?

A 'It seems to me that whatever reason people have for living together, it is a private matter. The state should have no say in it. If two people choose to live together, fine – it's up to them. It concerns them and no one else. We do not register our friends, why should we feel it important to register our lovers?'

B 'Couples need support. They need the support of other families and they need the support of society. Marriage does that. It shows couples that they don't just have to depend on their own emotions. Obviously, young passions die down and individual interests change, but marriage helps keep people together and protect their happiness. Besides, single-parent families are still not acceptable in this country.'

C 'I feel there are so many advantages to living by yourself. When I get home at night after a day's work I just love the feeling of being alone. That doesn't mean I'm lonely. Maybe an hour later I decide I want to go out, to be with somebody. But it's my own choice. It's not forced upon me. Therefore, even though it's expensive to live on your own, I prefer it.'

2 In groups, make a list of the advantages of the following states.

GROUP A
Living with someone you are not married to.

GROUP B
Marriage.

GROUP C
Living by yourself.

3 Work with students from other groups. Argue your group's point of view. Example:
'My group thought that it was better to live by yourself because . . .'

WRITING

Personal letters

1 Patty has written a letter to her friend Kate. The different sections of her letter have been mixed up. Decide on the correct order of the sections.

⑥ I haven't got much news. After a pretty exciting three weeks holiday, it's back to work non-stop. Steve and I hardly ever see each other at the moment. I've also taken to serious volleyball training: two hours every weekend evening, especially difficult as I have to get out of bed to be at the studios by 7a.m.! I was working evenings before Christmas, but I had to change to fit in the volleyball.

⑨ Hello, dear. Sorry I haven't written earlier. I've been meaning to but it seems every time I get a quiet moment to put pen to paper the phone rings and I have to go to help with some recording.

① 11th March 1991

④ Enough of me telling you how busy I am. The big question is when are you two coming to stay – we're dying to see you !? The spare room now has a bed so no excuses. Why don't you try and make it before the winter? Give us a ring anyway.

③ Love, Patty ✗

② Dear Kate,

⑧ Must rush – as always. 'Bye and please give Phil a hug from me. I miss you both a lot.

⑦ 11 Castle St.

⑤ PS Thanks for the card.

2   What is the main purpose of the letter?

3   In which paragraph is the main purpose:

a) to give personal information?
b) to make an invitation?
c) to bring the letter to an end?
d) to apologise?

4   From the letter, what do we know and what can we guess about:

a) Patty's working life?
b) how she spends her spare time?

5   What other ways are there of ending personal letters?

6   Look back at the semi-formal letter on page 54. In which ways is the personal letter on page 52 similar or different?

7   Which of these phrases would you *not* expect to see in a personal letter?

All the best.	I am grateful for your assistance.
I refer to your letter of the 19th March.	Look forward to seeing you!
It was so nice to hear from you.	I apologise for the delay in replying.
I'm sure it'll be OK.	When are you coming up?

8   Rewrite the formal phrases in Exercise 7 in a less formal way.

9   These are pictures of a man Kate has just met. She really likes him and is very keen to tell her friend Patty all about him.

Write Kate's reply to Patty's letter, describing the man. Make sure you include:
– an opening and closing greeting.
– an opening paragraph.
– the main information.
– a reply to Patty's invitation.
– the closing paragraph.

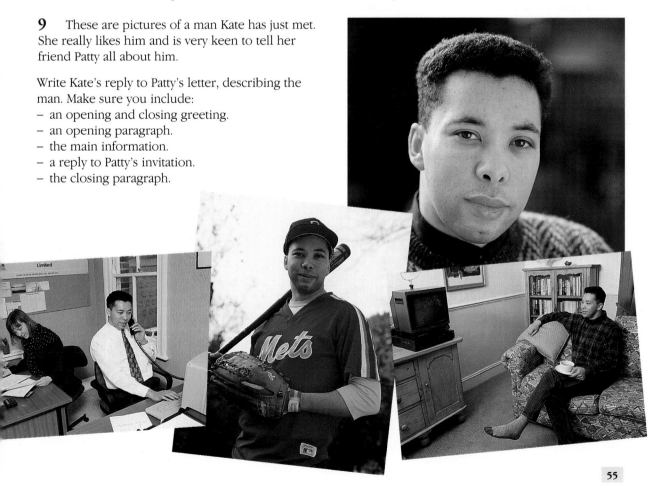

Language reference

1 Asking for descriptions

The structures *What (do / does) . . . look like?* and *What is / are . . . like?* are easily confused:
- *'What **does** Gloria **look like**?'* (asking about appearance) *'She's tall with brown hair.'*
- *'What**'s** / What **is** Jim **like**?'* (asking about personality) *'He's very quiet.'*

The structures are also often confused with the verb *like* and with the question *How is . . . ?*
- *'What **does** Gloria **like**?'* (asking about likes and dislikes) *'She likes coffee.'*
- *'How**'s** / How **is** Bruce?'* (asking about health and happiness) *'Not very well, I'm afraid. He says he's fed up with his job!'*

2 Adjective word order

This table is a guide to the order of adjectives before the noun.

OPINION	SIZE, AGE, SHAPE	COLOUR	PATTERN	NATIONALITY	MATERIAL	NOUN
a smart	young			French		man
a nice		brown	spotty			dog
a chic		red			silk	scarf

3 Possessive -s

Nouns and names have a possessive form, for which we add *-'s*:
 *'Whose eyes?' 'The boy**'s** eyes.'*
-'s is added to singular nouns ending in *-s* (*Charles**'s** career*) and irregular plural nouns (*the children**'s** school*).
With regular plural nouns add an apostrophe ('):
 a girls' school.
The pronunciation of *'s* or *s'* depends on the sound before it:
 /s/ if the sound is unvoiced: *cat**'s**, Frank**'s**, dentists'*
 /z/ if the sound is voiced: *girl**'s**, brother**'s**, dog**'s**, Jill**'s***
 /ɪz/ after /z/, /s/, /dʒ/, /tʃ/, /ʒ/ or /ʃ/: *Des**'s**, actress**'s**, judge**'s***
An alternative construction is with *of*:
 *the owner **of** the car* (= *the car's owner*).
This construction is usual when talking about a part of non-living things:
 The leg of the table (NOT ~~The table's leg~~).

4 Adverbs

Adverbs describe a verb (*He spoke **softly**.*), an adjective (*She's **really** happy.*) or another adverb (*They did it **extremely** well.*).
To form adverbs, in most cases add *-ly* to the adjective:
 *clever → clever**ly***.
In certain cases further changes are needed:
 *happy → happ**ily**; fantastic → fantastic**ally***.
However, some adjectives end in *-ly* (e.g. *friend**ly**, live**ly***) and some adverbs have the same form as the adjectives (e.g. *hard, fast, straight, far, early*): *a **hard** worker* (adjective); *He worked **hard*** (adverb).

5 Adverbs of manner

Adverbs of manner answer the question *How . . . ?* (i.e. in what manner?):
 *'How did he drive?' 'Very **carefully**, I'm glad to say.'*

6 Adverbs of degree

To make adjectives and adverbs less strong (express a small or medium degree) we can use:
a) *a bit / a little* (a small degree): *You're **a bit** quiet today, aren't you?*
b) *fairly* (a medium degree – often combines with words which are positive): *Lori plays squash **fairly** well.*
c) *quite* (in British English, it often means *better than expected*): *I like Lewis. He's **quite** amusing.*
d) *on the . . . side* (can mean *rather* or *too*): *His hair is **on the** long **side**.*
e) *rather* (a medium degree – often used with negative words): *Vicky's intelligent but **rather** lazy.*
f) *pretty* (often similar to *rather* – used in informal speech): *I thought the film was **pretty** awful.*

To make adjectives and adverbs stronger (express a high degree) we can use *very*. To give extra emphasis we can use *extremely, terribly, remarkably, really, incredibly*.
 *She's **extremely** mature for a nine-year-old!*
 *He did the job **incredibly** badly.*

A place to live

READING

Before reading

1 Tell your partner what kind of place you live in and what your favourite room is. Give your reasons.

2 Do rooms reflect our personalities? In what way would you decorate and furnish a living room or a bedroom?

Reading

1 Look at the photograph and read the text about Ivan Steward to find out what kind of place he lives in, and what kind of person he is.

A ROOM OF MY OWN

IVAN STEWARD IS A WINDOW CLEANER. Not only is window cleaning his bread and butter, it is also his inspiration, because some of his ideas on interior decoration came to him by looking through his customers' windows. He once saw a seaman's chest looking splendid in someone's room and he set his heart on finding a similar chest. He finally came across one in Bermondsey market. 'They told me it was an old chest that had been washed up on the shore – I wanted to believe that, so it's true as far as I'm concerned.' Now it's in the sitting room of his top-floor flat with its panoramic view of London.

If the room has a faintly Continental air, that's because while cleaning windows in Holland he noticed that Dutch people tended to have wooden floors rather than fitted carpets. 'They have all these different coloured woods, so I decided every time I came back I was going to bring back some wood.'

Ivan, now 41, is just under two metres tall, long-limbed – ideal window cleaner's physique – and soft-voiced, with a gentle manner but a considerable degree of drive and enthusiasm. As well as being a window cleaner, he is also an actor. Before he was either, he was a fireman.

Ivan bought the Persian rug in a carpet sale out of the money he was paid for playing Ambrose in the TV series 'Robin of Sherwood'. His role of Simkins in the film version of 'Porridge' paid for the sofa and the Victorian farmhouse chair. His mother, who died some years ago, gave him the cheese plant, and most of the other plants he bought in Columbia Road flower market. The television set stands on a cut-down Victorian table that he bought in Bermondsey market. He is devoted to dogs, and his girlfriend gave him the carved wooden dog on the television set. He also has a retriever called Sidney.

The African figure on his coffee table is one of three he bought in Dar es Salaam when he went to stay with a fellow drama student who lived in Africa. He came across the pair of boat paintings at a Sunday jumble sale in Essex.

Ivan keeps all his tips in the gin bottle and is hoping to buy his flat from the council.

(from the *Observer* colour supplement)

2 Answer the following questions.

a) Where does Ivan get ideas for decorating his flat?
b) What jobs does he do, and what other job has he done?
c) What is he saving money for?
d) Do you think Ivan is an interesting person? Give your reasons.
e) What do you think *bread and butter* in the second sentence means?

3 Where did Ivan get the following things from, and where are they in the room?

a) the seaman's chest
b) the Persian rug
c) the sofa
d) the Victorian chair
e) the plants
f) the television table
g) the wooden dog
h) the African figure
i) the pictures
j) the tips

Example:
Object: *the seaman's chest*
Where did he get it? *Bermondsey market*
Where is it in the room? *opposite the sofa, against the wall*.

4 Find five prepositional phrases (a phrase with a preposition and a noun) in the text. Each phrase should include one each of the following prepositions: *in, through, at* and *on*. Example: *He saw a seaman's chest looking splendid in somebody's room*.

5 Look again at the first paragraph of the text. The first sentence (*Ivan Steward is a window cleaner*) introduces the person under discussion. The second sentence (*Not only . . .*) gives some general supporting information about the subject of the text (i.e. his interest in interior decoration).

a) What does the third sentence (*He once saw a seaman's chest . . .*) add to the paragraph?
b) How does the last sentence (*Now it's in . . .*) help to link this paragraph to the next paragraph?

VOCABULARY

Making opposites

1 The adjectives in the box could be used to describe a room or things in a room.

| airy | practical | useful | tidy | colourful |
| romantic | tasteful |

a) Use the prefixes *un-* and *im-* and the suffix *-less* to make the opposites of the adjectives. Example: *airy → airless*
b) What other adjectives can you think of for describing a room (e.g. *cosy, spacious, formal*)?
c) Use some of the adjectives in this section to describe a room in your own home to a partner.

2 Make the opposites of the adjectives, adverbs (see Unit 7) and verbs in the box using the prefixes *dis-, un-, in-, ir-,* im- or *il-* or the suffix *-less*.

necessary	experienced	sensitive	like
agree	responsibly	patiently	pleasant
logically	tactfully	honest	married

3 Choose one of the words in the box above and make as many words from it (and its opposite) as possible. If necessary, check the words in your dictionary. Example:
necessary: *unnecessary – necessarily – unnecessarily – necessaries – necessitate – necessity*

4 Complete the following sentences, using the correct form (adjective, adverb or verb) of the word in brackets. Add a prefix or suffix where necessary. Example: *sensitive*
*She spoke **insensitively** and made her brother cry.*

a) The police said they were (*responsible*) parents for leaving their young children alone in the house.
b) Although it was her first job and she was (*experience*) she was willing to work hard.
c) I didn't like him, but he was always (*pleasant*) to me.
d) I felt that he was wrong so I had to (*agree*) with him.
e) He behaved (*honest*) by stealing his business's money.
f) I think he should have explained the situation more (*tactful*).

PRONUNCIATION

Syllables and word stress

1 Prefixes (*un-*, *dis-*) and suffixes (*-less*, *-ly*) are not normally stressed (*un'necessary*, *disa'gree*, *'tactless*, *'quietly*). Dictionaries often use the symbol (•) to show how a word divides into syllables (e.g. *ti•dy*) and stress marks (') to indicate which syllable is stressed (e.g. /'taɪdi/). Look at the dictionary extract below.

a) How many syllables has *information* got?
b) Which syllable is stressed?

> customs, etc., t... ...son who is studying them.
>
> **in·for·ma·tion** /infə'meɪʃən/ *n* (something which gives) knowledge in the form of facts, news, etc.
>
> ...for... ...on retrieval... the finding of stored infor-

2 In the boxes in the *Vocabulary* section on page 58 find at least *three* examples of: two-syllable words; three-syllable words; four-syllable words. Mark where the stress falls in each word. (Example: two syllables – *'tidy*)

LANGUAGE POINT 1

Saying where things are

1 [📼 8.1] Melanie and her friend are looking for a place to rent. Melanie is describing a flat she has just seen.

a) Listen to Melanie's description of the kitchen and make a list of the items of furniture she mentions. In pairs, check each other's spelling.
b) Copy the diagram below. Then listen again and label your diagram to show how Melanie describes the position of the furniture in the kitchen. Compare your diagram with a partner's.

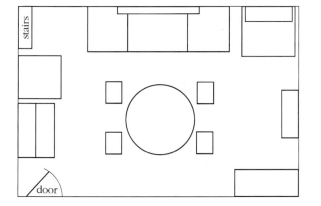

2 Melanie didn't describe the kitchen very accurately. Note down the differences between her description and what you see in the picture below. Example:
The washing machine isn't under the stairs, it's next to the freezer.

PRACTICE

1 Think of a room you are fond of and draw a square to represent it. In the square, label (in the places they are usually found):
– five items of furniture (e.g. *pine table*).
– five of your favourite possessions (e.g. *antique vase*).

2 Work in pairs, but don't show each other your pictures.

STUDENT A: Describe your room, saying exactly where your furniture and possessions are situated.

STUDENT B: Draw a square to represent Student A's room. Mark where each item is situated according to his/her description.

Discuss the differences between your drawings.

3 Tell each other where you got the furniture and possessions and what they mean to you. Example:
'I got the vase from my aunt for my eighteenth birthday. It always reminds me of her. Also I really like its colour and shape.'

LANGUAGE POINT 2

Making comparisons

1   Work in pairs. Are the following statements *True* or *False*? Change the false statements to make them true. Example:
Men live longer than women.   *False.*
'*Men live a **shorter** time than women.*'

Remember that *are* and *than* are pronounced weakly (/ə(r)/ and /ðən/) when they are part of a sentence. Remember also to emphasise the adjective or adverb which is contrasted, e.g. *shorter*

a) China is bigger than Russia.
b) The moon is nearer to the earth than the sun.
c) The North Sea is warmer than the Mediterranean Sea.
d) Prince Charles is older than Princess Diana.
e) The USA have a better football team than Brazil.
f) In Britain it becomes dark earlier in summer than in winter.

2   Complete the following sentences and then check with Section 3 in the *Language reference*.

– In adjectives or adverbs of one syllable the comparative is formed by adding _____ to the end of the adjective or adverb. This is followed by the word *than*.
– Some comparatives are irregular: for example *good* becomes _____ .
– Some adjectives and adverbs of two syllables also form the comparative with *-er*. For example, *early* becomes _____ .

3   Discuss the following statements with a partner and then agree or disagree, following the example below. Example:
Reading is more relaxing than watching television.
'*No, I don't agree. Watching television is more relaxing.*'

a) Parachuting is less dangerous than water-skiing.
b) Austria is more beautiful than Greece.
c) Washing-up is less boring than cooking.
d) Women are more intelligent than men.
e) English grammar is more difficult than English pronunciation.

4   Complete the following statement.

In most adjectives or adverbs of two or more syllables the comparative is formed by putting _____ or _____ in front of the adjective or adverb, and *than* after it.

Check with Section 3 in the *Language reference*.

5   Read these examples.
Learning English is as interesting as learning French.
Listening to a foreign language isn't as easy as speaking it.

Complete the following statement.

When you want to say that two things are equal you put _____ before the adjective or adverb and _____ after the adjective or adverb.

Check with Section 3 in the *Language reference* and find other ways of saying *not as . . . as*.

6   Read the following story.

> In 1900 Octavio Guillen met the girl who would one day be his wife. Two years later he announced his engagement to Adriana Martines and everyone said they made a lovely couple.
> They still made a lovely couple in 1969, when they cast caution to the winds and got married in Mexico City. They were both 82 and had been engaged for 67 years.

(from *The Book of Heroic Failures*)

a) Choose a title for the article from the examples in the box below. Discuss your choice with another student.

> The most cautious couple
> The best age to get married
> The worst age to get married
> The longest engagement
> The shortest engagement
> The least cautious couple

b) Complete the following statements.

The superlative form is made by adding *the* and _____ to adjectives and adverbs of one (or sometimes two) syllables. With adjectives or adverbs of three or more syllables you put *the* _____ or *the* _____ before the adjective.

Check with Section 3 in the *Language reference*.

PRACTICE

1 Make comparisons between the words in the circle, each time drawing lines between pairs of words. Make as many connections as you can.
Example:
*Yoga is **more relaxing than** ironing.*
*Dancing isn't **as tiring as** aerobics.*

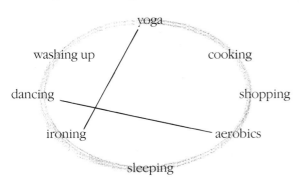

2 Imagine your house was on fire. Which five of the items below would you save? Why? Put the five in order of priority (e.g. Which is the most/least useful/precious/expensive? Which is the nicest?). Discuss your list with a partner.

a) your cat
b) jewellery
c) your computer
d) your favourite books
e) a very valuable sofa
f) your Persian rug
g) your best shoes
h) photographs
i) your passport
j) the television

3 Most languages have traditional sayings using *as . . . as*. Using the words in the box, complete the following to make idiomatic comparisons. Compare your answers with a partner's.

| a button   a post   nails   gold   a peacock |
| toast   a sheet   sin |

a) as warm as *toast*
b) as miserable as _____
c) as deaf as _____
d) as proud as _____
e) as white as _____
f) as hard as _____
g) as good as _____
h) as bright as _____

Write down some traditional *as . . . as* expressions translated from your own language(s). Explain them to your partner or to the other students in your class.

LANGUAGE POINT 3

Very / too / not enough

Look at these examples.

*This house is **very** small.*

*It's **too** small for my family. (This house is **not** big **enough** for my family.)*

*This house is **very** noisy.*

*It's **too** noisy to work in. (The house is **not** quiet **enough** to work in.)*

PRACTICE

Make sentences with *too* and *not enough*.

See **Use your grammar**, page 79, for further practice of comparisons, *very*, *too*, and *not...enough*.

SPEAKING

1   Look at these photographs. Which place would you most like to live in? Discuss the advantages and disadvantages of each place.

a tree house

a traveller's caravan

a houseboat

2   Imagine you are an estate agent. Work with your partner and try to 'sell' an unusual home to your partner. Your partner must think of all the objections. Example:

A: *An island house is just what you need. It is private and really quiet.*

B: *Yes, but it's very expensive, and what happens when the sea is rough?*

WRITING

Linking expressions

1   Some linking expressions join two clauses to make one sentence. Most can go at the beginning as well as in the middle of the sentence.

Although Ivan doesn't need the money, he likes being a window cleaner.

Ivan likes being a window cleaner, although he doesn't need the money.

Check with Section 5 in the *Language reference* for expressions which join clauses together and then use them to fill in the gaps in the following sentences.

a) _____ he was an actor or a window cleaner, Ivan was a fireman.

b) Ivan will buy his flat from the council _____ he has enough money.

c) He bought the wood for his floors _____ he was working in Holland.

d) The English prefer carpets _____ the Dutch prefer wooden floors.

2   Some expressions link ideas across sentences. They can have various positions in the sentence.

Ivan played Ambrose on TV. Afterwards, he was able to buy a Persian rug.

Ivan played Ambrose on TV. He was able to buy a Persian rug afterwards.

Refer again to Section 5 in the *Language reference*. Then fill in the gaps below.

a) Ivan is very gentle. He is enthusiastic _____ .

b) He wants to buy his flat eventually. _____ , he is renting it.

c) He fell off a ladder. _____ , he didn't hurt himself.

d) He left school early. _____ he decided he wanted to study drama, and went to drama school in the evenings.

3   Write a draft description of a house or a room that you really loved or hated. Make sure you include:

– factual information.

– human interest (what it reminded you of, how you felt about it, why you liked or disliked it).

– linking expressions (e.g. *but, after, also, however*).

– prepositional phrases of place (e.g. *in the corner of . . . , behind the . . . , on top of the . . .*).

Language reference

1 Prepositions of place

These are some of the prepositions of place you have met in this unit: *on, in, through, beside, next to, near, over, above, under, behind, between*.

2 Making opposites

Adding a prefix such as *un-* to the beginning of an adjective or adverb usually changes the adjective or adverb into its opposite: *pleasant → **un**pleasant*. Some other prefixes are: il- (**il**logical), im- (**im**practical), ir- (**ir**responsible), in- (**in**experienced), dis- (**dis**honest).
A common ending (or suffix) for an adjective is *-less* (use**less**, help**less**). The 'opposite' of these words usually ends in *-ful* (use**ful**, help**ful**).

3 Making comparisons

When we compare two things and say that one thing is *more* or *less* than the other we use a comparative construction.
He eats **more** / **less** quickly | **than** me.
                   | **than** I do.
My flat is **more** / **less** colourful **than** yours.
Ivan's flat is clean**er** / **less** clean **than** mine.
When the comparison is between three or more things we use a superlative.
You have **the biggest** house **in** the town.
The most unusual room **in** my house is the bathroom.
When we want to say that things are equal we can use *as . . . as*. Note that *as . . . as* is usually pronounced weakly (/əz . . . əz/).
He's **as** tall **as** his brother. (They are both 1m 50 tall.)
If we are talking about things that are not equal we can use either the comparative form or *not as . . . as*.
He's **less intelligent than** his sister.
He's **not as** intelligent **as** his sister.

FORM

After the comparative of the adjective or an adverb we use *than* (quieter **than**).
  Before the superlative we use *the*: She's **the** best swimmer **in** the world. (NOT ~~. . . of the world~~).
  If the adjective or adverb has one syllable, add *-(e)r* to form the comparative and *the* and *-(e)st* to form the superlative: *weak → weak**er** → the weak**est***.
  If the adjective or adverb has two or more syllables add *more* / *less* in the comparative (**more** / **less** slowly) and *most* / *least* in the superlative (**the most** / **least** interesting).
  Some two-syllable words (particularly those ending in *-y*) take *-er* in the comparative form: *early → earli**er**; pretty → pretti**er**.*
  With some two-syllable words (e.g. *clever, simple, tidy, stupid, gentle, handsome*) you can use either form: *clever → clever**er** OR **more** clever*.
  Some adjectives are irregular: *good → better → the best; bad → worse → the worst; old → older (elder) → the oldest (eldest); far → further (farther) → the furthest (farthest)*.
  Some adverbs are irregular: *well → better → the best*.

SPELLING

If the adjective ends with a single consonant after a single vowel, double the consonant: *big → bi**gg**er → the bi**gg**est*.
  For two-syllable adjectives ending in *-y* after a consonant, change to ***-ier*** and *the **-iest**: happy → happ**ier** → the happ**iest***.

4 *Very / too / not enough*

Very can be used with most adjectives to make them stronger.
This room is **very** small.
Too means *excessive*.
I'm not going to work today. I'm **too** tired.
Too + adjective can be followed by *to* + base form.
I'm **too tired to go** to work.
Too + adjective can also be followed by *for* and a noun or a pronoun.
This room is **too small for** all my books.
These shoes are **too small for** me.
Not (+ adjective) *enough* means *not as much as is needed*. It is followed by *to* and a verb in its base form. It can also be followed by *for* and a noun or a pronoun.
The house is **not** quiet **enough** (**for** me) **to work** in.

5 Linking expressions

(Some of these expressions were introduced in Unit 3.)
addition: *too, as well, and, also*
time: *afterwards, after, then, before, when, while, meanwhile, finally, later, as soon as, eventually*
contrast: *but, although, however, even though, nevertheless*
When opposites are contrasted (e.g. *She was tall whereas he was short.*) the following words and expressions can be used: *whereas, while, on the other hand*.

The following words and expressions link clauses together within a sentence: *although, even though, whereas, while, after, before, when, as soon as, but, and*.
He went home **as soon as** he finished his work.
And and *but* go in the middle of the sentence. The other expressions can go either at the beginning or in the middle.
Ivan is a window cleaner **and** he works as an actor.

Other words and expressions join ideas across sentences: *also, however, nevertheless, on the other hand, then, afterwards, meanwhile, too, as well, finally, eventually, later*. Apart from *too* and *as well*, which usually go at the end of the sentence, these expressions have various positions in the sentence. In general, it is safest to put them at the beginning.
He is a window cleaner. He is an actor **as well** / **too**.
He once fell off his ladder. **However**, he didn't hurt himself.

Reading the signs

LISTENING 1

Before listening

1   Listed in the box are some of the things British people think bring either good luck or bad luck.

Guess which bring good luck and which bring bad luck.

> a rabbit's foot   crossing fingers
> breaking a mirror   spilling salt
> a horseshoe   Friday 13th

2   Do you have the same superstitions in your country? Make a list of the things people in your country think bring:

a) good luck   b) bad luck

3   Compare your lists with another student's and discuss any similarities or differences.

4   Are you superstitious? Give your reasons.

Listening

1   Look at the pictures below. What are the people doing and why?

2   In ancient times, people thought that their itches were signs by which they could foretell the future. In which of the pictures do you think the person will have good luck?

3 [🔊 9.1]   Listen to the recording and check your answers.

4   According to the recording, which part of your body will itch if you are going to:

a) meet a male stranger?   c) have some good news?
b) receive a lot of money?   d) go on an unpleasant journey?

LANGUAGE POINT 1

Open conditionals: making predictions

Read this example.
If the itch is on the right side of your head, you will meet a female stranger.

a) Which of the following could be true about the first part of the sentence?
   i) It refers to a past action.
   ii) It refers to something which is generally true.
   iii) It refers to something that could possibly happen in the future.
b) What is the tense of the verb after *If*? Can we say: *If the itch **will be** . . . ?*
c) There are two clauses in the sentence. Which clause expresses a result?
d) Try to start the sentence with the clause: *You'll meet a female stranger if . . .* Is there a difference in meaning?

Check with Section 2 in the *Language reference* for words you can use instead of *'ll* (*will*).

PRACTICE

1   Make predictions from the following cues.
Example:
inside of the nose / problems follow
'If you have an itch on the inside of your nose, problems will follow.'
(When saying the sentences use the contracted form of *will*: . . . *problems'll follow*.)

a) hand itches / get rich
b) itchy tummy / somebody invite you out
c) want scratch right eye / see an old friend
d) lips / kiss someone soon
e) left ear / someone say rude things about you behind your back
f) right cheek / soon receive praise

2   Work in pairs. Make predictions for each other using some of the cues in the box. Add some cues of your own. Example:
'If you say "Touch wood", nothing will go wrong with your plans.'

walk under a ladder   see a pin and pick it up put an umbrella up indoors   see a black cat hang a bag of garlic around your neck get to the end of a rainbow   pull a wishbone

LANGUAGE POINT 2

Levels of certainty

Read about the predictions a fortune-teller made for a client.

> '(I think you'll get married again) fairly soon and you'll probably have at least two more children. I'm sorry to say, though, that you won't live to a very old age. As regards your career, it looks like you might become a journalist or something in the media. Anyway, you probably won't live in this country for long periods of time. You could become very rich and you may also be quite famous, although I'm not absolutely sure about that . . . '

Circle all the phrases which show the fortune-teller is either sure or not sure that something will happen. Match each prediction with the appropriate expression below. The first one has been done for you.

a) she's sure something will happen
   I think you'll get married again . . .
b) she thinks it's likely
c) she thinks it's possible
d) she thinks it's unlikely
e) she's sure something won't happen

PRACTICE

1   Think about your future life and write down:

a) four things you're sure will happen.
b) four things you're sure won't happen.
c) four things that could happen.

2   Work in pairs. Discuss with your partner your future lives.

VOCABULARY

Signs of illness

1 Complete the gaps in the following dialogues with words from the boxes. For speaker A, choose words from box A. For speaker B, choose words from box B. Use a dictionary if necessary.

A Symptoms

diarrhoea	pain	sneezing	sick	cough
faint	sore	bleeding	temperature	cut

B Illness

food poisoning	flu	tonsillitis	infection	
heart attack				

a) A: My throat's _____ . It hurts to swallow. But I don't _____ at all, even though I smoke fifty cigarettes a day.
   B: It sounds like _____ to me.

b) A: My nose is running and I can't stop _____ . I've also got a very high _____ .
   B: It's probably _____ . There's a lot of it about.

c) A: My mother feels very _____ after eating at that new restaurant. She has had terrible _____ for twenty-four hours!
   B: Oh no! That's the third person who's suffered from _____ after eating at that place.

d) A: I had this _____ in my hand last week. It was very deep and the wound wouldn't stop _____ . Now it's very painful again.
   B: I expect you've picked up some kind of _____ .

e) A: At the match yesterday, Brian felt very _____ and nearly fell over. He said he had a terrible _____ in his chest.
   B: Oh no! He didn't have a _____ , did he?'

2 Look back at Exercise 1. What advice would you give to each person for their illness. Use some of the words in the box if you wish. Example: *'Take an aspirin, and lie down and get some rest.'*

pastilles	hot lemon	suck	rub	aspirin
antiseptic lotion	doctor	plaster	tie	
keep warm	bandage			

Antonyms and synonyms

1 An antonym is a word which means the opposite or nearly the opposite of another word. Find antonyms in the box for each of the words in italics in order to complete the sentences below. Compare your answers with a partner's. Example: *The weather in May was **dry**, but in June it was **wet**.*

poor	thin	mild	hard	return	single
interesting	wet	dull	easy	heavy	sweet

a) I only drink *dry* wine. I hate _____ wine.
b) Do you prefer your cheese *strong* or _____ ?
c) Our exam was really *hard* but the other class had a(n) _____ one.
d) Put on a *thick* pullover if you're cold. That one is too _____ .
e) He's quite *dull*, but she's very _____ .
f) It's so *light* outside, but it's very _____ in the house because of the small windows.
g) You carry this bag – it's quite *light*. I'll take the _____ one.
h) Although she's very *rich*, he's quite _____ .
i) Our bed is quite *soft*, but my wife has a bad back so she'd prefer a _____ one.
j) A *single* ticket – or a _____ ?
k) I'm *married* but Sue's still _____ .

2 A synonym is a word which has a similar meaning to another word. What synonyms are there for the adjectives in the following phrases? Compare your answers with a partner's. Example: *an **untidy** room / a **messy** room*

a) an *attractive* man
b) an *amusing* story
c) a *nice* time
d) a *badly-behaved* child
e) a *quiet* voice
f) a *silly* answer

3 The following nouns can be found in Exercises 1 and 2 above. Think of as many adjectives as you can which go together with them naturally.

a) weather (e.g. **cold weather**, **wet weather**, etc.)
b) cheese
c) exam
d) bed
e) story

LANGUAGE POINT 3

Unless

Look at the picture and read the example sentences below. Then answer the questions.

If you don't turn that music down, I'll kill you!
Unless you turn that music down, I'll kill you!

a) Is the music loud?
b) Do the two sentences mean the same?
c) What can *unless* often mean?

Check your answers with Section 3 in the *Language reference*.

Promises and threats

1   Read these examples.
 i) *If you clean my car, I'll take you to a football match.*
 ii) *If you don't hurry up, I'll go without you.*
 iii) *Unless you increase my pay, I'll look for another job.*

a) Rewrite i) beginning: *If you don't . . .*
b) Rewrite ii) beginning: *Unless . . .*
c) Rewrite iii) beginning: *If you increase . . .*

2   Which of the six sentences above are promises? Which are threats?

3 [9.2]   'Is that a threat or a promise?' The tone of your voice is very important when making promises and threats. Listen to five sentences and say which are promises and which are threats.

Warnings

Look at the pictures and answer the questions.

'If you leave that broken bottle there, somebody could hurt themselves.'

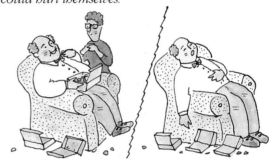

'If you don't stop eating so many chocolates, you'll have a heart attack.'

a) In each example, is it possible something bad may happen?
b) Do the speakers try to prevent it? How?

PRACTICE

1   Rewrite these sentences to make one sentence. Change as many words as necessary.
Example:
I might see him. If I do, I'll give him the money.
  (*If . . .*)
If I see him, I'll give him the money.

a) Slow down! I'll never let you drive again. (*If . . .*)
b) Stop that! I'll send you home. (*Unless . . .*)
c) Quieten down. I'll kick you out of here! (*If . . .*)
d) Clean up this mess! Then you can watch television. (*Unless . . .*)
e) I'll send it. First give me your address. (*If . . .*)

2   Practise saying the sentences above with a partner. Show how the tone of voice for promises is different from the tone of voice for threats.

3 Work in pairs.

a) What is the problem in each of these pictures?
What will the probable results be?

1

2

3

4

b) Suggest a warning for each of the pictures.

c) Which of the activities in the pictures do you
think is the most dangerous? Why?

> See **Use your grammar,** page 79, for further practice of
> *if* and *unless*.

LISTENING 2

Before listening

Work in pairs. Examine the palms of each other's
hands to find the four different lines.

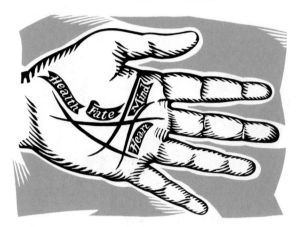

Fate line: The long vertical line that rises from the wrist to
the centre of the palm, towards the base of the middle finger.
Mind line: The second line down that runs horizontally
across the palm.
Heart line: The line from the edge of your hand below
your little finger that rises towards your index finger.
Health line: The line from the thumb side of the wrist
towards the little finger.

Listening

1 [9.3]   A woman is reading the signs on a
man's hand. Listen and find out which part of the
hand shows:

a) that he is a little unimaginative.
b) that his parents were unhappy.
c) that he might be a writer.
d) that he is stubborn.
e) that he suffers from chest infections.

2   Listen again and circle the correct alternative.

a) Outgoing / shy as a child
b) Calm / can be bad tempered
c) Attracted / not attracted to women
d) Close / not close to parents
e) Married in twenties / thirties
f) Headaches / backaches

3   Which of these does she predict?

a) He'll soon have another child.
b) He'll wear glasses.
c) He'll never be rich.
d) He'll get divorced.

4 Read the following to find out more about three of the lines on your hand.

Fate line Represents your career and way of life. A break in the line means a change of job. Branches rising up out of it mean success. Bars cutting the line indicate obstruction.

Mind line Represents the way you think. A straight line means you are logical. You are likely to be a mathematician or a scientist. A curved line means you are imaginative. You are good at dealing with people. If you have a straight line which develops a curve you have both sides to your personality. You would make a good doctor or teacher.

Heart line Represents passion and emotion. The nearer the line is to your fingers the cooler you are in romance. The lower the line starts, the sexier you are. If the line is short you may have trouble making relationships last. The opposite is true if the line is long.

5 Work in pairs. Look at your partner's hand. What can you discover about his/her personality?

SPEAKING

Story telling

Work in groups. You are going to tell a story about a man who was found unconscious in a tube train. Choose at least one of the words from both A and B below and one of the items in each of C and D and decide on your story line. Practise telling the story, adding as many ideas as you like.

A	B
blood stain first-aid kit bandage the 'kiss of life'	ambulance jogging police station reward

C

D

WRITING

Writing narrative

1 Group these sentences into three or four paragraphs to make a short story. The events are in the correct order.

Adam and Ben left university.
They both needed a job.
They decided to go on holiday together for the last time.
They stayed in a small hotel.
They didn't have much money.
It was the last day of their holiday.
On the way back from the beach they saw a fortune-teller.
Adam decided to visit the fortune-teller.
The fortune-teller predicted that Adam would soon get a good job, become rich and have a lot of children.
Adam was very pleased.
He told Ben about the fortune-teller's prediction.
Ben was jealous.
He pretended he didn't believe in fortune-tellers.
He didn't want to go to the fortune-teller.
Adam wanted to cheer Ben up.
Adam ran across the road to buy Ben a bottle of wine.
He didn't see a car coming round the corner.
Ben tried to warn him.
The car hit Adam.
He was badly injured.
In the night Adam nearly died.
Ben was by his bedside.
A week later, Adam started to recover.
Ben went back home.
He decided to go abroad.
He didn't tell Adam.
Two months later Adam came out of hospital.
He looked for Ben but couldn't find him.
Adam got a job as a waiter.
Ten years later Adam and Ben met by chance in London.
Ben had a good job overseas, was very rich and had four children.
He was working very hard but was not very happy.
Adam was very poor and couldn't find a job.
He was free and quite happy.
They decided to be friends again.

2 Write the story in three or four paragraphs, connecting the ideas and expanding the facts. Make the story as vivid as you can. Try to include linking words, adjectives and adverbs.

Language reference

A conditional describes something which must happen or be true before some other thing can happen or be true. Some conditionals are possible, e.g. *You'll burn yourself if you play with matches.* (You're playing with matches and I'm warning you.) Some are less possible or imaginary, e.g. *I'd buy a new house if I had enough money.* (Unfortunately, I have no money so I can't.)

1 Open (or 'first') conditionals

Open conditionals (sometimes known as the first conditional) normally refer to the future and are used for such things as:

a) making predictions: *If the weather is nice tomorrow, there will be a lot of people on the beach.*
b) promises: *If you pass your exam, I'll buy you a bottle of champagne.*
c) threats: *I'll tell the Principal if you don't behave yourself.*
d) warnings: *If you don't take more care, you'll have an accident.*

The condition is called 'open' because the future event (described in the *if*-clause) may happen (it's possible) but it may not. The result of the *if*-clause is expressed in the main clause.

With promises, threats and warnings in particular, your intonation helps to communicate your real intention.

FORM

AFFIRMATIVE
*If the weather **is** good, we **will go** for a walk.* *I'll phone her if I **have** time.*

NEGATIVE
*They **won't know** if we **don't tell** them.*

QUESTION
*What **will** you **do** if it **rains**?*

***If I win** the election, **I will** put up taxes.*
– Conditional clause: *If* + verb in the present tense: ***If I win** the election . . .*
– Main clause (describes the result of the condition): usually contains a modal, such as *will*: . . . ***I will** put up taxes.*
You can place the conditional clause after the main clause without changing the meaning.

2 Modal auxiliaries: levels of certainty

Will (see also Unit 5) is a modal auxiliary: *It'll rain. / It won't rain.* A modal is a verb which 'helps' a main verb (a 'fact' verb like *rain*) to show the speaker's opinion at the time of speaking. *Will / won't* expresses certainty, except when used with a word like *probably*, when it means something is likely or unlikely.
   *It'll **probably** rain. Why don't you take a coat?*
   *You **probably** won't live in this country for long periods of time.*
Modals which express possibility are *may*, *might* and *could*. In open conditionals they can be used instead of *will*.
   *If you get a taxi you **may** / **might** / **could** get there on time.*
   *If you don't get a taxi you **may not** / **might not** get there on time.*
Note that modals never change their form and do not have an *-s* form for the third person singular.
   *If he gets a new job, he **might** (NOT ~~mights~~) buy a car.*

3 *Unless*

Unless often means 'If . . . not'.
   ***If** you don't turn that music down, I'll kill you!*
   *I'll kill you **unless** you turn that music down!*
Unless can usually only be used when there is an idea of ending a situation that already exists.

4 Antonyms and synonyms

An antonym is a word which means the opposite or nearly the opposite of another word. Notice that because some words go together naturally the antonyms of adjectives can change in different phrases (***strong** coffee* / ***weak** coffee*; ***strong** wind* / ***light** wind*).

A synonym is a word with the same or nearly the same meaning as another word (*a **dull** person* / *an **uninteresting** person*). However, some words (e.g. *strong coffee*) go together (we say they 'collocate') in a way that sounds natural to a native speaker. Synonyms cannot always be put in their place. For example we don't say ***powerful** coffee* even though *powerful* is a synonym of *strong*.

Also, the feelings that are associated with one word – their 'connotation' – might be different from the feelings that might be associated with another word (*slim* and *skinny* mean *thin*, but *slim* has a positive connotation and *skinny* has a negative connotation).

A better life?

READING

Before reading

1 Life in the future.

a) Tell your partner about one of your hopes for the future. (*I hope I'll . . .* / *I hope to . . .*)

b) Do you think life in the future will be better or worse than now? Give reasons.

2 [🔊 10.1] What will houses in the future be like? Listen to David speaking.

a) Does he think houses will be big or small?

b) Will they be cheaper or dearer to heat? Why?

c) What kind of new electronic inventions will there be?

d) Where will the garden be situated?

e) How will we be able to change the size of the house?

3 Which of David's views do you agree or disagree with? Give your reasons.

Reading

1 Which of the things mentioned by David can you find in the picture below?

2 Read the article opposite and find at least three things that David didn't mention, but which are shown in the picture.

DOME SWEET DOME!

Weather-proof, solar-powered – and no housework to speak of!

1 Just imagine a house which cleaned itself, where robots prepared the meals, where dusting, ironing and DIY were things of the past. Imagine a house heated and powered by the energy equivalent to just one gas cooker ring, a house in which you could actually go *skiing* . . . Science fiction? Science fact!

2 The Home of the Future will be built *indoors*, for a start. Small groups of houses will nestle under gigantic glass domes surrounded by lush trees and shrubs. Tropical birds may flit across the rooftops in the constant, computer-controlled warmth.

3 The house itself will be any style or size you fancy. Being indoors, it will need only a tiny amount of energy to heat. Much power will come from solar panels in the dome – the round roof.

4 Forget front door keys. Your door will be opened as soon as it hears a voice it recognises. Your space-age butler – the ultimate home computer – will oversee security. This discreet electronic servant will control everything, from temperature, humidity and lighting to household gadgets and cleaning chores. He'll pay bills and order food, making sure it's delivered to your door. He'll book your holidays, order library books, even help you with the crossword!

5 Having a party? Make the living room larger by moving the walls. After your guests leave make it smaller again. Push a button and the walls will move backwards or forwards.

6 You'll be able to see what your guests are wearing *before* they arrive by calling them up on a video-phone in the hall. And the washing? Simply place it in the integrated laundry until it comes out ready to wear, thanks to the new, easy-care fabrics. What, no electric sockets? Instead each room will have a 'power wall' where you will be able to attach electric appliances.

7 Gone, too, will be the good old-fashioned duster – the air will be filtered and then scented with your favourite perfumes.

8 There will be plenty of room for fun! The leisure room door will be the entrance to a world full of endless adventure. When you get bored, simulators will provide any experience from canoeing to parachuting and skiing.

9 The garden will be in the loft. Roofs will be made of glass. This will allow flower borders, shrubs and lawns to grow well in that wasted space we normally use for rubbish.

10 Love them or loathe them, such homes of the future are on their way.

(from *Bella*)

3   Which of these developments are predicted in the article? Put a tick if it is predicted and a cross if it isn't. One has been done for you.

a) temperatures which never change ✓
b) no need for heating
c) no need for front doors
d) housework done by computers
e) no security problems
f) a TV screen which is hooked on the wall
g) clothes which don't need ironing
h) air with no smells

4   Which word in the article means:

a) very big (paragraph 2)?
b) fly lightly and quickly (paragraph 2)?
c) like (paragraph 3)?
d) be in control of (paragraph 4)?
e) uninteresting jobs (paragraph 4)?
f) space inside the roof (paragraph 9)?
g) hate very much (paragraph 10)?

5   The article comes from a weekly magazine. The style of the writing is informal and conversational. This style is achieved by using the imperative form (e.g. *Just imagine a house which cleaned itself*), asking shortened direct questions (e.g. *Having a party?*), the use of the impersonal *you* (e.g. *a house in which you could actually go skiing*), missing words (e.g. *Science fiction?*) as well as contracted forms and exclamation marks. In the text, underline at least one other example of each of the conversational features listed above. Compare your answers in pairs.

6   Would you like to live in the house described? Give your reasons. Describe your ideal house of the future.

LANGUAGE POINT 1

Time conjunctions

Time conjunctions are linking expressions which join together two clauses (e.g. *as soon as, after, before, until, when*).

a) Find an example of each of these conjunctions in the text above (paragraphs 4, 5, 6 and 8).
b) Which tense follows each of these time conjunctions? Does the tense refer to the present, past or future?

PRACTICE

1   Complete each of these sentences with one of the time conjunctions.

a) Let's wait here _____ it stops raining.
b) Close all the windows _____ you go out.
c) Please don't smoke _____ you're teaching.
d) I'll wash up immediately _____ you leave.
e) The phone rang _____ I got in the bath.

2   Use the time conjunctions to write sentences about your own life.

a) I think I'll . . . until . . .
b) When . . . I may . . .
c) I'm going to . . . before . . .
d) I'll . . . as soon as . . .
e) Before . . . I'll . . .

LANGUAGE POINT 2

If or when?

1   In some sentences *if* and *when* can mean almost the same thing. Example:
If/When you heat ice, it melts. (general rules or habits)

In other situations *if* and *when* have different meanings. For example, in which of the following sentences is the speaker sure that the other person will be bored? In which sentence is it just a possibility?
If you're bored, simulators will provide all the experiences you could wish for.
When you're bored, simulators will provide all the experiences you could wish for.

Check with Section 2 in the *Language reference*.

2   In which of these sentences is *if/when* used correctly? Correct the others.

a) We'll go for a walk when it doesn't rain.
b) If you wake up I'll be gone.
c) If you're ill tomorrow, don't go to work.
d) I'm going to be an actress if I grow up.
e) Don't worry if I'm late.
f) When you don't give me the money, I'll shoot!

LANGUAGE POINT 3

Future Passive

Read these examples.
Roofs will be made of glass.
The air will be filtered.

a) Do we know who will make the roofs and what will filter the air?
Is it important?
b) Which is the passive form: *will filter* or *will be filtered*?

Check with Section 3 in the *Language reference* for the use and form
of the Future Passive.

PRACTICE

1 Rebecca Lee is going to attend a conference on 'House Design in the Year 2500'. Read the letter she received from the conference organisers and find answers to the following questions.

a) Who will meet her at the airport?
b) What will she do before lunch?
c) Who will order her taxi?

2 Read the letter again.

a) Underline all examples of the Future Passive.
b) Why do you think the passive form was used in this letter?

3 Find some phrases that are typical of a semi-formal letter.
Example:
I note that . . .

Symposium

The Conference Specialists

15 Sydney Street,
Edinburgh.
Tel. 0131 236541
Fax 0131 236630

2 May 1995

Dear Ms Lee,

We are very glad to hear that you will be able to attend this year's conference to be held at the Metropole Hotel, Edinburgh.

I note that your plane arrives at 9 a.m. You will be met in the arrivals hall by one of our representatives and taken by car to our headquarters in Sydney Street. There you will be asked to complete the required formalities and will be given the necessary papers and information about the conference. After an opportunity to relax you will then be taken on a short sight-seeing tour of the city before meeting the conference organisers for lunch at a local restaurant, where we will be joined by the Director General.

We expect the conference to end by 5 p.m. If you want to leave on the 6 p.m. flight to Heathrow, a taxi can be ordered immediatley. Otherwise we will be delighted to have your presence at a dinner with the other conference participants.

We look forward to meeting you on the 15th. If there are any queries please do not hesitate to contact me.

Yours sincerely,

Edward Moller

Edward Moller
Conference Organiser

4 Active or passive? Look at the contexts (in brackets) below and tick the correct alternative in each case. One has been done for you.

a) (*Notice on the gate of a large house*)
We will prosecute trespassers.
Trespassers will be prosecuted. ✓

b) (*Hotel receptionist picking up the key*)
I'll show you to your room now.
You'll be shown to your room by me now.

c) (*Newspaper article*)
The rain forests will be better protected in the future.
Someone is going to protect the rain forests better in the future.

d) (*Girl to a friend before a driving test*)
I'll be bought a present by my parents if I pass.
My parents will buy me a present if I pass.

e) (*Guide showing tourists around a vineyard*)
At this stage the wine will be left for six months.
At this stage they'll leave the wine for six months.

f) (*Politician in a TV interview*)
The Government will not give the army a pay rise this year.
The army will not be given a pay rise this year.

g) (*Two brothers after a job interview*)
Do you think you'll be offered the job?
Do you think the interviewers will offer you the job?

h) (*A telephone call to a friend*)
We're holding a party tomorrow.
A party is being held tomorrow.

5 Work in groups. There is going to be a conference for teachers. You are on the planning committee.

a) Decide on:
 – the theme of the conference (Example: *Should we teach British-English or American-English?*).
 – where the conference will take place.
 – how long it will last.
 – the times of the programme.
 – the travel arrangements for participants.
 – social events.

b) In groups, write a welcome letter for participants. Use the passive form where possible.

LANGUAGE POINT 4

Making personal arrangements

Read these examples.
We're getting the 6 o'clock plane.
My mother is meeting us at 7.30.

When do we use the Present Continuous to talk about the future? Check your answers with Section 4 in the *Language reference*.

PRACTICE

1 Work in groups of three. You are going to the conference on Wednesday 15th June, but you want to meet up with your two friends on either the Monday or the Tuesday of that week. First make a note in your diary of at least three things you have to do on both Monday and Tuesday. Example:

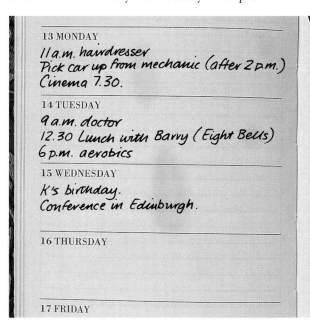

13 MONDAY
11 a.m. hairdresser
Pick car up from mechanic (after 2 p.m.)
Cinema 7.30.

14 TUESDAY
9 a.m. doctor
12.30 Lunch with Barry (Eight Bells)
6 p.m. aerobics

15 WEDNESDAY
K's birthday.
Conference in Edinburgh.

16 THURSDAY

17 FRIDAY

2 Find out what each other is doing at different times on these days. Find a time that you can all meet. Decide what you will do together (e.g. *go to the theatre, have a meal*). Use the Present Continuous as appropriate. Example:

A: *What are you doing on Monday evening?*
B: *Nothing really. I'm free after 6 o'clock.*
C: *Well, I'm going to the dentist's at 5.30, but I'm sure I'll be free by 7 o'clock.*
A: *OK. I'm busy until 6.45. What about meeting for a drink at 7.15 and . . . ?*

PRONUNCIATION

Vowels

Your dictionary can help you pronounce new words if you know the symbols used for the different sounds.

1 Look at the pronunciation chart on page 160 and make sure you can read the vowels in the chart. There are twelve of them.

2 Look at these two dictionary entries. How do you pronounce the vowels?

> **flirtatious** /flɜːˈteɪʃəs/ *adj* tending to flirt
> **flit** /flɪt/ *v* to fly or move lightly or quickly
> **float**[1] /fləʊt/ *v* **1** to (cause to) stay on the surface of a
> ~~quic~~ ~~out sinking~~

> ~~taste or smell~~
> **lush** /lʌʃ/ *adj* growing very well, thickly, and healthi-ly
> **lustre** /ˈlʌstə/ *n* the brightness of a shiny polished
> ~~face~~

3 [🔊 10.2]   The twelve words in the box each contain one of the vowel sounds of the English language. (In the case of *driver* we are interested in the vowel sound in the second syllable only.) Copy the words. Listen to the recording and write the correct vowel symbol next to each word, using your pronunciation chart as a reference. Example: *girl* /ɜː/

girl	driver	sad	fall	knee	flu
drink	when	good	fun	wash	farm

4 Write down one more example of each of the vowel sounds.

5 Decide which vowel sounds are used in these words. Copy and complete the pronunciation, then check in your dictionary.

a) taxi / 't __ ks __ /
b) dinner / 'd __ n __ /
c) necessary / 'n __ s __ sr __ /
d) tropical / 'tr __ p __ k __ l /
e) border / 'b __ d __ /
f) underneath / __ nd __ 'n __ θ /
g) afternoon / __ ft __ 'n __ n /
h) murder / 'm __ d __ /
i) naughty / 'n __ t __ /
j) rocket / 'r __ k __ t /
k) toothbrush / 't __ θbr __ ʃ /
l) woollen / 'w __ l __ n /

VOCABULARY

Phrasal verbs

Up and *down* often combine with verbs to form what are called phrasal verbs. In phrasal verbs *up* often expresses the idea of 'increase' and *down* the idea of 'decrease'. Example:
The television wasn't loud enough so I turned it **up**.
The radio was too loud so I turned it **down**.

1 Match the phrasal verbs in column A with their definitions in column B. (Note that some of these phrasal verbs have more than one meaning.)

A	B
1 grow up	a) do less of something
2 heat up	b) become happier
3 wind down	c) be quicker
4 cheer up	d) make slower
5 bring up	e) make less loud/hot/
6 turn down	noisy, etc.
7 cut down	f) rear/educate
8 hurry up	g) relax
9 slow down	h) go from childhood
	to adulthood
	i) make hotter

2 Fill in the gaps with appropriate phrasal verbs from column A in Exercise 1. In each case put the phrasal verb into the appropriate tense.

a) Why don't you try and _____ _____ your cigarettes to ten a day? Twenty is really far too many.
b) My parents died when I was young so my aunt _____ me _____ .
c) You seem a bit depressed. Is there anything I can do to _____ you _____?
d) We're going to be late unless you _____ _____ .
e) Yoga is a good way to _____ _____ if you find it difficult to relax.
f) The meal has gone cold, but I'll _____ it _____ for you.
g) I'm afraid I can't run very fast. My bad leg _____ me _____ .
h) Suzanne wants to be a computer analyst when she _____ _____ .
i) It's rather hot in here. May I _____ the heater _____?

SPEAKING

This is one artist's impression of what humans might look like in a few million years' time.

1   Why does the artist believe that human beings will look like this? Work in pairs and write as many reasons as you can. Example: *The person's arms are very thin because in the future machines will do all the heavy work and humans won't have to carry anything.*

2   How do *you* think men and women's physical appearance will change in the future? What kind of clothes will people wear?

3   Think of one more thing that will be quite different in the future (e.g. the car) and discuss what it will be like.

CREATIVE WRITING

1   Read this extract from a short story.

a) What kind of gadgets does the house have?
b) Why do you think there is no one at home?

2   What are some of the differences between the style of writing in the text *There Will Come Soft Rains* (TWCSR) and the magazine article *Dome Sweet Dome* (DSD)? Example: *TWCSR is a story (a narrative).*

a) _____ mainly uses the past tense.
b) _____ appears to talk directly to the reader.
c) _____ has one specific imaginary situation with absent characters.
d) _____ contains mainly future forms.

Can you find any other differences?

3   Discuss how you think the story continues. What has happened to the Featherstone family? Use your imagination. Agree on:

a) at least two things which will happen.
b) which characters you will introduce.
c) whether there will be any dialogue.
d) how the story ends.

4   In groups, write a draft of the story. Check your use of verb forms, time conjunctions and prepositions.

5   Write a neat version of your story and then read it out to the rest of the class. Vote on the most interesting story.

There Will Come Soft Rains

In the living-room the voice-clock sang, *Tick-tock, seven o'clock, time to get up, time to get up, seven o'clock!* as if it were afraid that nobody would. The house lay empty. The clock ticked on, repeating and repeating its sounds into the emptiness. *Seven-nine, breakfast time, seven-nine!*

In the kitchen the breakfast stove gave a hissing sigh and ejected from its warm interior eight pieces of perfectly browned toast, eight eggs sunnyside up, sixteen slices of bacon, two coffees, and two cool glasses of milk.

'Today is August 4, 2026,' said a second voice from the kitchen ceiling, 'in the city of Allendale, California.' It repeated the date three times for memory's sake. 'Today is Mr Featherstone's birthday. Today is the anniversary of Tilita's marriage. Insurance is payable, as are the water, gas and light bills.'

Eight-one, tick-tock, eight-one o'clock, off to school, off to work, run, run, eight-one! But no doors slammed, no carpets took the soft thread of rubber heels. It was raining outside. The weather box on the front door sang quietly: 'Rain, rain go away; rubbers, raincoats for today . . . ' And the rain tapped on the empty house, echoing.

Outside, the garage chimed and lifted its door to reveal the waiting car. After a long wait the door swung down again.

3

(from *There Will Come Soft Rains* by Ray Bradbury)

Language reference

1 Time conjunctions

Time conjunctions (*as soon as / after / before / until / when*) join clauses together to show the time at which something happens.

> Simply place the washing in the laundry **until** it comes out ready to wear.
> I'll tidy up **when** you leave.

When the sentence refers to the future, the time conjunction is usually followed by a present tense, not a future form.

> **As soon as** you speak, your voice will open the door. (NOT *As soon as you will speak . . .*)

2 *If* or *when*?

In sentences which express a present condition (a general rule or a habit) *if* and *when* can mean the same thing. Notice that the present tense is used in both clauses.

> **If / When** it snows, this road always gets blocked. (It always happens.)

But when *if* means *if it is true that . . .* and expresses possibility we cannot use *when*.

> Don't worry **if** (NOT *when*) I'm late. (I'm not sure that I will be late.)

If we are sure something will happen, we use *when*.

> I'm going to be an actress **when** I grow up. (I'm sure I will grow up.)

3 The passive

USE

In active sentences, the subject of the verb is the person or thing doing the action.

> I'll meet Rebecca at the airport. (*I* is the subject; *Rebecca* is the object.)

In passive sentences, we are often more interested in the action than who is doing the action. An object in an active sentence would be the subject in a passive sentence (see Unit 19).

> Rebecca will be met at the airport. (By me, but that's not important!)
> Roofs will be made of glass. (It's not important who makes them.)

The passive is often used when we want to distance ourselves from the subject. It is often used in formal and semi-formal situations (e.g. semi-formal letters).

FORM

In this unit we have only looked at the Future Passive, formed by the future form of the verb *be* + the past participle.

> The house **will be cleaned** by computer.

4 Future personal arrangements

In English it is very common to use the Present Continuous to talk about future personal arrangements which are already planned.

> We**'re doing** our Christmas shopping on Saturday. Do you want to come? (We've already planned it for the future.)
> He**'s meeting** me at nine o'clock.

The Present Continuous refers to the future only in the context of personal arrangements. It is usually necessary to include a time adverbial (*on Saturday*, *at nine o'clock*) to make it clear that we are talking about the future and not the present.

> What **are** you **doing** this evening?
> What **are** you **going to do** this evening?

Both of these questions are asking about personal plans made before now and so refer to the future from the point of view of the present. There is no real difference in meaning between the two questions above. Native speakers use them interchangeably. This is not the case in the following two questions.

> **Is** it **raining**?
> **Is** it **going to rain**?

Raining is not a personal arrangement and the Present Continuous cannot be used here to talk about the future. *Is it going to rain?* refers to the future; *Is it raining?* refers to the present.

5 Phrasal verbs

A phrasal verb is a group of words containing a verb that acts like a single verb. One type of phrasal verb consists of a verb + adverb particle (e.g. *turn up*).

Phrasal verbs are very common, especially in informal English, and may cause you difficulty, particularly when the phrasal verb has a meaning which seems different from the meanings of the two words looked at separately. (For example: *to **keep** somebody **up*** can mean *to stop someone from going to bed*.)

Phrasal verbs sometimes have several meanings. Two of the meanings of *bring up* are:

a) mention (*Don't **bring** that **up** now!*)

b) educate and care for a child (*I was **brought up** not to speak during meals.*)

However, the adverb particle can sometimes help us understand the meaning. For example:

up often expresses the idea of increase: *hurry up, heat up, turn up*

down often, but not always, expresses the idea of decrease: *calm down, cut down, settle down*

When a phrasal verb with an adverb particle is followed by a noun object the adverb particle can come either before or after the object.

> **Turn down** the television.   **Turn** the television **down**.

Note, however, that if the object is a pronoun, the object must come before the adverb particle.

> **Turn it down**. (NOT *Turn down it*.)

Use your grammar

UNIT 6

Defining relative clauses

Work in pairs. There has been a bank robbery.
STUDENT A
Look at page 154.

STUDENT B
You are a police officer. Student A and the men in the pictures committed the crime. They all did different things: one carried a gun; one tied up the bank manager; one blew up the safe; one put the money in the bags; one drove the car. They have hidden the money in a house.

a) You have arrested Student A. Look at the pictures and write questions to ask him / her. Use *who / that, which / that* or *where*. Example:
Is this the man /carried the gun …?
Is this the house /you hid the money …?

b) Ask Student A your questions.

UNIT 7

Describing people

Work in pairs.
STUDENT A
Look at page 154.

STUDENT B
You are at this official reception. The people you know are named. Answer your partner's questions about them. Then describe the people you don't know to your partner and find out their names. Example:
B: *Who's the woman at the back with the long, blond hair?*
A: *That's Helena Acton.*

Senator Jackson

Hans Niemann

Mr Simpson

Mrs Simpson

Buddy Coran

Françoise Bertrand

UNIT 8

Comparisons

a) Work in groups. Compare these things. Use the adjectives in the box or any others you know.

1

2

3

interesting	fast	bad	filling	light	elegant
spicy	practical	slow	exciting	tasty	heavy
comfortable	nice	hot	environmentally-friendly		
good	delicious				

b) Which do you prefer? Why? *I like...best because...*
I don't like...because it's very / too... / not...enough.

UNIT 9

If and *unless*

Work in groups. Steve has to get up at 7.00 am.

a) If he oversleeps, what will happen? Put the events in the box in order.

oversleep   his boss / be angry   lose his job
be very poor   fall in love with an American woman
be late for work   emigrate to the USA   miss the train
Anne / not marry him

b) Take it in turns to say a sentence beginning with *If...* to tell Steve's story. Example:
If Steve oversleeps, he'll miss the train.

c) Tell the story again. This time begin your sentences with *Unless...* You will need to change some of the verbs. Choose verbs from the box below. Example:
Unless Steve wakes up, he'll miss the train.

keep   be on time   be rich   wake up   catch
be pleased

UNIT 10

Time conjunctions

Work in pairs.

STUDENT A
Look at page 155.

> STUDENT B
> **a)** You are going to invite your partner out to the cinema. Choose one of the cinemas on the map below but don't show your partner where it is. Invite him / her to the cinema and agree to meet there. Give directions from his / her house using expressions like: *as soon as, after, before, until, when.*
> Example:
> *When you come out of your house, turn right.*
>
> **b)** Now your partner is going to invite you out to a restaurant. Agree to meet there. Follow his / her directions from your house on the map.

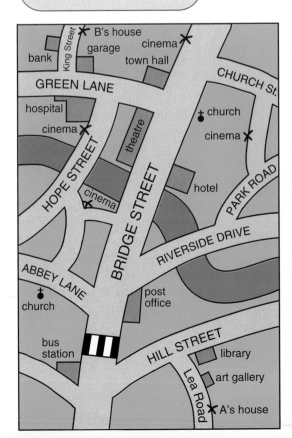

Is the service good enough?

SPEAKING

1   Look at the pictures and discuss the following in pairs.

a) Which of these places would you prefer to stay the night at? Why?
b) List three things you look for in overnight accommodation?
   Example:
   a comfortable bed
c) Which three things do you hate most? Example:
   no shower in the room

2   Work in groups.

a) Would you be prepared to spend a lot of money on a good hotel? Give your reasons.
b) Look at the two lists of services provided at a hotel in Tokyo. The first list tells you what is available in the hotel as a whole. The second list tells you about the services in each room. Choose five services which you feel are important from each of the two lists. Discuss the reasons for your choices and put the services you have chosen in order of priority.
c) Put a cross next to any services in the two lists which you think are not important.
d) Are there any services you think are missing from the two lists?

CITY HOTEL • TOKYO • JAPAN

Services

Hotel
Swimming pool
Games room
Mini-gym
Sauna/solarium
Good restaurants
Ironing facilities
Baby-sitting facilities
Car park
24-hour laundry service
Free newspapers
Telefax

Room
Radio / Colour TV
Direct dial telephone
Hairdryer
Electric trouser press
Bathrobes
Mini-bar
Private bathroom
24-hour room service
Tea- and coffee-making facilities
Air-conditioning
Writing desk

LISTENING

1 [📼 11.1] Listen to this phone conversation. A woman is booking a room at a hotel. Imagine you are the receptionist. Fill in the registration form as you listen.

Mermaid Hotel
Luton

Registration form

NAME: _____

PHONE NUMBER: _____

TYPE OF ROOM REQUESTED: _____

DATES: _____

SPECIAL REQUESTS: _____

CAR REGISTRATION: _____

TIME OF ARRIVAL: _____

2   Listen again and complete the sentences.

a) _____ how much that'll cost?
b) _____ your name, please?
c) _____ to leave my car with you?
d) _____ reserve you a place for eight days.
e) _____ the number and make of your car, please?
f) _____ book me another room at the same time, could you?
g) _____ now.

LANGUAGE POINT 1

Requests and offers

1   Which of the sentences in *Listening* Exercise 2 are: i) requests?   ii) offers?

2   Notice that when we think a request is difficult, unusual or inconvenient it is often better to sound less confident and use a polite form.
'I wonder if you'd mind lending me your car.'
(The speaker thinks the request is difficult and unusual and is not confident that the request will be accepted.)
Which of the request forms in *Listening* Exercise 2 are the most polite?

3   The following expressions were used by a hotel guest to members of staff. Decide on the two most polite and the two least polite expressions.

a) Send my breakfast to my room, *will you*?
b) *I don't suppose you could* open the bar early, *could you*?
c) *Put* the mattress on the floor.
d) *Do you think you could possibly* find me an interpreter?
e) *Can you* give me a quieter room, *please*?
f) *Would you mind helping me* with my suitcases?

4   Do you have a similar way of asking for things in your language?

5 [📼 11.2]   Your intonation can make any of the above request forms sound either polite or impolite. Listen to the recording. In which of the requests does Speaker A sound as if he/she knows the task is inconvenient or difficult for the other person?

a) A: *Could I* have some ice, *please*?
   B: Yes, of course. I'll send some up at once.
b) A: *Would you mind* sending champagne and chips to my room at 4 a.m., *please*?
   B: I'll try, sir, but on Wednesdays the kitchen staff leave at midnight.
c) A: *Can you* show me to my room, *please*?
   B: Certainly, sir.
d) A: *I'm terribly sorry, sir, but would you mind not* smoking in the foyer, *please*? It's one of our rules.
   B: Of course not. I didn't realise.
e) A: *I was wondering if* I could borrow a dressing gown.
   B: No, madam, I'm afraid we don't lend items of clothing. There's a big department store next door. They might be able to help you.

LANGUAGE POINT 2

Agreeing to / Refusing requests

When we can't agree to a request it is often polite to apologise and give a reason, make an excuse or give some helpful advice. In each of the dialogues above what expressions does Speaker B use to agree or not agree to a request?

See **Use your grammar**, page 77, for further practice of requests and offers, agreeing and refusing.

PRONUNCIATION

Using intonation

1 [11.3]   Listen to dialogues a) to d) and match them with the pictures below.

2   What's happening in each dialogue?

3   Listen to the dialogues again. Which people in the dialogues sound:
i) polite?   ii) impolite?   iii) sarcastic?

4   Which speaker's voice starts at a high pitch? Why?

5   Practise saying the following sentences, according to the instructions in brackets.

a) Put the kettle on, please. (*Politely*)
b) Put the kettle on, please. (*Impolitely*)
c) Would you mind closing the window?
   (*A colleague in the classroom has just opened it. You are irritated.*)
d) I'm sorry to trouble you. Could you do me a favour? (*Your car has broken down and you want a stranger to help you push it to the garage. Be as polite as possible.*)
e) Do you think you could just sign this little piece of paper? (*You are a nervous insurance salesman.*)

PRACTICE

1   Work with a partner and decide which of these people uses: a) very formal request forms; b) direct imperatives. Invent and practise each dialogue.
Example (*picture 1*):
'*Would you mind not talking, please?*'
'*Sorry, but I had a problem with my homework.*'

2   What requests would you make in the following situations?

a) You want your bank manager to increase your overdraft.
b) You ask a middle-aged stranger the way to the post office.
c) You ask your boss if you can leave early.

3   Work in pairs. Student A should ask Student B for three things. Student A should consider how polite to be and whether to give a reason for each request. Student B should agree or refuse, depending on how he/she feels.

to pass you the salt
to lend you his/her new motorbike
to make you something to eat
to take your dog for a walk in the rain
to play you some of his/her CDs
to stop humming
to stop swearing

READING

1 Read the following extract about Julian Payne, who used to be the manager of the Ritz Hotel in London.

WHAT THE MANAGER SAW . . .

1 'YOU GET ALL SORTS of requests, and the mark of a good hotel is to provide whatever is asked for without sounding surprised. If a client asks for rubber gloves, you don't ask why. You say, "No problem, pink or yellow?"

2 'There have been some requests which, much as I would have liked to comply with them, I couldn't. A Japanese businessman thought I was like a captain of a ship and asked me to marry him and his fiancée. On another occasion, we did help out. A young lad thought that if he proposed to his girlfriend at the Ritz she would say yes. He asked us to put the ring in the pastry – I think it was in the strawberry tart – and she accepted.

3 'Top hotels are used more and more to impress. They are used for doing business and romancing. If you've got something to sell, take your clients to the best hotel where the surroundings are so conducive to saying yes. A friend of mine working at the Savoy tells the story about a man who gave him £5 to say, "Good morning, Mr Smith" when he walked through the door with two other men. This he did, and could hear Mr Smith saying, "I do wish they would leave me alone at this place." '

4 According to Julian Payne, the most powerful people in any top hotel are the porters. 'They can do almost anything. They can get tickets on Concorde when Concorde is fully booked. They can get you tables at the best restaurants or tickets for "Phantom of the Opera". Don't ask me how they do it or what their deal is because I don't know. Most of them have been there for years. They retain their jobs for a long time and they know more about the history of the hotel and the guests than anyone else. They are invaluable. A head porter will come in on his day off so he can greet someone he remembers visiting the hotel years ago.'

(from *The Observer*)

2 Complete the following sentences.

a) A good hotel gives its customers _____ .
b) A Japanese businessman wanted _____ .
c) A young lad asked the hotel to put a ring in the pastry because _____ .
d) Businessmen and lovers _____ .
e) 'Mr Smith' gave a man at the Savoy £5 because _____ .
f) Porters are very powerful because _____ .

3 In pairs, write short dialogues between the hotel staff and each of the following people referred to in the text above. Include the request mentioned in the text.

a) a client asking for rubber gloves
b) the Japanese business man
c) the 'young lad'
d) Mr Smith
e) a customer wanting a ticket for 'Phantom of the Opera'

Practise your dialogues and present some of them to the rest of the class.

VOCABULARY

Hotels

The following people work in a hotel. Say what they do. The first one has been done for you.

a) porter: *A porter is someone who is in charge of the entrance to a hotel.*
b) doorman
c) receptionist
d) chambermaid
e) cashier
f) telephonist

Can you think of any more hotel jobs? Say what the people in these jobs do.

Verbs to nouns

1   Three common endings for nouns are *-ion*, *-ment* and *-ation*. Change the verbs in brackets into nouns using these suffixes and then complete the sentences.

a) The waiter told us about the menu but we couldn't follow his (*explain*).
b) We had a long (*discuss*) about which wine to choose.
c) After some (*hesitate*) we decided to order red wine.
d) It was a difficult (*decide*), but we chose a French wine in the end.
e) The service was rather slow, but it didn't spoil our (*enjoy*) of the meal.
f) To my (*embarrass*) I found I had forgotten my purse.

2   The verbs in brackets below form nouns in a different way from the verbs in Exercise 1. Complete the sentences.

a) My (*choose*) of dessert was very popular.
b) I decided to make a (*complain*) about the service.
c) On our (*arrive*) at the restaurant the waiter took our coats.
d) On balance, the meal was a great (*succeed*).
e) As an actor, Carl was a total (*fail*).
f) I didn't much like the (*appear*) of the hotel; it seemed too old-fashioned.
g) Violent (*behave*) at football matches has been a disaster for the sport.

SPEAKING

1   Read the text.

nd   ended up at the newsagent.   Th;

A BRITISH DISEASE?

ack   Why is it that British people are so
DS   bad at service? Why is it that I
to   always have to interrupt shop assis-
d-   tants' conversations in order to get
he   served? They are much more inter-
is   ested in gossiping than selling! In
)n   restaurants waiters are either off-
as   hand or obsequious and *hate* being
S   told there is anything the matter
   with the food. In supermarkets and
a   banks cashiers close their tills down
1   as soon as you approach with not so
t   much as an 'I'm sorry'. It's imposs-
;   ible to make an appointment with
)   the gas board so you have to take a
1   day off work and sit there waiting
,   until they bother to turn up! I could
1   go on and on. Does anybody else
-   have these problems? Is it a problem
;   unique to Britain?

a) Write down three pieces of advice you would give to waiters and shop assistants in Britain.
b) What aspects of service make you angry in your own country? In what ways is the service good?
c) Compare your answers with another student's.

2   In a restaurant.

a) How do you attract the waiter's attention? Put a tick in the box next to each of the methods you would use. Put a cross next to the methods you definitely wouldn't use.

whistle   tap your wine glass   hiss
click your fingers   clap your hands
catch his/her eye   say 'Excuse me'

b) What other methods are there? Which methods are considered rude in your country?
c) If possible discuss your answers with someone who is from a country other than your own.

3   In restaurants in your country, how much money do you leave the waiter as a tip?

4 Look at the menu. Decide what you would choose for the: first course; main course; dessert. Are there any dishes you would definitely *not* choose? Example:
'I wouldn't choose any of the meat dishes because I'm vegetarian.'

MENU

First course

Sardines in garlic butter	£4.25
Liver paté with toast	£4.50
Seafood with a savoury dip	£5.75
Fresh celery and onion soup	£3.25
Chilled melon	£2.55
Chicken pieces in a spicy sauce	£4.50

Main course

Trout fillets poached in wine	£7.25
Mixed fish grill with garlic butter	£7.00
Lamb chops with mint jelly	£6.75
Half a roast duckling with orange sauce	£8.00
Fillet steak with mushrooms	£9.75
Vegetable lasagne	£5.75
Steak and kidney pie	£5.75
Escalope of veal with tomatoes	£7.50

Vegetables

Chips or new potatoes	£1.80
Vegetables or mixed salad	£2.50

Desserts

A choice of gateaux	£3.75
Fresh fruit salad	£3.20
Coffee with cream or pot of tea	£1.80

5 Roleplay. Work in small groups. One of you is a waiter. The others are customers. Each customer must order three courses.

> WAITER
> The chef is ill. Not all the items are available for the first course or the main course. (*Select which items are available.*)

> CUSTOMERS
> It is a special occasion for one of you. (*Decide who it is and the occasion.*) There are some things you don't like on the menu. (*Which?*) Each of you has only got a certain amount of money to spend. (*How much?*)

WRITING

Notes and messages

1 Look at this note.

a) How are the important words emphasised?
b) Which words are missed out?
c) What punctuation is typical of notes and messages?

2 Look at each of the messages below.

a) What is the situation and what is the purpose of the message?
b) How do we know the relationship between the two people?

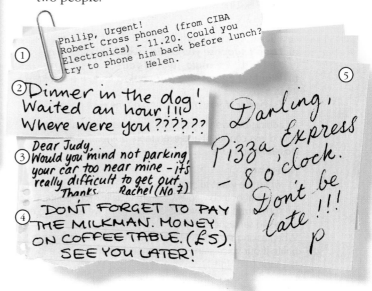

① Philip, Urgent! Robert Cross phoned (from CIBA Electronics) – 11.20. Could you try to phone him back before lunch? Helen.

② Dinner in the dog! Waited an hour!!! Where were you??????

③ Dear Judy, Would you mind not parking your car too near mine – it's really difficult to get out. Thanks. Rachel (No 7)

④ DON'T FORGET TO PAY THE MILKMAN. MONEY ON COFFEE TABLE. (£5). SEE YOU LATER!

⑤ Darling, Pizza Express – 8 o'clock. Don't be late !!! p

3 [📼 11.4] Listen to the answerphone messages and write them down in note form.

Language reference

1 Requests

Politeness usually depends on who we are speaking to and the kind of language expected in a situation. In most cultures we are normally expected to be more polite to strangers than to people we know. In British English, speakers are usually less direct (and use more complex phrases) when they want to be more polite. Intonation can make requests friendly or rude.

The most direct forms of request are:
a) The imperative: **Put** the mattress on the floor. **Don't** talk. **Stop** talking. The word please can come at the beginning or end to 'soften' the command: **Please** don't talk.
b) The imperative with a tag: Put the mattress on the floor, **will you**?
c) Saying what you want or need, which in Britain is often thought to be rude: **I want** that mattress on the floor. (I'd like . . . is usually more acceptable than I want . . .)

Less direct forms (i):
a) **Will you** bring me breakfast in my room, please?
b) **Can you** give me a quieter room, please?

Less direct forms (ii):
a) **Could you** give me a quieter room?
b) **Do you think you could** help me with my suitcase? **Do you think you could** stop talking?
c) **Do** / **Would you mind** bringing me champagne and chips? **Do** / **Would you mind not** touching the fruit?
(See Review Unit 1 for the form of some less direct questions.)

Less direct forms (iii):
a) **I don't suppose you could** / **would** lend me some rubber gloves, **could** / **would you**?
b) **Would it be possible (for you) to** bring me breakfast in bed?
c) **I wonder if you'd mind** helping me with my bags?

By adding the word possibly to a request, you can make it sound less confident and even more polite: Could you **possibly** bring me . . . ?

Note that:
a) when we want to show we think a request is difficult, unusual or inconvenient we are usually more polite.
b) sometimes when we use a polite form we are joking or being sarcastic.
When asking strangers to do things it often sounds more polite if our voice starts at a high pitch than if it has a low, flat tone (see Unit 1).

2 Agreeing and offering

After agreeing to a request, we often make an offer:
Yes, certainly. / Yes, of course. (agreeing)
Sure. It'll be done immediately. (an offer, e.g. in an hotel)
OK, I'll do that straightaway. (personal offer)

3 Refusing requests

In order to refuse a request, we often apologise and make an excuse:
Sorry. I'm afraid I can't. I didn't realise . . . (it was so late).
I'm terribly sorry (I'll try) but . . . (I'm really busy).

4 Verbs into nouns

Some typical endings for nouns that come from verbs are:
  -ion: discuss**ion**, promot**ion**, deci**sion**
  -ment: enjoy**ment**, disappoint**ment**
  -ation: explan**ation**, imagin**ation**
However, there are many less common endings:
arrive → arrival; choose → choice; complain → complaint; succeed → success.

Money, money, money

LISTENING

Before listening

1 This person holds 1,199 credit cards – the world record! What are the advantages and disadvantages of using credit cards a lot?

2 Read this newspaper extract about an old lady who left £500,000 when she died.

a) What is strange about the way the old lady lived?
b) Why do you think she chose to live like that? Give your opinions.

When she died she had lived alone in a six-bedroom home for fourteen years, and dressed in second-hand clothes from jumble sales. She only went out twice a day – early in the morning, to look for useful things on the beach to take home, and then for a session on the fruit machines later on.

Among the rubbish found in her house after her death were her diaries. She had written down every penny she spent, including jumble sale bargains, and anything she won on the fruit machines.

Grocer, George Bumstead, 70, says: 'Every Monday she used to come into my shop and buy her weekly order of six eggs, seven bananas and seven pounds of potatoes. The order never changed, and all she had to cook with was an old gas cooker with two rings – the oven didn't work.'

The irony of the story is that this eccentric old lady, who used to love watching American soap operas, could have lived in the extravagant style of her favourite soap opera, *Dallas*, if she had wanted to.

(from *Titbits*)

3 Do you prefer to spend or to save money? Give reasons, and say: *either* what you spend your money on; *or* what (if anything) you are saving your money for.

4   *-aholic* (or *-oholic*) is a suffix which means *addicted to* or *dependent on*. (For example, a *chocaholic* is someone who is addicted to chocolate.) What do you think a *'shopaholic'* could be?

Ask these questions to find out which students in the class are 'shopaholics'. Tick *yes* or *no*, as appropriate.

Are you a *'Shopaholic'*?

Do you . . .   yes   no

a) always pay cash when you go
   shopping?   ☐   ☐

b) feel guilty when you spend a lot of
   money?   ☐   ☐

c) only go shopping when you have
   something specific to buy?   ☐   ☐

d) usually know how much you have in
   your purse/wallet?   ☐   ☐

e) sometimes waste money?   ☐   ☐

f) often owe people money?   ☐   ☐

g) always pay off credit card bills in full
   at the end of the month?   ☐   ☐

h) have overdraft facilities at the bank?   ☐   ☐

i) save money regularly?   ☐   ☐

j) sometimes go shopping intending to
   spend a lot of money?   ☐   ☐

k) hide what you bought from your
   partner/parents/flatmate?   ☐   ☐

SCORE

Score 1 point for each of the following answers:

a = No	e = Yes	i = No
b = No	f = Yes	j = Yes
c = No	g = No	k = Yes
d = No	h = Yes	

8–11: You are a 'shopaholic' and need help!
4–7: Sorry! You have some problems.
0–3: You are careful with money.

Listening

1 [📼 12.1]   Listen to the first song extract.

a) Does the singer have a job?
b) Is she rich or poor?
c) What does she hope to do? Why?
d) What does she think is 'funny' and 'sunny'?
   Do you agree?

2 [📼 12.2]   Listen to the second song extract.

a) Is the singer rich?
b) What doesn't he want to do?
c) What would he build if he were rich?
d) Where would he build it?

3   Discuss some of these questions.

a) In your opinion, which song shows the stronger desire for money?
b) Which song do you think expresses an impossible dream?
c) Which song seems close to your point of view?
d) Which of the songs do you prefer? Why?

VOCABULARY 1

Money expressions

Choose words from the box to complete the sentences below.

wealthy	afford	on	cost	bargain
broke	overdrawn	lends	earns	owe

a) An idiomatic expression for *to have no money* – to be _____ .

b) Another expression for *to be in the red* – to be _____ .

c) I got a really good _____ at the sale. A pullover for only £5!

d) Another adjective for *rich* is _____ .

e) You can borrow money from a bank. In other words, a bank _____ people money.

f) I can't _____ to buy a new car. They're too expensive.

g) I _____ the bank £3,000.

h) We spend lots of money _____ food.

i) She's quite rich now – she _____ lots of money in her new job.

j) I'd like a new coat, but they _____ too much.

LANGUAGE POINT 1

Imaginary situations

1 [📼 12.3] 'Imagine you had all the money you wanted. What would you do with it?' Listen to Keith, Sue, Ben and Norma's answers to this question. Use the words in the box to write sentences about what they would do. Example: *Keith would buy a new car (if he had all the money he wanted).*

luxurious hotel	business	car	doctor

2 What would *you* spend the money on?

3 Look at this sentence.
If I had all the money that I wanted, I'd give up my job.

a) Is Sue talking about the past, present or future?

b) Do you think she will get all the money she wants? Is the situation likely, or is it imaginary?

4 Read this short dialogue.

ANN: I really hate my job. What would you do if you were me?

BILL: If I were you, I'd look for a new one.

a) Is Bill talking about the past, present or future?

b) Is the situation (*If I were you . . .*) likely, or imaginary?

c) Which form of *be* comes in the *if*-clause?

Check with Section 1 (Pronunciation) in the *Language reference* and then practise saying the dialogue above.

5 Possible or imaginary?
If I give you all the money that you want, what will you do with it?
If I gave you all the money that you wanted, what would you do with it?

a) In which of the sentences above is it more possible that the speaker will give the other person the money? Think of a situation for that sentence.

b) In which sentence is the past tense used to talk about the future?

6 Which two of the following sentences are *not* correct?

a) If someone will scream in the house next door, I'll call the police.

b) I wouldn't tell her if she asked me.

c) I wouldn't be surprised if somebody were listening to our conversation.

d) I might go and see him if he wanted me to.

e) If the money market would collapse I wouldn't lose all my savings.

Check with Section 1 in the *Language reference*.

PRACTICE

1   Say whether you think the following future situations are possible or imaginary. Then say what you *will* do or what you *would* do in each situation.
Examples:
Your boyfriend phones you this evening. (*Possible*)
If my boyfriend phones me this evening, I'll tell him I've got a headache.
You are poor. (*Imaginary*)
If I were poor, I'd live in a cheaper house.

a) You see a bank robbery in the street.
b) The police stop you for driving too fast.
c) Someone asks you to marry them next week.
d) You go to live abroad.
e) The weather is fine at the weekend.
f) You become President of your country.
g) You lose your job.
h) You oversleep.

2   Look at the following situations and compare your ideas with your partner.

What would you do if . . .
a) someone was following you down a dark street?
b) you saw a pool of blood in your living room?
c) you saw the furniture moving on its own?
d) you heard a noise downstairs at 2 a.m. and you were alone?
e) you were trapped in a lift?
f) you ran out of petrol miles away from anywhere?

3   Complete each of the following sentences with an appropriate form of the verb.

a) If it (*be*) warmer in Britain, people wouldn't go abroad so much.
b) You (*be able to*) run a lot faster if you were slimmer.
c) If she (*stop*) smoking, her cough would get better.
d) I would check your change if I (*be*) you.
e) What a pity I haven't got my car. If I had, I (*take*) you to the airport.

4   Complete the following sentences from your own experience.

a) I'd be very miserable if . . .
b) I'd be terrified if . . .
c) I'd leave the country if . . .
d) I might not speak to you ever again if . . .
e) I'd be very happy if . . .

LANGUAGE POINT 2

Wish

1   Wish is often used to express a desire for things to be different. Example:
I wish I didn't sleep so much. (But I do.)

a) Complete the sentences in the speech balloons.

b) Which tense is used after *wish* to talk about something you want (to happen) (in the present or future) which is not happening?

2   Rewrite the sentences above using *if* . . .
Example:
I wish I didn't sleep so much because if I didn't I could get to work on time.
(Note that *could* can be used to mean *would be able to* or *was able to.*)

3   Complete these sentences.

a) I wish it were Friday because . . .
b) I wish I could get up early in the mornings, so . . .
c) I wish I were . . . because . . .
d) I wish I had . . .

See **Use your grammar,** page 115, for further practice of the second conditional and *wish*.

VOCABULARY 2

Theft

1   Complete the following sentences with words from the box.

> burglary   robbery   mugging   pickpocket

a) When you steal money or a large amount of goods from a bank or a shop the crime is called _____ .

b) Somebody who steals from your bag or pocket (usually in a crowded place) is called a _____ .

c) When somebody breaks into your home and steals something, the crime is called _____ .

d) When somebody steals money from you and uses violence it's called _____ .

2   What is the person called who commits:

a) a burglary?   b) a robbery?   c) a mugging?   d) a theft?

SPEAKING

1   Read the comments made by three teenagers about their attitudes to stealing.

a) Where possible, decide which of their comments you agree or disagree with and write down any comments of your own.

b) Do you sympathise with any of the young people? Is stealing more acceptable if you're poor? Discuss your views in groups.

c) Read what the young people said again and find two colloquial expressions which mean *steal*.

2   Put the following crimes in order depending on how serious you think they are. (1 is the most important, 6 is the least important.) Discuss in groups.

a) Taking clothes from a large shop without paying.

b) Mugging an old lady and taking £2 from her.

c) Stealing from your mother's purse.

d) Taking home things like pens and sellotape from where you work.

e) Selling stolen goods.

f) Stealing £3 million from a bank.

Andrew

'If somebody pinches something from a big shop or a business or something like that and they get away with it, I say good luck to them. What does it matter? It's not the same as stealing off a friend or knocking down a poor old lady and running off with her purse.'

Tina

'I've nicked loads of pens, sellotape and things from work. The employers nick things and cheat, don't they. If you don't do it they will.'

Janet

'My father was done for selling stolen goods and went to prison. But what else can you do when you're unemployed and you've got a family to bring up?'

CREATIVE WRITING

1   The person in the photograph is a 'shopaholic'. Discuss the questions below.

a) What do you think has happened?
b) How do you think she feels?
c) What sort of things do you think she has bought?
d) How did she get the money?
e) How could she break the habit?

2   This is a short magazine article which accompanied the photograph.

The new disease of our time

After splashing out three hundred pounds on ten pairs of shoes a young girl found that shopping developed into an obsession which left her with debts totalling over fifty thousand pounds.

This condition, known as 'shopaholism' is on the increase all over the country. It often begins in quite a small way, as it did with Diane (the girl in our picture). She used to go shopping to cheer herself up whenever she was depressed. It began with small items of underwear or bath products and make-up, and developed into buying complete outfits, and clothes she didn't need.

The current trend for making credit easily available and tempting young people to get credit cards and store cards is largely responsible, according to the government, who are trying to crack down on easy credit for under-18s.

Withdrawing credit cards can help, but for serious 'shopaholics' the need to buy remains, and the habit can only be broken by treating the symptoms in the same way as a drug addict or an alcoholic.

a) Imagine that Diane wrote a letter to the 'Problem Page' of a women's magazine, explaining her problem and asking for advice. Work in small groups and write the letter that she wrote. Begin and end like this:

> Dear Mavis,
>   I am writing to you for advice because I really don't know who to turn to. It all began

> What shall I do?

b) Pass your letter to another group, who will write a reply to the letter. You must do the same for another group. Use expressions of advice such as:

Why don't you . . . ?   *If I were you I'd . . .*
Couldn't you . . . ?   *You should . . .*

c) Read out some of the letters which ask for advice and some which give advice. The class should decide on the best ones.

Language reference

1 The second conditional

USE

The second conditional is used to talk about imaginary situations in the present and the future. Note that some of the imaginary situations are actually impossible.

> *If I were a rich man, I wouldn't have to work hard.* (It's imaginary – it's very unlikely I will get rich.)
> *If I were you, I'd leave the country.* (It's impossible because I'm not you.)

By contrast, in first (or open) conditional sentences the future event is possible (see Unit 9).

FORM

AFFIRMATIVE
If you **asked** her she **would be** furious. **I'd drive** you to the airport if I **had** my car.

NEGATIVE
I **wouldn't go out** if I **were** you. If you **didn't ask** her she**'d be** furious.

QUESTION
If I **spoke** French, **would** you **give** me the job?

If is usually followed by the Past Simple (or sometimes the Past Continuous).

> *If someone **screamed** in the house next door (I'd call the police).*
> *If you **were helping** me (I'd get the job done more quickly).*
> *If I **were** you (I'd look for a better job).*

Note that *were* is often preferred to *was* for all persons (including *I*, *he*, *she*, *it*), particularly in more formal English. In the main clause the structure is usually:

would / should / might / could + base form.

Note also that you can place the *if*-clause after the main clause.

> *I'd look for a better job if I were you.*

PRONUNCIATION

Note that the pronunciation of *were* in conditional sentences is usually weak (/wə/), and *would* is usually contracted ('*d*), except in questions and short answers.

> *If I **were** you I'**d** leave the country.* (/wə/, /aɪd/)
> ***Would** you go if you had enough money?* (/wʊd/)
> *Yes, I **would**. I'**d** go at once.*

2 *Wish* + past tense

USE

Wish + past tense is used to talk about something you want to happen (in the present and the future), which is not happening now. It expresses dissatisfaction with present states or events.

> *I wish I were / was young.* (But I'm not.)
> *I wish I had a new car.* (But mine is old.)

FORM

Like the *if*-clause in the second conditional, *wish* is followed by the Past Simple (or sometimes the Past Continuous) and *were* is often preferred to *was* for all persons.

> *I wish I **didn't sleep** so much.*
> *I wish it **were** Friday because then we could go home.*

3 *Could*

The modal *could* (see Unit 9 for more information on modals) is the past tense of *can*. It is often used in second conditional or *wish* + past tense sentences.

> *I wish I **could** get up earlier in the mornings.*
> *If I were rich, I **could** stay in the Hilton in Los Angeles.*

4 Giving advice

Some ways of giving advice are:

> *If I were you I'd . . .*
> *You should . . .*
> *Why don't you . . . ?*
> *Couldn't you . . . ? / You could . . .*

Layabout

READING

Before reading

1   Look at the headlines in A and the newspaper story in B. Tick the appropriate column in the table below as in the example.

A

Love-struck gardener married a lettuce

TV star Anne's secret love

World's laziest slob – hasn't been up since 1932

B

Parliament to investigate secret payments to MPs

THE OWNER of a parliamentary company which seeks to influence government decisions is to be questioned about secret payments to MPs . . .

	A	B
a) Large headlines	✓	
b) Politically important story/stories		
c) Factual language		
d) Wants to shock		
e) Humour and gossip		

2   The headlines in A come from 'popular', tabloid newspapers. The story in B comes from a 'serious' newspaper. Which newspapers in your country have headlines like the headlines in A? Which newspapers in your country have stories most like the story in B? What kind of people read each kind of newspaper and why?

Reading

1   Decide which of the headlines in the *Before reading* section goes with the story opposite. Then find the paragraphs which tell you:

a) how John eats without leaving his bed
b) what world events he has missed
c) who looks after him
d) his plans for the future
e) how it all began

2   Look again at the text. Find the phrase or sentence which shows us that:

a) John did not have to buy the farm. (paragraph 2)
b) Bessie is very loyal to John. (paragraph 3)
c) John's room is very dirty. (paragraph 3)
d) John enjoys his comfortable life. (paragraph 5)

3   Which of the alternatives below do you think is most correct? (If you don't agree with either, write your own opinion.)

a) *after staying in bed for an incredible 56 years!* (paragraph 1)
  i)   The newspaper is impressed. (It admires John.)
  ii) It pretends to be shocked but really wants us to laugh at John.
b) *and dozed through a world war* (paragraph 1)
  i)   John fell asleep in 1939 and woke up in 1945.
  ii) The newspaper is exaggerating.
c) *can't be bothered to prop himself against the pillows* (paragraph 4)
  i)   The newspaper feels sympathy for John.
  ii) It wants to give the impression it has an unfavourable opinion of him.

4   Are these sentences *True* or *False*?

a) The adjectives help to make us interested in the situation.
b) The language used to describe John is meant to make us laugh at him.
c) The story is of great social importance.

What do your answers tell you about the kind of newspaper the story is from?

5 Answer these questions in pairs.

a) Do you like this kind of story or do you find it unpleasant? Give your reasons.
b) Do you believe the story? (Give a reason.)
c) What do you think about John? (For example, is he intelligent? Do you admire him?)
d) What good reasons can you think of for someone staying in bed for 56 years? Did it have any advantages for John?

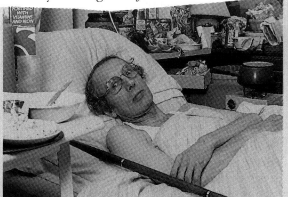

1 **EASY-GOING John Richards last night claimed the title SUPER SLOB ... after staying in bed for an incredible 56 years!** Now aged 72, John has SNORED through ten governments, KIPPED while men landed on the moon and DOZED through a world war.

2 Bone-idle John, who has never done a day's work in his life, hasn't bothered to get up since he turned in for a kip in 1932. He was just 16 when he announced to his family: 'I'm going upstairs – I may be some time.' He lives the life of luxury thanks to the farm his parents left to him and which his sister looks after even though the layabout never lifts a finger to help.

3 Munching chocolate bars in the same sheets and pyjamas he crawled into 56 years ago, John groaned, 'I can't be bothered to get up. I haven't been on my feet for so long I think I've forgotten how to walk,' he added from the bug-infested bed. Grimy John's devoted sister, Bessie, pops in once a week to give him a quick wash and brush up. But even she puts on rubber gloves, a plastic apron and wellies before entering the smelly room.

4 The cat-nap expert has turned his cramped room into an amazing live-in larder, with boxes of goodies within easy reach of his bed; a hotplate by his side means his food never goes cold. A whole wall is lined with cans of beans, potatoes and peas, bags of crisps, popcorn and candy, while empty burger cartons and sweet wrappers are strewn all over the sticky carpet. He even discovered a half-eaten cheese sandwich which fell under the bed TEN years ago! 'Bessie takes the rubbish away but she must have missed that one,' confesses the lazybones, who can't be bothered to prop himself against the pillows.

5 The whacked-out wimp, who is permanently tired, has not sat up since 1942 or rolled over on his side since 1960. 'I just don't seem to have the energy to do anything. I've been here for 56 years and I'm worn-out just thinking about it,' he admitted. 'People may think my life's not very exciting but at least it's easy,' he said from his mouldy mattress in Ohio, in the American mid-west. 'I'm just going to stay here, in my own home, in my own bed for-ever,' he added defiantly.

(from the Sunday Sport)

VOCABULARY 1

Colloquial language

Colloquial language is language which is only used in informal situations (for example, in personal conversations). Example:
*I couldn't sleep a **wink**. / I didn't get a **wink** of sleep last night.*
The word *wink* is used in this colloquial expression when we want to say someone couldn't sleep for even a short period.

Slang
Slang is colloquial language which is often not polite. It is not suitable for more formal writing but is frequently found in the 'popular' newspapers. It is marked as slang (*sl*) or informal (*infml*) in the dictionary and should be used with great care.

1 In paragraphs 1, 2, 4 and 5 John is referred to by an impolite slang word. In the first paragraph the article calls him a *slob*. Check the dictionary extract below. Now find the other three slang words referring to John and check them in your dictionary.

> drink made in SE Europe from PLUMS
> **slob** /slɒb/ *n infml* a rude, lazy, dirty, or carelessly dressed person: *When are you going to get out of bed, you fat slob?*
> sloe /sləʊ/ *n* a small bitter kind of PLUM with dark purple skin

2 The words in the box are all from the text and are all used in colloquial English. Use a dictionary to help you group each of the words under these headings: *Sleep*, *Laziness* or *Dirt*. If you want to put a word in more than one group, give a reason.

kip	doze	smelly	grimy	bone-idle
snore	slob	worn-out	layabout	
sticky	lazybones	turn in	cat-nap	
mouldy				

3 Which of the words above do you think are slang and should be used with care?

4 Do you know any other colloquialisms in English? Which of them are slang?

VOCABULARY 2

Looking up idiomatic expressions

Idiomatic expressions are a combination of two or more words which together have a special meaning. Often the meaning cannot be guessed from the individual words. Example:
*He never **lifts a finger** to help.*

1   *Lift a finger* is an idiomatic expression. Which is the most important word in the expression?

If you look up that word in the dictionary, it gives you the meaning, the way it is used and an example.

so as to make it work as well as possible
fin·ger[1] /ˈfɪŋɡə(r)/ *n* . . . **10 lift/raise a finger** (*usu. in negatives*) to make any effort to help when necessary: *He was the only one who lifted a finger to help the victims.* **11 pull/take/get one's finger** out *BrE*

If you look up the wrong word, a dictionary will sometimes refer you to the other word.

to which a person gives the whole of a life
lift[1] /lɪft/ *v* . . . **10** [T (UP)] *lift* to make (the voice) loud, e.g. in singing – see also **lift a finger** (FINGER[1])
lift[2] . . . [C] an act of lifting: *One more* . . . .

2   Work individually and then compare your answers with a partner.

a) Decide on the most important word in each of the idiomatic expressions (in *italics*) below and look them up in a dictionary.

b) Complete each sentence in an appropriate way.
   i) I *turned a blind eye* when . . .
   ii) He *hit the nail on the head* when . . .
   iii) It *drives me mad* when . . .
   iv) We've *run out of* . . .
   v) I think I've *put my foot in it*. I've . . .
   vi) I'm a bit *hard up* so . . .
   vii) He's really *on the ball* today. He . . .
   viii) My knee *is playing up*, so I'm afraid I can't . . .
   ix) *Keep this to yourself* because I don't want . . .
   x) He was always *letting her down*, so eventually she decided . . .

c) Is it possible to translate any of the expressions above into your own language word for word, or do you have to find another expression? Find another way of saying some of the expressions in English.

LANGUAGE POINT 1

Unfinished past: *since/for*

1   Look at each of the examples carefully and answer the questions.

*John hasn't sat up **since** 1942.*
a) When did John start lying down?
b) Is he still lying down now?
c) How long has he been lying down?

*He's stayed in bed **for** 56 years.*
a) Is he still in bed?
b) When did he go to bed?
c) How long has he been in bed?

2   Which is the correct ending to each of these sentences?

a) For a specific point in the past when something began (e.g. *last year* / *1932*) we use the word:
   – *for*
   – *since*
b) For a length of time (e.g. *56 years* / *an hour*) we use the word:
   – *for*
   – *since*
c) When we ask questions about length of time we begin:
   – *How much time . . . (have you been here?)*
   – *How long . . . (have you been here?)*

PRACTICE

Make sentences with *since* or *for*. Example:
Helen / want / be / doctor / she was very young.
*Helen has wanted to be a doctor **since** she was very young.*

a) He / have / beard / two years.
b) I / not eat / seafood / I had food poisoning two months ago.
c) He / not get out / bed / 28 years.
d) He / not have / more than four hours sleep a night / he became Prime Minister.
e) I / not take / sleeping pills / ages.
f) A: How long / you / be awake?
   B: . . . / three o'clock, dear.

LANGUAGE POINT 2

Present Perfect Continuous

Look at how the Present Perfect Continuous is used in these examples.

*He's **been wearing** the same pyjamas for 56 years.*
*He's **been sleeping** in the same sheets since 1932.*

It is also possible to use the Present Perfect Simple (e.g. *He's **worn** the same pyjamas for 56 years.*) but the continuous form is preferred where the focus is on:

– an unbroken routine in progress.
– the activity itself.

Remember, however, that many verbs are not usually used in the continuous form (see Unit 2).

PRACTICE

1   Rewrite these sentences using *for* and *since*.

a) He moved to Spain in 1978. He's still living there. *He's been living in Spain . . .*
b) He started working for us two weeks ago.
c) She bought the coat 25 years ago. She still has it.
d) They first met the Smiths in 1960. They still know them.

2   Write down some questions to ask John Richards or Bessie, using the following question words at least once: *How long . . . ? When . . . ? Why . . . ? What . . . ? Have you . . . ?* You may use the cues below, but try to think of some questions of your own as well. (Use the Past Simple, the Present Perfect or the Present Perfect Continuous.)

a) live on the farm
b) change sheets
c) decide not to come back downstairs
d) miss
e) have many visitors
f) decide to wear rubber gloves

Help each other to correct any mistakes and then roleplay the interviews in groups of three. One of you is John Richards, one of you is Bessie and one of you is a journalist.

> See **Use your grammar,** page 116, for further practice of the Present Perfect Continuous with *for* and *since*.

PRONUNCIATION

Sentence stress

In English sentences, some words are spoken with extra force (i.e. they are stressed) in order to show their importance. Example:
*Can I have another **sandwich**?* (In most cases *sandwich* would be the most important word to the speaker, so it is stressed.)

Stressed words are usually 'content words' like *table* or *cinema* and not 'grammar words' like *is, the* or *to*. Stressed words are the kind of words we use when we want to save space, such as in telexes, newspaper headlines and short postcards.

1   Say whether each of the following items is a *telex, newspaper headline* or a *postcard.*

a) Arriving Heathrow 10 p.m. flight. Please meet.
b) New spy scandal. Minister resigns.
c) Father very ill. Return immediately.
d) Having wonderful time. Weather amazing. Visited Niagara Falls – visiting Hollywood, Tuesday.
e) Famous actor arrested. Wife found dead.

2   Which words have been missed out in the items in Exercise 1? Try to make complete sentences.

3 [▣ 13.1]   Listen to some possible answers to Exercise 2.

4   Guess which is the stressed word in each of these sentences.

a) He was walking down the street.
b) I'm going to the cinema with her.
c) She was holding a red coat.
d) Why don't you try taking two aspirin later?
e) She's got a very strong personality, hasn't she?

5 [▣ 13.2]   Listen and check your answers.

6   Practise saying each sentence with a partner.

SPEAKING

1 [🔊 13.3] Work in groups. Listen to these extracts from two different radio programmes. What are the differences between: a news broadcast on a 'popular' radio station; a news broadcast on a more 'serious' radio station? Discuss, for example:
- the use of music.
- the tone of voice and speed of delivery of the newsreader.
- the kind of language used.
- how the news items are constructed (e.g. Are the facts presented first? Is there an interview?)

2 Work in two groups. Group A should read article A. Group B should read article B. Underline the most important facts of the story. (You may need to look up some of the vocabulary in your dictionary.) Examples:
A   Police . . . found the body of Grace Slan.
B   David Morris . . . failed to get any cash.

3 You are going to prepare a radio news broadcast (as you did in Unit 5) about either Grace Slan or David Morris. Decide:
- who is to be the newsreader.
- which interviews you are going to include (for example, with article A: a neighbour or a relative; with article B: a shop assistant).
- whether your broadcast is for a popular or a more serious radio station. (One group could be popular, another more serious.)

4 Rehearse your broadcast, making sure you use the language and style appropriate to the type of radio station that you have chosen.

5 Present your broadcast to the other group.

WRITING

Summary writing

1 Work in the same groups as in the *Speaking* exercise above. You are going to write a summary of your news broadcast. Agree on the facts and make a note of them. (Use the information from the interviews.)

A

Tragedy of 'timewarp' woman

POLICE stumbled into a timewarp when they found the body of Grace Slan.

For the 81-year-old spinster had died as she lived – alone in a one-bedroomed flat unchanged since the start of the First World War.

There was no bathroom, no electrical appliances. Instead there was an old kitchen range with a kettle hanging above, gas lamps, period furniture and newspapers with headlines about the General Strike of 1926.

All the china and crockery dated from 1914 to the 1920s – and nothing had been cleaned since Miss Slan's father died 30 years ago.

None of Miss Slan's neighbours at Scott Ellis Gardens, Westminster London, knew anything about how she lived. 'She would shout and swear if anyone offered help, advice or friendship,' said PC Tiney.

(from the Daily Mail)

B

Robbery bluff was notable failure

AN UNEMPLOYED man killing time before a date decided to turn to crime to ease his money problems. He wrote out a note reading: "I've got a gun in my pocket and I'll shoot it off unless you hand over the money."

But David Morris, aged 21, failed to get any cash in spite of going into three shops in London Road, West Croydon.

At a chemist's a girl assistant refused to accept the note, believing it contained an obscene suggestion. Next door, in a hardware shop, the Asian assistant said he could not read English.

In desperation, Morris, of High Road, Beckenham, Kent, went to a takeaway food shop, but the assistant could not read the note because he did not have his glasses.

Morris told police: "I've been a twit. When the judge hears about this he won't believe anyone could be so stupid. I only pretended to have a gun."

2 Individually, draft the story in a factual way. Do not use emotional language or show your opinions. Do not copy sentences from the newspaper article. (Your introduction might start: *An 81-year-old woman, Grace Slan, . . .* Your next paragraph might include quotes from what the interviewees said.) Finally, comment on each others' drafts before rewriting.

Language reference

1 *Since/for*

Both *since* and *for* make clear how long something has been happening.

Since refers to the beginning of the period.

> John hasn't got out of bed **since 1932**.
> We have been waiting **since 12 o'clock**.

For refers to the length of the period.

> He hasn't been to bed **for three nights**.
> We have been waiting here **for two hours**.

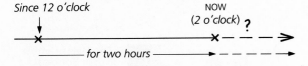

For (but not *since*) can be used with any verb forms (not just the Present Perfect) to describe a period of time.

> **I'll be** there **for** two weeks.

2 Present Perfect Simple

We can use the Present Perfect Simple to talk about actions and activities which began in the past and which have continued up to the present. (See Unit 4 for other uses of the Present Perfect Simple.)

> **I've studied** English for the last three years.

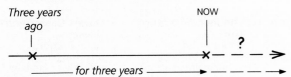

This means 'I started studying English three years ago and I'm still studying it'. The activity is incomplete. It might continue into the future. We don't know.

3 Present Perfect Continuous

USE

We can also use the Present Perfect Continuous to talk about an 'unfinished past' when we want to focus on the activity or situation itself and/or emphasise that it has been in progress throughout the period.

> He**'s been wearing** the same pyjamas for 56 years.
> She**'s been staying** in my flat since last Saturday.
> 'How long **have you been studying** English?' 'Two years.'

Remember that verbs that refer more to states and experiences (stative verbs) do not normally take a continuous form (see Unit 2).

> How long **have you had** that car? (NOT . . . ~~have you been having~~ . . .)
> **I've hated** you for years. (NOT . . . ~~I've been hating~~ . . .)

FORM

Have / has been + *-ing* form of verb.

AFFIRMATIVE
I / You / We / They**'ve** (**have**) **been working** here for six months. He**'s** / She**'s** (**has**) **been working** here for six months.

NEGATIVE
We **haven't been working** here for very long. She **hasn't been working** here for very long.

QUESTION
How long **have** you **been working** here? How long **has** she **been working** here?

Leisure

LISTENING

Before listening

1 Look at these advertisements for holiday breaks. Where in Britain can you go if you want to:

a) learn how to act?
b) know how to solve murders?
c) take better photographs?
d) do watersports?
e) walk in beautiful countryside?

Learning and adventure holidays for all ages

The Dales Centre, North Yorkshire
Walking holidays in the Dales and Lake District from Mar to Oct. £350 for 7 nights full board in hotels.

Yelden House Hotel, Lancashire
Good food and wine tasting weekends. 10 Jan – 20 May. £150 – £200 for 3 nights half-board.

Millfield College of Education, Somerset
6-night flower-arranging and gardening courses in April and May. £150, including B&B.

Chichester Guest House, Cornwall
One-week photography courses in spring and autumn. £200 for 5 nights full board.

The Bee Inn, Northumberland
One-week bee-keeping courses Jun–Sept. £180 for 6 nights half-board.

Beech Hill Hotel, Lake District
Murder weekend. 1 Feb £160 for 2 nights half-board.

British Theatre Association, London
Adult summer school in Cheltenham from 8–17 August. Practical acting and directing classes. Age 18+. £400 for 9 nights full board.

Outdoor Adventure, Norfolk
7-night watersport courses: canoeing, windsurfing, surfing (from beginners to advanced). Apr to Nov £300 approx. Full board included.

Mortimers Cross Inn, Bath
Parachuting, flying and gliding courses all year round. Tuition provided. Beginners welcome. £20 per night B&B. Parachuting from £60 per flight, flying £50 per hour in air, gliding courses from £70 to £300.

Dorset Coast Centre, Dorset
6 and 7 night birdwatching and wildflower holidays April–July. From £200 half-board.

(from *Activity and Hobby Holidays*)

2 Which of the holidays above would you *most* like to go on? Which would you *least* like to go on? Give your reasons.

3 Which of the hobbies above would be unusual for people in your country?

Listening

1 What are the hobbies shown in the photographs? Which of the holidays in the adverts on the left would be suitable for people who have these hobbies?

2 [📼 14.1] Listen to Mike, Julie and Bruce talking about their hobbies, and match the speakers to the activities in Exercise 1.

3 Copy the table and make notes about Mike, Julie and Bruce's hobbies.

	HOBBY	ADVANTAGES	DISADVANTAGES
Mike Julie Bruce			

4 Which of these hobbies, if any, would you enjoy doing?

VOCABULARY

Words which are often confused

1 Underline the correct word in the pairs of words below. Example:
*She spent the day **lying**/laying on the beach.*

a) Will you *take/bring* my gloves here, please? They're on the shelf in the kitchen.
b) I am sure he understands how you must feel. He's a very *sensible/sensitive* person.
c) Can you *borrow/lend* me £5 until tomorrow? I'm broke.
d) Don't forget to *check/control* the oil in your car before you leave.
e) I used to drive an Escort but I don't *now/actually*. I've got a new Rover.
f) 'Where is Sheila?' 'She's *expecting/waiting for* James outside.'
g) I think I'll spend the evening *watching/seeing* television.
h) Speak up! I can't *listen/hear* very well.
i) Every time I buy an umbrella I *loose/lose* it.

2 Choose at least three of the words you *didn't* underline above and write a sentence to show how they are used. Example:
*I decided to help my parents by **laying** the table.*

LANGUAGE POINT 1

Obligation and permission (1)

1 When Mike was interviewed about learning to fly earlier in the unit he talked about what he was *obliged* to do, what he was *not obliged* to do, what he was *prohibited* from doing and what he was *permitted* to do. Copy the table below. Then look at the sentences opposite and put the expressions in *italics* under the correct headings as in the example.

a) You *needn't* do the written exams until you are ready.
b) You're *not allowed to* go solo until you've got your air law exam.
c) And you *have to* do a lot of exams.
d) You *can* pay for each lesson as you go along.
e) Of course you *can't* fly unless you're fairly fit.
f) You *don't have to* pay all at once.

OBLIGATION	NO OBLIGATION	PROHIBITION	PERMISSION
		can't	

2 Check your answers with Sections 1 to 4 in the *Language reference* before doing the practice activities.

PRACTICE

1 Talk about some of the things you:
i) *can't / are not allowed to* do
ii) *have to* do
iii) *can / are allowed to* do
iv) *don't have to / needn't* do

a) when you are learning to drive.
b) in prison.
c) in a church/mosque/synagogue.
d) when you're on a diet.
e) in hospital.
f) before you go abroad.
g) when you visit a tropical country.
h) when you get married.

Example: a) when you are learning to drive.
*In Britain you **have to** do a practical test before you get a licence.*
*You **aren't allowed to** drive on the motorway.*
*You **can** do an intensive driving course, if you want to learn very quickly.*
*In Britain you **don't have to** do a written test.*

2 Jill is staying in somebody's flat while they're away. This is a list of instructions which was left for her.

a) What does Jill have to do? Example:
  She has to feed the cat twice a day.
b) What isn't she allowed to do / can't she do? Example:
  She can't park outside the neighbour's house.

1. Please feed the cat twice a day.
2. Do not park outside my neighbour's house - he'll be very rude to you!
3. Put rubbish out on a Thursday - dustbinman day.
4. No smoking please.
5. Please avoid sticking things on the wall in the bedroom - it's just been decorated.
6. Please send all mail on to 68 Lanark Street.
7. Pay the milkman on a Friday.

LANGUAGE POINT 2

Obligation (2)

When we want to give advice to someone we often use *should* or *shouldn't*. Example:
You've been drinking too much. I think you should take a taxi.

For stronger advice to yourself and others we sometimes use *must* or *mustn't*. Examples:
I really must see that film soon.
You mustn't drive. You must give me the car keys.

1   Match the statements in group A to the contexts in group B.

A
a) Visitors must not take photographs.
b) Do you think we should check if he's OK?
c) I really must remember to post that letter before five o'clock.
d) You shouldn't worry so much. They are caused by tension.
e) Books must be returned before the end of the month.
f) You must take this prescription to the chemist's.
g) Don't forget. You really must get a present for your daughter today.

B
1 A sign in a school library.
2 A reminder. He always forgets her birthday.
3 Instructions from a doctor.
4 The closing date for the job application she's written is tomorrow.
5 The baby is crying.
6 A sign in a museum.
7 He gets bad headaches.

2   Complete the following speech bubbles using expressions of obligation or prohibition. One has been done for you.

3   What might you say in the following situations?

a) You haven't any food in the fridge and the shops close soon. (*I . . .*)
b) Your aunt wants a dog, but they are prohibited in flats. (*You . . .*)
c) Remind your room mate that playing loud music after 11 p.m. is forbidden. (*You . . .*)
d) It is necessary to wear a uniform at your school, but a new student doesn't know. (*You . . .*)
e) Give very strong advice to a friend who works too hard and is ill as a result. (*You . . .*)

LANGUAGE POINT 3

Must or *have to*?

Must and *have to* have very similar meanings and sometimes either form can be used. With *have to* the obligation is usually external (i.e. it comes from somebody or something else). Examples:
I know it tastes horrible but the doctor says you have to take it.
I can't fly solo yet. I have to have a medical exam.

Must is used when the feeling of obligation comes directly from the speaker, who feels she or he wants to emphasise its importance. Examples:
Sorry, I can't leave yet. I must finish my work.
You must learn to arrive on time.

Check with Section 1 in the *Language reference* for more information on the use and form of *must*, and the difference between *must* and *have to*.

PRACTICE

1   Complete these sentences using *must* or *have to* and discuss your answers with a partner.

a) I'm afraid I can't come to your party. The boss has told me I _____ go away on business.
b) The house looks awful! I really _____ find time to clean it.
c) You really _____ stop driving so fast or you'll have an accident.
d) This is going to be an expensive month because I _____ pay the telephone bill.
e) I hear that in England you _____ get a licence if you have a TV. It's the law.
f) I _____ go to bed now or I won't be able to get up for work.

2   Use *mustn't* or *don't have to* to complete the sentences.

a) 'It's OK. You *don't have to* wear fancy dress to the party if you don't want to.'

b) 'You _____ smoke in Bill's car. He gets really angry if you do.'

c) 'Now don't forget. You _____ walk on the grass.'

d) 'You _____ do that. I'll do it later.'

LANGUAGE POINT 4

Obligation and permission (3)

1 [📼 14.2]   Listen to Jenny talking about the advantages and disadvantages of university life when she was a student, and fill in the gaps in the text.

'One of the things I liked most about being at university was living away from home, and the, and the freedom it gave me. So I __(1)__ stay out as late as I wanted – I __(2)__ explain to anyone where I'd been, and although we obviously __(3)__ do some work in order to get through the exams, well we __(4)__ go to all the lectures if we didn't want to. It was incredibly relaxed; we __(5)__ to do whatever we wanted, within reason.'

2   Write down the past forms of:
a) *have to*   b) *must*   c) *don't need to*
d) *can*   e) *are allowed to*

Check your answers with Sections 1 to 3 in the *Language reference*.

PRACTICE

1   Ask questions to find at least one person in the class who at the age of twelve:

a) didn't have to go to bed early.
b) could choose their own clothes.
c) had to eat certain kinds of food.

2   Ask other people about their lives at the age of twelve.

See **Use your grammar**, page 116, for further practice of obligation, prohibition and permission.

SPEAKING

You are a representative on a committee which is helping to plan *The Paradise Centre*, a new luxury leisure centre near your home. On the right are some photographs of what it will look like.

If *The Paradise Centre* is successful it will provide a place where people will be able to go not only to play sports but also for general entertainment and to meet people with similar hobbies. It also aims to be a health and beauty centre. It intends to cater for all ages – from 5 to 85 – and all tastes!

1   Work in groups. Look at the poster headings below and discuss what facilities you want to offer. Be as original as you can. Remember your aim is to please a wide variety of people with different interests and of different ages.

2   Make decisions about what rules and regulations there will be, as well as practical matters such as how much it will cost to be a member, and what the opening hours will be.

3   Appoint a chairperson to organise the discussion and record any decisions taken. Then design a poster advertising *The Paradise Centre*.

4   Compare your plan for *The Paradise Centre* with other groups' plans, and vote on the best one.

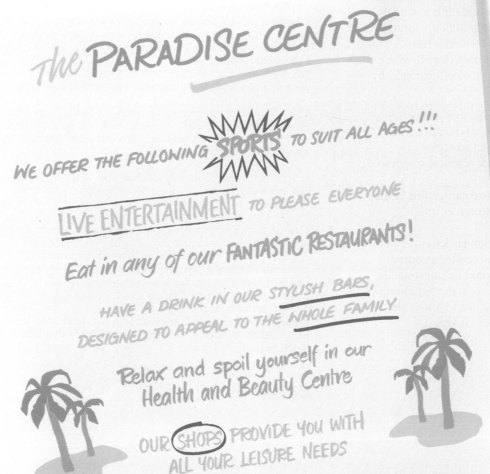

The **PARADISE CENTRE**

WE OFFER THE FOLLOWING **SPORTS** TO SUIT ALL AGES!!!

LIVE ENTERTAINMENT TO PLEASE EVERYONE

Eat in any of our FANTASTIC RESTAURANTS!

HAVE A DRINK IN OUR STYLISH BARS, DESIGNED TO APPEAL TO THE WHOLE FAMILY

Relax and spoil yourself in our Health and Beauty Centre

OUR SHOPS PROVIDE YOU WITH ALL YOUR LEISURE NEEDS

WRITING

Opening and closing a letter

1 For each of the following openings say:
– whether the letter is personal or semi-formal.
– what the purpose of the letter is.
Choose from the ideas in the box. One has been done for you.

> job application   complaint   asking for information
> sympathy   congratulations   ordering goods   thanks

a) I am writing to complain about the service I received . . . (*semi-formal – complaint*)
b) I was so sorry to hear about your accident.
c) Thanks for the lovely present.
d) With reference to your advertisement in the *Evening Post*, I would like more details . . .
e) Following our telephone conversation of yesterday I would like to place an order . . .
f) Great to hear the news about the baby!
g) I should like to apply for the post of . . .

2 Which of the following would be suitable ways to close:
i) a semi-formal letter?   ii) a personal letter?
Suggest a context for each one.

a) I enclose a stamped addressed envelope and cheque for . . .
b) I look forward to hearing from you at your earliest convenience.
c) Hope you're keeping well.
d) I hope you can settle this matter to my satisfaction as soon as possible.
e) Best wishes.
f) I apologise for any inconvenience this may have caused.

3 Asking for information. Mike wrote a letter to the place which advertised flying holidays (at the beginning of the unit). The paragraphs of his letter are in the wrong order. In which paragraph does he:

a) talk about his flying experience?
b) say why he is writing?
c) ask for more advice?
d) speak about practical matters?

4 Put the five paragraphs of the letter into the correct order.

5 Write a similar letter applying for a weekend course which you would be interested in. (Use the adverts at the beginning of the unit if you like.) Follow the format of Mike's letter.

Dear Sir or Madam,

1 I wonder if it would be possible to begin with 2 days gliding instruction and then have 2 days parachuting instruction followed by 2 days flying. I would also like your advice on how many days you would recommend for beginners to get an idea of gliding and parachuting and what combination you would suggest.

2 I would prefer to come the week of April 7th–14th (7 nights) and I would be grateful if you could tell me how much this will cost, giving more details about living accommodation, etc.

3 I look forward to hearing from you and to receiving the booking forms. I enclose a stamped addressed envelope.

4 I am writing after seeing your advertisement in the newspaper for parachuting, flying and gliding courses. I am interested in having further information about these courses.

5 I have had 25 hours flying instruction in a Cessna 152 at an aerodrome near my home and I have passed my exams in air law and meteorology. I have had no experience at all, however, of parachuting and gliding.

Yours faithfully,

Mike Jefferies

Language reference

1 Obligation

a) *Have to*

Have to expresses obligation but usually describes what other people, not the speaker, require (i.e. it is external obligation).

> You **have to** wear a tie if you go to that nightclub. (It's one of the rules.)
> I **had to** go away on business last week. (My boss told me to.)

It is sometimes used when you are being polite and want to make excuses.

> I'm sorry but I **have to** wash my hair this evening.

Have got to is often used instead of *have to*. It is nearly always used in the contracted form.

> I**'ve got to** pay the phone bill this week.

FORM

NEGATIVE
You **don't have to** go.
I **haven't got to** finish it.

QUESTION
How old **do you have to** be to drive?
What **have we got to** do?

The past form of *have to* and *have got to* is *had to*.

PRONUNCIATION

In connected speech *have to* is usually pronounced /hæf tə/. In short answers and at the end of sentences *to* is strong.

> I don't want to, but I have **to**. /tu:/

When *have got to* is used in connected speech *I* and *have* are usually contracted to *I've*, and *to* is weak (/tə/). *Got* often joins up with *to* and is pronounced /ˈgɒtə/.

> I've **got to** go.

b) *Must / mustn't*

When we think something is important and we want to give strong, direct advice to someone, we can use *must* or *mustn't*. Depending on intonation, *must* can sound like an order. *Mustn't* is used to tell people *not* to do things.

> You **must** take these tablets four times a day.
> You **mustn't** worry so much.

(Note that the imperative is often more common in everyday language:

> **Take** these tablets four times a day, **please**.)

We often use *must* when we want to describe what we think is important for ourselves.

> I **must** go home. I want to write some letters.

Must can only be used to refer to the present and the future. *Had to* is used to refer to the past.

PRONUNCIATION

Notice the weak pronunciation of *must / mustn't*, and the frequent omission of the /t/.

> I must go. /ˈmʌs gəʊ/
> You mustn't say that! /ˈmʌsn/

c) *Should / shouldn't*

Should / shouldn't is also used for advice but is less strong than *must / mustn't*.

> You **shouldn't** smoke so much.

2 Absence of obligation

There are several ways of saying that it is *not necessary* to do something.

a) *Don't have to / haven't got to*

> You **don't have to** go to lectures. Nobody checks.
> You **haven't got to** wear a tie.

b) *Don't need to / needn't*

> You **don't need to** wear a uniform.
> We **needn't** hurry. The film doesn't start for ages.

Notice that *needn't* is not followed by *to* (NOT ~~We needn't to hurry.~~)

When talking about the past the most common expressions to use are *didn't have to* and *didn't need to*.

> I **didn't have to** go to bed early when I was ten.
> She **didn't need to** come in early at night.

3 Prohibition

Prohibition is expressed by *not allowed to, can't* and *mustn't*. The first two expressions generally refer to external prohibition, whereas *mustn't* is usually a direct order.

> You **aren't allowed to** photocopy this book.
> You **can't** fly unless you're fairly fit.
> You **mustn't** walk on the grass.

When talking about the past the most common expressions are *wasn't / weren't allowed to* and *couldn't*.

> I **wasn't allowed to** have pocket money.
> He **couldn't** drive because he wasn't insured.

4 Permission

Permission is expressed by *allowed to* and *can*.

> You **are allowed to** smoke in this room only.
> You **can** borrow my car if you like.

Allowed to usually suggests that permission is being given by someone else, not the speaker.

A meal or murder?

READING

Before reading

1   Look at the photographs of the two girls and read the headlines and captions. Do you agree with Kerry, who thinks that 'it is natural for humans to eat meat' or with Helen who feels 'guilty after eating meat'? Give your reasons.

To One Girl A Burger Means A Meal

'It's natural for humans to eat meat'

Kerry

To Another It Means MURDER

'I felt so incredibly guilty after eating meat'

Helen

2   What is the name for:
– somebody who doesn't eat meat?
– somebody who doesn't eat any animal products?

Reading

1   People who share Kerry's ideas should read Text A. People who think like Helen should read Text B. See if your guesses about Kerry or Helen's point of view were correct. Then answer the questions following the text that you have read.

Text A

Helen's point of view

1 Helen has been a vegetarian for a year and a half. 'It happened all of a sudden,' she says. 'I just couldn't eat meat any more. It made me feel sick. I suddenly thought of it as eating an animal, like a piece of cow, instead of a piece of beef. I did have a few meat meals during the first few weeks, but I felt so incredibly guilty and ashamed afterwards that I soon stopped. I wouldn't eat meat now if you paid me.

2   'When I told my mum I wanted to be a vegetarian, she went, "No, no, no." But I talked to dad and he said I could; I got round them by telling them I'd probably be sick if they gave me meat. Mum took me to the doctor who gave me loads of advice, and I've felt fine ever since. I've got thinner, but that's OK by me. I gave up meat because I think it's wrong to kill animals. Chickens and turkeys are the worst – it's easier to imagine them as whole animals. I eat eggs and cheese, but we have our own chickens so the eggs are free-range. Some vegetarian foods annoy me, like when they're called vegetarian beef or something, because that's imitating meat which is nearly as bad as having the real thing. I don't find vegetarian food boring, though. School's no problem either because they always have a soya meal for the vegetarians.

3   'I do get a bit of stick from my friends about my beliefs. They say, "I'll get you a pig's heart for Christmas." But I can be a bit annoying sometimes because I'm always trying to convert them. I try not to, but it's difficult.

4   'I feel so strongly about vegetarianism and I'm convinced it's a healthier way of life.

5   'I feel really proud because turning vegetarian is a big decision to make. You do feel so much better inside for doing it, though. To be honest, I don't know how people can't feel guilty tucking into a big, juicy steak.'

Complete these sentences.

a) Helen became a vegetarian because . . .
b) She persuaded her parents to agree by . . .
c) She eats . . .
d) She feels that being a vegetarian . . .

Now work with somebody who read about Kerry's point of view to find out:
1 why Kerry feels that eating meat is healthier.
2 if she eats all kinds of meat.
3 if she wears fur.
4 how she can eat animals when she's an animal lover.

Text B

Kerry's point of view

1 'A diet with meat in it is a lot healthier than a vegetarian one,' says Kerry. 'Vegetarians always look a bit skinny and I should imagine a lot of them miss out on their protein. I mean, you don't get much protein from vegetables and fruit, do you? And lots of them need to take vitamin tablets and things.

2 'I've never considered becoming a vegetarian. I love meat and I'll eat any kind – except possibly rabbit. That's because I see rabbits as pets, whereas a cow isn't, and my father brings a lot of rabbits home to chop up and eat and that puts me off a bit. I'd eat rabbit if it was already chopped up and came in a packet, but I don't like seeing animals killed.

3 'I think being a vegetarian is a bit half-hearted, to tell you the truth. A bit hypocritical. You should either be a complete vegan or a meat-eater. Lots of vegetarians wear leather and it seems to me as if they can't make up their minds. The only stand I make is not to wear fur. I'd never wear a fur jacket because certain animals are killed for their fur and nothing else. If you kill a cow, you eat the meat and wear the skin. That's OK because it's natural for humans to eat meat. Animals kill animals and humans are animals – so they kill animals to stay alive.

4 'Vegetarians tend to learn all there is to know about vitamins and all that, but I don't really think about food that much. I just eat what my parents eat. I can understand people wanting to save animals, because I love animals myself, but killing animals for meat doesn't strike me as being wrong. It's not as if the animals are tortured or anything – it's just one shot. That's it.

5 'Anyway, I don't see an animal on a plate when I have some meat. I don't think of it like that. I just like my meat that's all.'

(from *Just Seventeen*)

Complete these sentences.

a) Kerry thinks it's healthier to eat meat because . . .
b) She won't eat rabbit, unless it's chopped up, because . . .
c) She thinks vegetarians are hypocritical because a lot of them . . .
d) She feels strongly about fur because . . .
e) She is happy to eat meat because . . .

Now work with someone who read about Helen's point of view to find out:
1 when Helen gave up eating meat, and why.
2 what her parents said and did.
3 what kind of animals she thinks are the worst to eat.
4 what kind of food she eats.
5 how she feels about being vegetarian.

2 In each text find one example of language we normally use more in conversation than in writing. Example:
I mean, you don't . . . do you? (Kerry, paragraph 1)

VOCABULARY

Deducing words in context

1 Find the following words or phrases in the texts in the previous section. (Look at both texts, not just the text *you* read.) Try to work out from context the most likely meaning of the words in **bold** from the alternatives provided.

Text A
a) *It happened all of a sudden* (paragraph 1)
  i) without anyone noticing
  ii) quickly and unexpectedly
b) *I do get a bit of stick from . . .* (paragraph 3)
  i) something to hit somebody with
  ii) unfriendly comments
c) *I'm always trying to convert them* (paragraph 3)
  i) have a conversation with them
  ii) change what they believe in
d) *. . . and I'm convinced it's . . .* (paragraph 4)
  i) completely certain
  ii) not sure if
e) *. . . feel guilty tucking into a . . .* (paragraph 5)
  i) eating enthusiastically
  ii) refusing to eat

Text B
a) *. . . miss out on their protein* (paragraph 1)
  i) something in food that builds up the body
  ii) lunch
b) *. . . is a bit half-hearted* (paragraph 3)
  i) not making much real effort
  ii) very sad
c) *A bit hypocritical* (paragraph 3)
  i) too worried about their health
  ii) dishonest in their feelings
d) *. . . as if they can't make up their minds* (paragraph 3)
  i) invent something
  ii) reach a decision
e) *. . . the animals are tortured or anything* (paragraph 4)
  i) caused great pain and suffering
  ii) killed quickly

2 Work with a student who has not read your text and try to agree on your answers.

3 Look at these dictionary definitions of two of the phrasal verbs in the text.

a) *get round* (Text A, paragraph 2)
Which of these definitions of *get round* is correct in this context?

> **get round** (prep) [I] (of news, etc.) to spread: *The story soon got round.* **2** [T] (**get round** sthg.) to avoid; GET **around**: *They got round the immediate problem by borrowing a lot of money.* **3** [T] (**get round** sbdy.) to persuade (someone) to accept one's own way of thinking: *Father doesn't want to let us go. but I know I can get round him.*

> *verb + preposition* Here the particle *round* is a preposition so the direct object must come after the preposition: *I got round my parents.* (NOT ~~I got my parents round~~.)

b) *that puts me off* (Text B, paragraph 2)
Which of these definitions of *put off* is correct in this context?

> *...port; the boat put into Sydney for supplies.*
> **put off** (adv) [T] **1** (**put** sthg./sbdy. ↔ **off**) to move to a later date; delay: [+ obj/v-ing] *I'll have to put off my visit/put off going until next month.* **2** (**put** sbdy. ↔ **off**) to make excuses to (someone) in order to avoid a duty: *I put him off with a promise to pay him next week.* **3** (**put** sbdy. **off** (sthg.)) to discourage (someone) (from something): *She was trying to make a serious point, but people kept putting her off (her speech) by shouting. | Don't talk, it puts her off her game.* **4** (**put** sbdy. **off** (sthg./sbdy.)) to cause (someone) to dislike (someone or something); REPEL: *His bad manners/bad breath put me right off (him).* **5** (**put** sbdy. ↔ **off**) to stop and allow (someone) to leave a vehicle or boat
> *put on phr v [T] **1** (**put** sthg. ↔ **on**) to cover (part*

> *verb + adverb* Here the particle *off* is an adverb. It can go before or after the direct object: *It put the man off* or *It put off the man.*

PRACTICE

Work in pairs. For each of these sentences decide:
– which is the direct object.
– whether the particle (e.g. *up, off, after*) can also come after the object.

a) I gave up smoking ages ago.
b) I took off my coat.
c) He looked after the baby.
d) I turned up the music.
e) She's thinking about going to college next year.

Check your answers in a dictionary.

LANGUAGE POINT

Quantity

1 Andrew and Brigitte were interviewed by a market research company and asked about the kinds of food they buy. However, there are six grammatical mistakes in each of the transcripts of what they said. (Example: *I buy **lots of meat**.* NOT ~~I buy much meat~~.) Underline and then correct the words you think are wrong. Compare your answers with a partner. The first one has been done for you.

Andrew
What sort of things do I buy? Well, I buy <u>much</u> meat because it makes me feel full of energy. . .and it's nice. I buy very few other fresh food, though. I prefer my meals out of the freezer. But I do like fruit, so on Thursdays I go to the market and get any apples, bananas, melons. . . things like that. I know I don't eat much vegetables. The trouble is there aren't some vegetables I really like. Anyway, I have hardly some time for cooking these days.

Brigitte
Well, I can't eat food with additives – no any at all – so when I'm in a supermarket I have to spend a lot of time looking at labels. Actually, I, I don't eat many tinned food. Or, or even frozen food. I prefer everything fresh. And as for sweet things, they're not very good for you so I never have some chocolates – or things like that in the house – although sometimes I, I do buy a little home-made biscuits from a friend. What else? Oh, I like dairy products, particularly milk and yoghurt. And, oh yes, every Saturday I buy a few cheese as a treat. I try not to eat too much eggs, though. I don't want a heart-attack!

2 [🔊 15.1] Listen to the recording of what Andrew and Brigitte actually said and check your answers to Exercise 1.

3 Which of the two people is most like you? Give your reasons.

4   Underline the correct alternative and then fill in the gaps with the correct alternatives. Then check your answers with Section 1 in the *Language reference*.

a) *some/any*
 i) We use *some/any* in affirmative sentences:
    I want _____ bread.
 ii) We use *some/any* in sentences with a negative meaning:
    I never drink _____ alcohol. I don't want _____ mineral water, thanks.
 iii) In requests and offers when we want the answer *Yes* we use *some/any*:
    Would you like _____ cake?

b) *much / many / a few / a little*
 i) We use *much/many* and *a few / a little* with uncountable nouns:
    'Is there _____ wine left?'
    'No, there's only _____ .'
 ii) We use *much/many* and *a few / a little* with countable nouns:
    There are not _____ cans of beer left and there are only _____ cartons of orange juice.

PRACTICE

1   Go round the class as in the example below. Each person has to repeat what was said before and add on another item. Try not to say the same quantity more than once. Example:

*'I went to the shops and bought **some cakes**.'*
*'I went to the shops and bought **some cakes and a kilo of** . . .'*
*'I went to the shops and bought **some cakes, a kilo of** . . . **and a few** . . .'*

2   Write down what you eat and drink at mealtimes and for snacks in a typical day. Then interview a partner and add details of his/her eating habits.

3   Work with another pair and give details about yourself and your partner. Say:

a) how much meat or fish you eat on a typical day.
b) how many sweet things you eat.
c) how much you drink.
d) what you eat a lot of.
e) what you eat a little of.
f) whether you think you have a healthy diet. (Give reasons.)

4   Look at the *Checklist for Healthy Eating* and the examples below. Discuss in groups. What do you think you eat too much of? What do you think you don't eat enough of? Example:

*Paul eats chocolate all the time. He eats **too much** chocolate.*
*He hardly ever eats any fruit. He **doesn't eat enough** fruit.*
*He eats chips everyday. He eats **too many** chips.*

CHECKLIST FOR HEALTHY EATING

Each day aim to eat most of these:
1 portion (4oz/125gm) potato or rice
4–6 slices wholewheat bread or 2 slices and a portion of wholemeal pasta
½ pint (300ml) skimmed milk
1 portion (4oz/125g) green leafy vegetables such as spinach, cabbage or lettuce
1 portion (4oz/125g) pulse vegetables such as peas, baked beans or lentils
1 portion (4oz/125g) other root vegetables such as carrots and turnips
2 pieces of fruit
1 portion high fibre breakfast cereal such as muesli or porridge

Each week try to include:
1 portion (6oz/175g) white fish such as cod and haddock
2 portions (4oz/125g each) lean meat
1 portion (4oz/125g) oily fish such as sardines and tuna
1 portion (4oz/125g) poultry and 3–4 eggs
2oz/50g hard cheese or 4oz/125g cottage cheese
1 portion (4oz/125g) liver or kidney

Each week have no more than:
4oz/125g butter/margarine
2oz/50g chocolate/jam/sweets
1 portion fried food
1 pastry / slice cake
2 sweet puddings

Of course, the portion sizes given are averages and individual needs vary.

5 Give each other advice about eating habits.
Example:
*'I think you eat too much cheese. Why don't you
eat more cereals?'*

6 Work in groups of three. Each person should
take one of the roles below.

> STUDENT A
> You are a vegan. You strongly disagree
> with people eating meat, fish, eggs, cheese
> or milk.

> STUDENT B
> You are a vegetarian. You do not eat fish or
> meat but see nothing wrong in eating dairy
> products.

> STUDENT C
> You are a gourmet. You love good food,
> including meat, fish and dairy products.

a) Work out from the checklist the things you can
and can't eat.
b) Compare your diets and try to persuade each
other of your point of view.

> See **Use your grammar**, page 116, for further practice
> of quantity expressions.

PRONUNCIATION

Consonants

1 Read Section 2 in the *Language reference* to
find out the difference between voiced and
unvoiced consonants.

2 [📼 15.2] The consonants in the box often
cause problems because some of them are voiced
(e.g. /z/) and others are unvoiced (e.g. /s/). Listen to
the recording and practise saying the words. Then
divide the consonants into two equal groups
according to whether they are voiced or unvoiced.

> **zoo** (/z/)   **six** (/s/)   **jam** (/dʒ/)
> **church** (/tʃ/)   **shoe** (/ʃ/)   **usual** (/ʒ/)
> **this** (/ð/)   **both** (/θ/)

3 [📼 15.3] The dialogues below have been
specially written to contrast pairs of voiced and
unvoiced consonants. Listen to the recording and
decide which consonants are being practised in
each dialogue. (For example, the first dialogue
contrasts /z/ and /s/.) Practise the dialogues in pairs.

a) A: Pass the scissors, Susan.
   B: Say 'please', stupid. Or else!
b) A: Jim and Charles chose a large gin with a
      cherry.
   B: Charming! Put cheap ginger jam on their
      cheese.
c) A: I usually wear short, beige shirts.
   B: With your shape, you should wear something
      less casual and fashionable!
d) A: Thank your mother and father for their
      sympathy.
   B: I don't think it's worth bothering either of
      them.

SPEAKING

1 You are going to do a survey about eating. Find out about the people in your class using the following questionnaire. Cross out or add any questions you like, depending on what you think the important and interesting issues are.

> ## EATING
> **1** Have you ever been on a diet?
> **2** Do you avoid food which has additives?
> **3** Do you have a lot of salt with your food?
> **4** Do you take vitamin supplements?
> **5** Do you or your parents spend a lot on food?
> **6** Do you eat between meals?
> **7** Do you 'live to eat'?
> **8** Do you eat frozen and ready-prepared meals?

2 Copy the vertical and horizontal scales of the example graph and add bars to show the number of students who answer *Yes* to each of the questions in your survey.

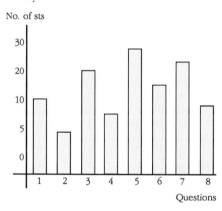

3 Can you draw any conclusions about the eating habits of people in your class?

WRITING

Writing a report

1 Read the report below and underline expressions connected to quantity. The first one has been done for you.

According to a recent Health Authority survey, eating habits among <u>the great majority of</u> teenagers are changing for the better. However, the habit of eating too many sweet foods still persists.

The report found that a third of 11-year-old boys and two-thirds of 11-year-old girls are on a diet. However, two out of three boys still eat fried food at least every other day, although a staggering seventy-five per cent now prefer to eat healthier cereal and wholemeal bread for breakfast rather than the traditional British 'fry-up'. In addition, almost all young people appear to be cutting down on food such as hamburgers and sausages. Nevertheless, over half of those interviewed still eat meat every day.

The report concluded that, despite much more awareness of healthier eating among the 11–16 age group, sweet snacks are still the weakness for most young people. Four out of five teenagers still find fizzy drinks, crisps and chocolate irresistible, and hardly any of the teenagers said they would give them up.

2 Write a sentence to summarise the main argument in the report.

3 In the second paragraph circle the linking expressions which connect the ideas in one sentence with the ideas in another.

4 Write a short report using the information you collected in your *Eating* survey. Begin like this:

In a survey of . . . (*say how many*) people from . . . (*say which countries or how many countries*) on . . . (*say what the survey was about*) we found that in our class . . . (*give a brief summary of the results*).

Use expressions from the example report and any of the following expressions.
most of us / most people
nearly all of us / nearly everybody
none of us / nobody
hardly any of us / hardly anybody
a few people / some of us
about half / a quarter / a third

Language reference

1 Talking about quantity

Countable nouns are nouns which normally have both a singular and a plural form: e.g. *a packet / packets, a can / cans. Uncountable* nouns (sometimes known as 'mass nouns') are nouns which normally have a singular but no plural: e.g. *some milk, lots of spaghetti, information, a piece of information* (NOT *some informations*).

How we talk about the quantity of a thing depends on whether the thing in question is countable or uncountable. Some quantity words can be used with both countable and uncountable nouns; others can be used with only one or the other.

WITH COUNTABLE	WITH UNCOUNTABLE
no	no
none	none
hardly any	hardly any
some / any	some / any
a few / many / a lot (lots) of	a little (bit of) / much / a lot (lots) of
(very) few / not many	(very) little / not much
too many / not enough	too much / not enough

a) *No / none*

No means 'not a' or 'not any'.
> There are **no** yoghurts left.
> There's **no** steak on the menu.

None means 'not one' or 'not any'.
> **None** of us eats fish. **None** at all.

b) *Some / any*

The words *some* and *any* refer to an indefinite amount. We use *some* in affirmative sentences as well as in requests and offers when we are positive.
> There are **some** eggs in the fridge.
> Would you like **some** cheese? (I expect you would.)

We usually use *any* in sentences with a negative meaning.
> They haven't got **any** yoghurt left.
> He never has **any** money.

c) *Much / many; a little (bit of) / a few*

We use *much* and *a little* with uncountable nouns.
> 'Is there **much** wine left in that bottle?' 'No, there's only **a little**, I'm afraid.'

We use *many* and *a few* with countable nouns.
> 'How **many** cans of orange juice are there?' 'I'm afraid there aren't **many** left.' / 'I'm afraid there are only **a few** left.'

A little (bit of) / a few are normally used in affirmative sentences. *Many* is normally used in negative sentences and questions. *Much* is generally not used in affirmative sentences.

There are several ways of making *much* and *many* stronger: *very much / so much, very many / so many.*

d) *Little / a little; few / a few*

Little / few have a negative meaning (i.e. 'not much' / 'not many'). *A little* means 'a small amount'. *A few* means 'a small number'.
> We eat **little** meat. (not much)
> We eat **a little** meat. (a small amount)
> **Few** people in the class eat a big breakfast. (not many)
> **A few** of us eat fish. (a small number)

e) *A lot of / lots of*

A lot of / lots of mean 'a large quantity of'. Both can be used with countable and uncountable nouns.
> There are **a lot of / lots of** bottles outside the front door.

f) *Too (much / many) / not enough*

Too means 'excessive'.
> You drink **too much** beer.
> **Too many** children eat sweets.

It is important not to confuse *too much / many* with *very much / many* (= 'a lot').
Not enough means 'not sufficient'.
> You do**n't** eat **enough** vegetables.

g) *Hardly any*

Hardly any means 'almost no'.
> I drink **hardly any** alcohol. I just don't like it.

h) *A half, a third, the great majority*

> About **a half** of the students take vitamin supplements.
> **The great majority** of students are worried about additives.

Note that you can also say: About **half** the students . . .

i) *No one, nobody / everyone, somebody, everybody / someone, most of us*

Note that all of these indefinite pronouns take a singular verb, apart from *most of us.*
> **No one** in our class gets much exercise.
> **Most of us** have a snack between meals.

2 Voiced and unvoiced consonants

Voiced consonants (e.g. /z/, /dʒ/, /ʒ/, /ð/) are produced with a movement of the vocal cords. You can feel the vibration by placing your hand on the front of your throat.
Unvoiced consonants (e.g. /s/, /tʃ/, /ʃ/, /θ/) are produced without the vibration of the vocal cords.

Use your grammar

UNIT 11

Requests and offers, agreeing and refusing

Work with a partner.

STUDENT A
Look at page 155.

> **STUDENT B**
> **a)** You had to go into hospital yesterday. It was an emergency, and you will be there for two weeks. Ask your partner to do the things in the pictures for you. Remember to be very polite if you think it's a difficult request. Use expressions like *Can / Could / Will / Would you (mind)…?* or *I was wondering if…?*
> **b)** Your partner is going on holiday. He/She asks you to do things for him / her. However, you hate cleaning and are frightened of snakes. Agree to the requests or refuse . If you refuse, make an excuse *(I'm sorry, but…)* and offer to do something else instead *(Shall I…? I'll…)* .

buy / newspapers / magazines

video / favourite programmes

phone / friends

wash / clothes

UNIT 12

Second conditional

You are going to live on a desert island for a year. You can take five things with you. Choose one thing from each category: food; drink; music; videos; possessions you can't live without.

a) Make a list of your five choices. Examples: *lots of pizza, my guitar, etc.*
b) Ask four people in the class what they would choose. Make notes and ask for their reasons. Example:
If you could take only one video, which would you choose? Why?
c) Report back to the class. Who could you not share your desert island with? Why not?

Wish and the past tense

You can make three wishes. Think about your job / work, family, home, nationality, appearance, personality, friends, politics and the things you would like to own.

a) Write a wish on three different pieces of paper. Use expressions like *I wish I had / could / were / didn't…* Example:
I wish I could play the violin.
b) Work in groups. Put the pieces of paper in a pile. Take turns to choose a piece of paper and guess who made the wish.
c) The person who made the wish should give his / her reasons. Example:
I wish I could play the violin because I'd like to join an orchestra.

115

UNIT 13

Present Perfect with *for* and *since*

a) Look at the painting. Work in pairs and give your opinions about these questions.

1 Where is the woman?
2 What is she thinking about?
3 What do you think has happened?
4 How long has she been there?
5 What has she been doing?
6 What is she going to do next?

b) Work in groups. Tell each other what you think has happened / is going to happen.

c) Decide on the best version, and write it as a story.

UNIT 14

Obligation, prohibition, permission

STUDENT A
Look at page 155.

> STUDENT B
>
> It's your first day at a residential summer school. Think of questions to ask your partner, who has already been at the school for a week. Use the words below and expressions like *have to / can / are allowed to*. Example:
> Use the phone in the Student Common Room?
> *Can we use the phone in the Student Common Room?*

1 Students / use these computers / photocopiers?
2 Go to / all lessons?
3 Visitors / meals?
4 Bring / own towels?
5 Change traveller's cheques / at school?

UNIT 15

Quantity

You have just moved into a new house and you are planning a housewarming party. There will be eighteen people at the party: two old people, four young children, two teetotallers (people who don't drink alcohol), three teenagers, three men and four women (one vegetarian)

a) Work in pairs. Make notes about what you will need to buy. Think about music, food, decorations and drink. Don't worry about the exact quantities. Use words like *some, any, a few, a little, lots / a lot of*.

b) Work in groups. Compare your lists. Agree and disagree with the people in your group. Example:
I agree we need some balloons. But we only need to buy a little bread.

Beastly tales

VOCABULARY 1

1   Some people have very strange pets.

a) Use the words in the box to name the animals in the photographs above.

> bat   rat   crocodile   snake   ferret   tiger

b) Do people keep pets in your country? What kinds of pets?

c) Why do you think people choose to keep pets like the ones above?

2   In the texts below the children are talking about pets.

a) While you are reading write down the names of the pets they have, and the ones they would like to have.

b) Which animals are not typical pets?

Hammy

Martin, 5

I've got a hamster called Hammy. He's 16. I give him lettuce and some toast. I want a kitten, as I'd like its purring. I might get one when I'm a man.

Lewis, 7

I would like to have a squirrel because I like their tails. I would like an alligator, too. I'd put it in a big pool. When my sister went in she would get gobbled up.

Rosemary, 6

I've got four baby worms. I keep them in a worm house in the garden. I'd like a tiger. I'd call it Furry. I'd feed it four pork chops and keep it in the shed.

(from *Woman*)

LISTENING

Before listening

Look at the photograph of Ann Webb above.

a) What is the name of the type of spider she is holding?

b) How would you feel about holding a spider like that?

c) Imagine that you are going to interview Ann Webb about her spiders. Write down at least five questions that you would like to ask her and compare with a partner. Example:
How many spiders do you have?

Listening

1 [📼 16.1] Listen to the first part of the interview with Ann Webb and tick any questions you wrote down that were asked. Put a cross next to the questions that weren't asked. Did anything surprise you about what she said?

2 Listen again and choose the correct answer based on the recording.

a) Ann Webb has _____ spiders.
  – 18 – 80

b) Ann and Frank Webb bought their first spider:
  – in 1982. – in 1962.

c) Her husband Frank:
  – loves all animals, but not spiders.
  – loves all animals, including spiders.

d) Ann Webb:
  – studies spiders for scientific research.
  – treats them as part of the family.

e) The spiders:
  – only eat house crickets.
  – eat lots of different insects.

f) To get house crickets Ann Webb:
  – breeds them herself. – goes to a pet shop.

g) She feeds the spiders:
  – every week. – every six months.

h) When they are in the wild tarantulas:
  – hunt for food themselves.
  – wait for food to arrive.

3 [📼 16.2] Listen to the second part of the interview.

a) There are six factual mistakes in the summary of the radio interview below, which was published in a magazine. Underline the mistakes, and then compare what you have found with someone else. The first one has been done for you.

b) Correct the factual errors and if necessary listen again to check your answers.

> **M**rs Webb told me that while she was holding a spider <u>she often felt too afraid to speak</u>. She said that 60 per cent of the population would also be terrified. However, she said that films such as James Bond films had given spiders good publicity. She said that tarantulas could sting a human being like a bee if they felt like it and, although they were not naturally aggressive, they would kill a person if necessary. She said she liked their beauty and their exciting life-style but she didn't know why she was so passionate about them.

LANGUAGE POINT 1

Reported statements

1　Look at how Ann Webb's words were reported. Notice that the Present Continuous changes to the Past Continuous and the Present Simple changes to the Past Simple.

Ann Webb's actual words: 'While I *am* holding a spider I often *feel* too afraid to speak.'

This was reported as: '*Mrs Webb told me that while she was holding a spider she often felt too afraid to speak.*

Look at the other examples below and check what happens to the following when they are reported: *would, have, can, will.*

- '60 per cent of the population *would* be terrified.'
  She said that 60 per cent of the population would be . . .
- 'James Bond films *have* given spiders good publicity.'
  She told me that James Bond films had given spiders . . .
- 'Tarantulas *can* sting a human being like a bee.'
  She said that tarantulas could sting . . .
- 'They *will* kill a person if necessary.'
  She told me that they would kill . . .

2　Look back at the examples in Exercise 1. What do you notice about the difference between the construction which follows *say* and the construction which follows *tell*?

PRACTICE

1 [🔊 16.3]　Listen to the extract from the radio news about Fred the tortoise.

Fred gets £26,000

2　Complete the newspaper report about Fred.

FRED the tortoise inherited a fortune yesterday when his devoted owner, Dolly Duffin died. His new owner, the old lady's closest relation, Susan Kirkwood, said that Dolly __(a)__ her only £ __(b)__ and a photo album. Even the old lady's cats __(c)__ got any money. Obviously, she __(d)__ to leave all of it to Fred. She told reporters that Dolly __(e)__ very eccentric and so the family __(f)__ surprised, although it was ironic that her family __(g)__ have to go on living on her pension while Fred __(h)__ be able to have a life of luxury.
　She finished by saying that she __(i)__ look after Fred as well as she __(j)__, although perhaps not as well as her aunt __(k)__.

(from the *Daily Mail*)

LANGUAGE POINT 2

Reported questions

1　After the interview with Ann Webb the radio interviewer told his editor what he and Ann had talked about.

'I asked her how many spiders she had. Then I wanted to know when she had bought the first one. She asked me if I liked spiders.'

What were the exact words that the interviewer and Ann used to ask their questions? Example:

INTERVIEWER: *'How many spiders do you have?'*

2　Look at this example carefully and tick the correct alternative in each of the statements below.

'How many spiders do you have?'
I asked her how many spiders she had.

a) When questions containing question words (*what, how,* etc.) are reported they:
　– take the auxiliary *do/does/did.*
　– do not take the auxiliary *do/does/did.*
b) The reported question:
　– is a statement.
　– remains a question.
c) The word order of the reported question:
　– changes.
　– doesn't change.
d) The verb in the reported question:
　– usually changes into the past.
　– always stays in the present.

3　How are *Yes/No* questions reported? Check with Section 2 in the *Language reference.*

PRACTICE

Write to somebody in your class.

a) Take three pieces of paper and write the name of a different student in your class at the top of each sheet. On each piece of paper write a different question to each person.

b) Give your questions to each of the three students, who should write a reply and return the sheet to you.

c) Tell another person about each of the questions you asked and the replies you received.
Example:
'I asked Carmen what she was doing tonight and she told me that she was washing her hair.'

LANGUAGE POINT 3

Reported imperatives

1   After the interview Ann Webb tried to get the interviewer to become more friendly with her spider, Cleo!

a) Match each of the sentences below (i–iv) with an appropriate reporting verb from the box. Practise saying each sentence in direct speech with the appropriate intonation. Example:
'Go on, stroke her. She's quite safe.' (persuade)

tell   ask   persuade   invite

   i) 'Go on, stroke her. She's quite safe.'
  ii) 'Don't drop her, or she'll hurt herself!'
 iii) 'Pick her up if you want to. It's OK.'
  iv) 'Give Cleo that insect to eat, would you?'

b) Change each sentence into reported speech.
Example:
*Ann **persuaded** him to stroke Cleo.*

2   Look at the example reported sentence from Exercise 1.
Ann persuaded him to stroke Cleo.

What is the word order for reported imperatives? Complete the gaps using the words from the box, and then check with Section 3 in the *Language reference*.

object   reporting verb

AFFIRMATIVE
subject + _____ + _____ + *to* + base form

3   Look at the example of a reported negative imperative and note the word order.
She told him not to drop Cleo.
Then complete the gaps below, using the words from the box.

not   reporting verb   object

NEGATIVE
subject + _____ + _____ + _____ + *to* + base form

4   Notice that *tell* is used for reported orders (*He **told** me **to** open the window.*) as well as for reported statements (*I **told** him **that** I was coming.*). *Ask* is used for reported requests (*I **asked** her **to** meet me.*) as well as for reported questions (*I **asked** her **what** she was doing.*). Check with the *Language reference* Section 3 for different constructions with *tell* and *ask*.

PRACTICE

Complete the second sentence in each example so that it becomes a reported version of the first sentence. Use reported statements, questions and imperatives.

a) 'Why has the shop closed already?' he asked the woman.
   He asked . . .

b) 'You will meet a tall dark stranger, and fall madly in love,' the fortune-teller said to me.
   The fortune-teller told . . .

c) 'You must avoid alcohol and cigarettes for a month,' the doctor said to him.
   The doctor told . . .

d) 'I've just seen a very strange animal,' said Susan.
   Susan said . . .

e) 'Peter, open the window, could you, please?' asked the teacher.
   The teacher asked . . .

f) 'Don't go!' they said to me.
   They tried to persuade . . .

g) 'Why don't you stay for dinner?' Richard said to Christine.
   Richard invited . . .

h) 'The tennis match hasn't finished yet,' said Jennifer.
   Jennifer said . . .

See **Use your grammar**, page 151, for further practice of reported speech.

VOCABULARY 2

1 Look at these idomatic expressions with *like*.

a) Match the two parts of the phrases in columns A and B to make idiomatic expressions. Discuss with a partner what you think they mean.
Example:
'To swim like a fish' means 'to swim very well'.

A		B
swim		a dog
have eyes		a horse
work	LIKE	a fish
drink		a hawk
eat		a fish

b) In each case think of an equivalent expression in your own language, and translate it into English word for word. If possible, discuss your translation with someone who does not speak your language.

2 What kind of people are the following?

a) Match the idiomatic expressions in column A with the definitions in column B. One has been done for you.

b) Do you know anyone who fits any of the descriptions?

A	B
A person who . . .	*is . . .*
is catty	shy/quiet
is batty	arrogant/conceited
is sheepish	sly/spiteful
is ratty/crabby	arrogant/conceited
thinks he/she's the cat's whiskers	self-conscious/ embarrassed
is mousy	irritable
thinks he/she's the bee's knees	mad/crazy

SPEAKING

1 Do you know any traditional stories about how the leopard got its spots?

2 Read the text. In pairs, expand it by answering the questions in brackets and using your imagination as much as possible.

3 Compare your stories in groups and decide on your final version.

4 Tell your own story about how another animal became the way it is now. Some possible titles are:
– How the elephant got its trunk.
– Why ants are so small.
– Why giraffes have long necks.

How the leopard got its spots

One day, ant's mother died (*How?*), and all the animals decided to accompany him to the funeral. (*Which animals were his friends? Where was the funeral going to be held?*).

As they went along the road from the village they passed a farm full of . . . (*What animals were on the farm?*). The leopard was very fond of . . . (*What?*) and his mouth watered. He passed the farm very . . . (*How?*) until he was at the back of the procession. When he was alone he rushed into the farm. (*What did he do there?*)

After the leopard had rejoined the other animals the farmer came rushing after the animals. (*What did he do and say?*) Of course, the animals denied it but the farmer said they must stand trial to see who was guilty. He made a . . . (*What did he make?*) and asked the animals to jump over it. He said the guilty one would fall in.

One by one, the animals jumped over. When it was the leopard's turn he hesitated but eventually he had to go. (*What happened to him?*) The animals were amazed and called him a thief. He had to crawl home ashamed, and to this day he has his spotted coat as a reminder of his greed.

(from *Tales of an Ashanti Father*)

CREATIVE WRITING

1   Look at this photograph of a cobra and the one of the leopard (in the previous section) and write down as many words or phrases as you can to describe the two animals. Use words from the box if you want to. (You may want to check some of the words in your dictionary.)

gentle   venomous   cruel   elegant   graceful   regal
beautiful   terrifying   cunning   affectionate   dangerous
playful   impassive   unpredictable   hypnotic   deadly
vindictive   powerful   evil   fast   muscular   fascinating
proud   arrogant

2   Read the two poems below.

a) Write down the adjectives and verbs that are used in the descriptions of the animals. Do you agree with the way the writers have described the animals?

Leopard

Gentle hunter
his tail plays on the ground
while he crushes the skull.

Beautiful death
who puts on a spotted robe
when he goes to his victim.

Playful killer
whose loving embrace
splits the antelope's heart.

(from *Yoruba Poetry*)

The Snake Song

Neither legs or arms have I
But I crawl on my belly
And I have
Venom, venom, venom!

Neither horns nor hoofs have I
But I spit with my tongue
And I have
Venom, venom, venom!

Neither bows nor guns have I
But I flash fast with my tongue
And I have
Venom, venom, venom!

Neither radar nor missiles have I
But I stare with my eyes
And I have
Venom, venom, venom!

I master every movement
For I jump, run and swim
and I spit
Venom, venom, venom!

(by John Mbiti)

b) What is interesting about the way the writer has described the leopard in the first line of each verse?

c) What are the different ways a snake defends itself? How do tortoises, hedgehogs and crabs defend themselves?

3   Think of an animal.

a) First write down as many words and expressions as you can to describe the animal. Think of its appearance, its behaviour, its personality and how it moves.

b) Write a short poem or description. You might want to use some of the words in the box in Exercise 1. If you like you can copy one of the patterns used in the poems in Exercise 2. Examples:

EAGLE   ELEPHANT
I am king of the world . . .   *Heavy steps, heavy thoughts . . .*

Language reference

Reported speech (sometimes known as *Indirect speech*) is used when we tell one person what another person said without repeating the actual words used.

> *'How many spiders do you have?'* (direct speech)
> *I asked her how many spiders she had.* (reported speech)

1 Reported statements

A *reporting verb* is a verb like *tell* or *say*. *Tell* has to be followed by an object (e.g. *me*).

> *She **told me** (that) **she** had about 80 spiders at the moment.* (NOT ~~She told she had~~ . . .)

Say is not followed by an object.

> *She said (that) **she** had about 80 spiders at the moment.* (NOT ~~She said me she~~ . . .)

The word *that* is optional.

When the reporting verb is in the past tense, the tense in the reported statement often moves one tense back in the past.
a) Present Simple changes to Past Simple:
> *'They're all tarantulas.'* (direct)
> *She **said** (that) all her spiders **were** tarantulas.* (reported)

b) Present Continuous changes to Past Continuous:
> *'We're leaving for Canada.'* (direct)
> *Kate **told** me they **were leaving** for Canada.* (reported)

c) Past Simple sometimes stays as Past Simple or changes to Past Perfect:
> *'I went to the pet shop.'* (direct)
> *Joanne **said** she **went** (**had been**) to the pet shop.* (reported)

The Past Perfect is used when we want to emphasise the fact that one thing happened before another. (There is more information on the Past Perfect in Unit 18.)

d) Past Continuous can stay as Past Continuous or change to Past Perfect Continuous.
> *'I was reading all morning.'* (direct)
> *He said he **was reading** (**had been reading**) all morning.* (reported)

e) Present Perfect changes to Past Perfect:
> *'I have just bought a new car.'* (direct)
> *He said he **had** just **bought** a new car.* (reported)

f) Some modal verbs also change:
> *'I'll help you.'* (direct)
> *She **said** she **would** help me.* (reported)
> (Note that *will* changes to *would*.)
> *'I can't swim.'* (direct)
> *Richard **said** he **couldn't** swim.* (reported)
> (Note that *can* changes to *could*.)
> *'I must go.'* (direct)
> *Julia said she **had to** go.* (reported)

Would, *should*, *could* and *might* remain the same.

In spoken language people sometimes do not change the tenses in the reported statement, especially when the statement is still true at the time of the reporting.
> *'I'm very happy.'* (direct)
> *He **said** he's very happy* (reported) (. . . *and he's still happy*).

If the reporting verb remains in the present tense (which is common in informal speech), the reported statement usually does too.
> *'I'm going to Dublin next week.'* (direct)
> *She says she's going to Dublin next week.* (reported)

Sometimes time and place words from direct speech have to be changed in indirect speech, depending on the context.
> *'We're leaving for Canada tomorrow.'* (direct)
> *Kate said they were leaving for Canada **the next day**.* (reported)
> *'It's here!'* (direct)
> *He said it was **there**.* (reported)

Quotation marks are not used in reported speech.

2 Reported questions

When a question is reported the new sentence is no longer a question. The auxiliary *do*, *does* or *did* and the question mark are not necessary and the word order changes from question word order to statement word order. Reporting verbs include *ask* and *want to know*. Compare word orders:

> **Q   V   S**
> *'How   are   you?'*
> (direct = **Q**uestion word + **V**erb + **S**ubject)

> **Q   S   V**
> *He asked me   how   I   was.*
> (reported = **Q**uestion word + **S**ubject + **V**erb)

Use *if* or *whether* when reporting *Yes/No* questions (i.e. questions beginning with *Do / Does*, *Is / Are*, etc.).
> *'Are they poisonous?'* (direct)
> *He **wanted to know if** / **whether** my tarantulas were poisonous.* (reported)

3 Reported imperatives

Requests and *commands* are reported with verbs like *tell*, *ask*, *persuade* and *invite*. The sentence pattern is usually:
Subject + **R**eporting Verb + **O**bject + *to* + **B**ase form.

S	**R**	**O**	**to**	**B**	
She	*told*	*him*	*to*	*be careful.*	*('Be careful!')*
She	*persuaded*	*us*	*to*	*hurry up.*	*('Hurry up!')*

Notice the word order in negative imperatives.
> *'Don't speak to her like that!'* he told us. (direct)
> *He told us **not to speak** to her like that.* (reported)
> (NOT . . . ~~to not speak~~ . . .)

Tell can be used for reported statements and reported orders (see above).

Ask can be used for reported questions and reported requests.
– *'Who have you seen?'* he asked. (direct question)
> *He **asked** me who I had seen.* (reported question)
– *'Can you pass me the salt, please?'* (direct request)
> *He **asked** me to pass (him) the salt.* (reported request)

What are you afraid of?

READING

Before reading

1   A phobia is a strong unnatural fear of something. Usually there is no obvious reason for the fear. Some people, for example, are frightened of open spaces. Others are afraid of spiders. How many phobias can you think of?

Reading

1   Look through this article and underline the different types of phobias.

2   Read the passage again more carefully and make notes under the following headings: *Causes, Symptoms, Treatment.*

3   Work in pairs. Compare your answers and discuss the following questions.

a) Which sufferers do you have most sympathy with?
b) Do you know any other ways of dealing with phobias? Give details.
c) Do you know anybody who has suffered from a phobia? Can you describe what happened?

FOR YEARS, Ken Sell had a strange problem – he was terrified of touching things or of being touched. "I sat in a chair for six years, only moving to go to bed. For a short while I actually lost the use of my legs," he says.

For the estimated one in twelve people who suffer from a phobia, life can be governed by their irrational fear. The range of symptoms phobics suffer includes breaking out in a cold sweat, rapid pounding of the heart, a rise in blood pressure, nausea, faintness or a paralysing weakness of the limbs.

What causes a rational fear to develop into a phobia is largely a mystery. Sometimes it may be depression or a shocking event but often there seems to be no explanation.

One London man left his job because his terror of pigeons stopped him going out in daylight. Another told a BBC radio phone-in programme: "I'm terrified of leaves, especially rhubarb. I can't go near them. If I come close, my heart thumps and I go all shaky."

Cases are recorded of people being terrified by telephones, knives, swallowing food, cigarette smoke, white shirts and by tunnels or bridges. Those with severe phobias will go to extreme lengths to avoid contact with whatever terrifies them. One woman jumped out of a moving car when she spotted a spider.

Ken Sell, who now works for the charity Phobic Action, cured himself by suddenly forcing himself to touch things all the time. A more gentle programme is set out in *Living with Fear*, a book by Professor Marks of the Institute of Psychiatry, London. In his exercises, first the fear itself is faced, then, gradually, the victim learns to face it in a calm frame of mind. He has been successful with a wide range of problems including agoraphobia, fear of animals or objects, fear of sex and fear of being dirty which leads people to wash hundreds of time a day.

(from *The Independent*)

rhubarb: a sharp-tasting garden plant whose stems are cooked and eaten

VOCABULARY

Adjectives into verbs

1   Divide the words and expressions in the box into two categories: *Fear* (e.g. *terrified*) and *Symptoms* (e.g. *sweating*).

> frightened   feeling sick   going white
> scared   sweating   terrified   shaking
> screaming   petrified   trembling   fainting

2   Put the *Fear* words in order of strength. (There is more than one possible order.)

3   Write down a verb (or verbs) which correspond(s) to the words in the *Fear* category. Example: *terrified: terrify, terrorise*

PRONUNCIATION

Diphthongs

1 [📼 17.1]   A diphthong is a vowel sound made by pronouncing two vowels quickly one after the other. Listen to the following words. Each contains one of the diphthong sounds in English.

> sounds   go   way   fly

2   Look at the pronunciation chart on page 160 and find the pronunciation symbols for the above sounds. Example: *sounds /aʊ/*

3   Write the pronunciation symbols across the top of a sheet of paper as headings for a table with four columns. Put the words *sounds*, *go*, *way* and *fly* into the correct columns.

4 [📼 17.2]   Listen to the following sentences and find words with diphthong sounds that correspond to each of the four pronunciation symbols in your table. Write the words in the correct columns.

'My friend's child is afraid of the phone ringing. If it rings loudly she puts a pillow over it and hides until it stops.'

5   Add some other words you know to each column. Compare your lists with a partner.

LANGUAGE POINT 1

The -ing form

1   Underline all the *-ing* forms in this passage.

'Travelling by train makes me into a nervous wreck. I don't know why it is exactly but a moving train sends shudders down my spine. Last night I was driving home from doing the shopping when the car packed up and I had no choice but to get a train. It was absolutely terrifying. I tried all the boring tricks I knew to calm my nerves: gripping the side of my bag, putting on dark glasses, eating whole bars of chocolate. But they didn't work . . . '

2   *Travelling by train* is the subject of the verb *makes*. In *a moving train* the word *moving* is an adjective. Find an example of an *-ing* form which is like a noun.

PRACTICE

1   Tell your partner what makes you:
– nervous. (Example: *'Flying makes me nervous.'*)
– scream.
– angry.
– emotional.

2   Complete the following sentences. One has been done for you.

a) Why do you watch television? I think it's a waste of time.
   *I think **watching television** is a waste of time.*
b) Who is going to order?
   Who is going to do . . . ?
c) You must give dogs plenty of exercise. It's important for their health.
   Giving dogs . . .
d) She's still preparing her lecture. Don't speak to her. Wait for her to finish.
   Don't speak to her until she finishes . . .
e) I don't like it when people tell me what to do.
   I can't stand people . . .
f) You can't sleep in the park at night. It's forbidden.
   . . . is forbidden.
g) Have you been to the shops?
   Have you done . . . ?
h) Please be quiet.
   Do you mind . . . ?

LANGUAGE POINT 2

-ing or to?

1   Some verbs (e.g. *enjoy*, *can't stand*, *admit*) are followed by verbs in the *-ing* form (see Review Unit 1). Example:
I enjoy reading.
Other verbs (e.g. *hope*, *agree*, *decide*) are followed by *to* + base form. Example:
I hope to see you tomorrow.

Divide the verbs in the box into two groups: those followed by *to* + base form and those followed by an *-ing* form. There are five verbs in each group.

offer	miss	feel like	deserve	deny
refuse	give up	learn	mean	put off

Check your answers with Section 2 in the *Language reference*.

2   Complete the sentences by changing the words in brackets to either *to* + base form or an *-ing* form.

a) When I saw the car coming towards us so fast I expected it (*hit*) us.
b) I'm vegetarian so I always avoid (*eat*) meat or fish.
c) The terrorists were afraid and wanted (*escape*).
d) Have you finished (*read*) that book?
e) When I saw his new haircut, I couldn't help (*laugh*).
f) Have you managed (*find*) what you were looking for?

3   Some verbs can be followed by either an *-ing* form or *to* + base form with little change in meaning. How many of the following sentences can you change to the alternative form? Example:
I promised not to be late.
This CANNOT be changed to *I promised not being late.*

a) I hate getting up early.
b) It began to rain.
c) I refused to go to his party.
d) Why don't you offer to help her?
e) They denied seeing him.
f) They continued playing even though the light was bad.
g) I put off leaving until I had to.
h) I'd love to come to your party.

PRACTICE

1   Work in pairs. Student A and Student B should each choose verbs from the box to make short exchanges. Some of the verbs are followed by an *-ing* form (e.g. *avoid*) and some are followed by *to* + base form (e.g. *decide*). Student A should use the cues and Student B should respond as he/she likes. Example:
A: *You must **avoid walking** home in the dark.*
B: *Don't worry! I've **decided to take** a taxi.*

dislike	avoid	decide	arrange	agree
want	manage	enjoy	promise	try
can't stand	don't mind			

a) walk home in the dark
b) restaurant(s)
c) travel by train
d) film(s)
e) buy a portable phone

2   Which alternative is correct?

a) Ruth threatened *putting* / *to put* him in a tank of crocodiles.
b) I know Bruce planned *helping* / *to help* but he forgot.
c) I'm getting too old. I'm going to give up *running* / *to run*.
d) Has Gill learnt *playing* / *to play* the flute yet?
e) I couldn't help *wondering* / *to wonder* what you were thinking.
f) Imagine *seeing* / *to see* you here!
g) Why do you always pretend not *understanding* / *to understand* what I'm talking about?
h) I don't fancy *going* / *to go* for a swim in weather like this.

3   Continue the following sentences.

a) When I finish this course I intend . . .
b) In the summer I prefer . . .
c) I don't mind . . .
d) I can't afford . . .
e) Next week I have arranged . . .
f) I find it very difficult to give up . . .
g) I think teachers deserve . . .

Compare your answers in pairs.

See **Use your grammar,** page 151, for further practice of *-ing* and *to*.

SPEAKING

Before speaking

1 What kind of phobia does this headline refer to? What effect do you think this fear has on the sufferer's life?

2 Work in groups of three (Students A, B, and C). You are going to take part in a TV programme on phobias.

SHIVERING, SHAKING, SICK . . . AT THE SIGHT OF A BUTTON

> **STUDENT A**
> Read Text A about Sue Mahoney. Imagine you have the phobia you read about and you have decided that you need help.

> **STUDENT B**
> Read Text B. You are Professor Marks. What advice will you give Sue Mahoney?

> **STUDENT C**
> You are a TV interviewer. You are going to:
> – introduce the programme. (*How will you introduce it?*)
> – interview Sue Mahoney. (*Write some of the questions in note form.*)
> – interview Professor Marks to ask his advice. (*Write some of the questions in note form.*)
> – bring the programme to an end. (*What will you say?*)
> If necessary, scan the texts quickly to find out anything you want to know.

Text A (Student A)

Southend hairdresser Sue Mahoney has suffered from a button phobia for as long as she can remember.

'Ever since I was a child I have hated buttons,' says 23-year-old Sue with a shudder.

'Now I won't tidy the tops of cupboards, in case I reach out and touch a button by mistake. And I lift clothes from drawers using a pen.

'Obviously I don't buy any clothes with buttons on them – and I have the fastenings at the top of skirts altered so that I don't have to see a button-hole.

'My gran's great – she knits me loads of cardigans without buttons. And my boyfriend,

Text B (Student B)

HELP YOURSELF TO A NEW LIFE OF FREEDOM

If you suffer from extreme anxiety about something you might be able to cure yourself by following these guidelines designed by Professor Isaac Marks.

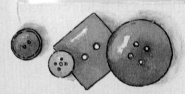

Colin, knows I prefer him to wear T-shirts . . . although, when we first met, he thought I was a bit reserved because I would run away from him if he tried to cuddle me while wearing a shirt with buttons on it.'

(from *Chat*)

1. Write down precisely what frightens you. For example: *I worry about dirt and germs so I wash my hands all day.*
2. For each fear, write clearly what you want to achieve: *I want to be able to touch things without washing my hands.*
3. Write down the benefits to your life of achieving these aims: *I can hug my children without being frightened of giving them germs.*
4. Write some statements on small cards to help you cope when you feel frightened: *I must tense all my muscles as much as I can, then relax them until I feel easier. I must breathe slowly and steadily and learn to deal with the situation.*
5. Make a firm decision not to run away from the situation. Start to imagine the situation and refer to the cards when necessary. Write down what you do and feel each time.
6. When you build up enough confidence, try putting yourself in the situation that frightens you and repeat the exercise.
7. Carry on until you find those things that used to terrify you have become a bit of a bore and you have forgotten what you used to feel.

(from *The Independent*)

Speaking

1 Plan the TV programme and have a rehearsal.

2 Present your programme to the other groups (or record it and then present it). Finally, vote on whose programme was the most interesting. (You are not allowed to vote for your own.)

WRITING

Linking words and expressions

1   Complete the gaps in this personal letter with the linking words
and expressions below.

Dear Simon,
    Thanks for your letter. It's always lovely to hear from
you, and I know how busy you are. 1_____, I've
been pretty busy myself in the last few weeks – my exams
are in a fortnight.
    2_____, I don't think I'm going to do very well
in them because every time I think about them I get a
terrible attack of nerves. I don't know what I'm going
to do about it. 3_____, things often turn out
unexpectedly, don't they? And you sometimes do well
without expecting to. 4_____ Louise will do
brilliantly as always – I should imagine that 5_____
she will get a first class degree.
    6_____, the main reason for writing to you
was to ask if Louise and myself could come over and
stay for a week when the exams are over. 7_____,
if you would rather not, or if you have other plans,
don't worry. 8_____ we will look after ourselves
if we come and we won't be any trouble!
    9_____, write and let us know, will you?
Perhaps we'll meet up before then 10_____ – at
a show in London or something?
    Take care. Lots of love to Margaret.
                        Keith

1 a) Personally   b) After all   c) Mind you
2 a) Unfortunately   b) By the way   c) On the other hand
3 a) In other words   b) Having said that   c) Besides
4 a) What's more   b) Of course   c) Personally
5 a) apparently   b) in my opinion   c) eventually
6 a) Well   b) Firstly   c) In the end
7 a) Because   b) After all   c) Obviously
8 a) Naturally   b) Also   c) Meanwhile
9 a) At last   b) In the end   c) Anyway
10 a) after all   b) in any case   c) finally

2   What advice would you give Keith for his nervousness
about exams?

Language reference

1 The -*ing* form

The -*ing* form is added to the base form of verbs to make:
- the continuous / progressive form of the verb:
  go → **going**
- an adjective: a **frightening** film
- a noun: Who does the **shopping** in your house? **Flying** makes me nervous.

See Unit 2 for the spelling changes which are sometimes necessary when making an -*ing* form (e.g. shop → sho**pping**). Notice that countable nouns with -*ing* can often have a plural (e.g. *feelings*).

2 *To* + base form and -*ing*

Many verbs which are followed by *to* + base form express a concern with the future, in particular verbs of hopes, offers and plans.

I **hope to see** you tomorrow.
She **offered to help** me later.
He **wants to visit** us next week.

Examples of verbs followed by *to* + base form:

| She | agreed   arranged   can't afford
decided   deserved   expected
hoped   intended   learnt
managed   meant   offered
planned   pretended   promised
refused   threatened   wanted | *to play* the piano. |

Examples of verbs followed by -*ing*:

| He | admitted   avoided   couldn't help
couldn't stand   denied
didn't mind   disliked   enjoyed
fancied   finished   gave up
imagined   missed   put off
suggested | *eating* lots of meat. |

3 Verbs followed by *to* + base form OR -*ing*

Some verbs can be followed by either *to* + base form or -*ing* with little change of meaning.

| She | began   continued
hated   liked   loved
preferred | *playing* / *to play* with spiders. |

However, *to* + base form sometimes suggests an action on a specific occasion while -*ing* sometimes suggests a general statement.

I would **like to see** you tomorrow. (specific)
I **like seeing** you. (general)

4 Pronunciation: diphthongs

There are eight diphthongs in English (see page 160 for a list). Those practised in this unit are:

/aɪ/	/aʊ/	/eɪ/	/əʊ/
fly	sounds	way	go

Tales of the unexpected

READING

1 The title of the text you are going to read is *Uncle Arthur's Smoke Signals*. The pictures below are clues to what the story is about. Make guesses about the story.

2 Read the text to find out the connection between the pictures and the story. Then fill in the gaps with words from the box below.

however	but	because	until	after that	when	so	and

UNCLE ARTHUR'S SMOKE SIGNALS

We knew that my husband's uncle had left us some money in his will ___(a)___ he had told us about it before he died.

___(b)___ after he died, at the age of 92, we heard nothing, ___(c)___ we thought he had changed his mind and we forgot all about it. ___(d)___, a year after his death my husband noticed the smell of his uncle's pipe wafting through our house.

Over several years the strange, smoky smell returned – ___(e)___ one evening it was terribly strong ___(f)___ I saw Uncle Arthur standing there, quietly telling us that he *had* left us something in his will. ___(g)___ I got a copy of it I discovered that he had in fact left us £2,000. When asked, a relative made the excuse that the cheque had got lost in the post. A replacement cheque arrived and ___(h)___ we never smelt smoke or saw Uncle Arthur again.

(from *Chat*)

3 Answer these questions.

a) What were the couple expecting when Uncle Arthur died?
b) Why did they think this?
c) What did they think when they didn't get any money?
d) Why did Uncle Arthur return?
e) Why didn't they receive the money at first.

4 Discuss your answers with another student.

LANGUAGE POINT 1

Past Perfect

Read the example, and then decide which of the two statements below is correct.
*Uncle Arthur said he **had left** us something in his will.*

a) We only use the Past Perfect to talk about things which happened a long time ago.
b) We use the Past Perfect when we are already talking about a past event and we want to go back to an earlier time (before this past event).

PRACTICE

1   Put the following sentences into the correct order to make a paragraph.

A mystery reunion

a) When I arrived I realised the impossibility of finding them in such a big place.

b) It took me about thirty seconds.

c) However, I was feeling very cheerful because I had just given a good lecture, so instead of panicking I just relaxed and let my feet take me to them.

d) One day in Los Angeles I arrived at Disneyland to meet my wife and kids.

e) The problem was we hadn't decided on a specific place because we hadn't realised Disneyland was so huge!

(from *She*)

2   Complete the following sentences.

a) They didn't arrange a place to meet because . . .
b) He was feeling cheerful because . . .

> See **Use your grammar**, page 152, for further practice of the Past Perfect.

LANGUAGE POINT 2

Past Perfect or Past Simple?

1   Read the sentence below. Which of the two events happened first – *feeling cheerful* or *giving a good lecture*?
*I was **feeling cheerful** because I **had given** a good lecture.*

2   What is the difference in meaning between these sentences?
When he arrived I had already gone to bed.
When he arrived I went to bed.

Now look at the following sentences.
He saw the bull. He ran away.
As soon as he saw the bull he ran away.

We can say *As soon as he **had seen** . . .* , but in this particular case the Past Simple is preferred because:
a) one action (*ran*) happens as a result of the other (*saw*).
b) the time expression *as soon as* makes the sequence of actions clear.

PRACTICE

Connect the following sentences.

a) I saw him. I fell in love with him. (*As soon as I . . .*)
b) Judy didn't want to read his latest novel. She wanted to read his others first. (*Judy . . . until . . .*)
c) They opened the drawer. They found the money. (*When . . .*)
d) She told him the news. He left at once. (*After . . .*)

LANGUAGE POINT 3

Past Perfect Continuous

The Past Perfect Continuous is used when we want to focus on activities which were in progress up to or near the moment in the past we are already talking about. Example:
*When I met her she looked very tired. She'd **been travelling** all night.*

a) Was she still travelling when I met her?
b) Did the travelling happen over a period of time?

PRACTICE

1   Last year Kevin and Susan had a great time on holiday. This is an extract from a postcard they wrote towards the end of their holiday.
We'll be sorry to leave. We've been swimming every morning before breakfast.

Look at the pictures and say what they had been doing on their holiday. Example:
'Kevin and Susan didn't want to leave the holiday resort. They'd been swimming before breakfast every morning.'

1 before breakfast

2 every morning

3 at lunchtimes

4 in the afternoons   **5** nearly every evening

2   Choose the Past Simple, the Past Perfect or the Past Perfect Continuous for each of the base forms in brackets.

a) When I (*leave*) my house this morning I was amazed! It (*snow*) during the night and everything outside was white.
b) Kevin (*not begin*) cooking the meal until he (*see*) the end of the film.
c) I (*not go*) out before I (*feed*) the dog and (*water*) the plants.
d) When I (*leave*) Poland in 1984 I (*work*) there for over five years and (*make*) a lot of friends.
e) The taxi driver (*not know*) the way so when we (*arrive*) the play (*start*).
f) He (*be*) asleep for over two hours when Janet (*get*) home.

3   Continue these sentences using your own imagination. For each example, say what happened next. Example:

I hardly recognised my teacher when I saw him. (*Why? What had happened to him? What happened next?*)
   He had put on a lot of weight and lost most of his hair and he was also wearing spectacles, which he hadn't done before. When I recognised him I asked him lots of questions about what he had been doing, and introduced him to my husband.

a) She was pale and shaking as she left the churchyard. (*Why? What had she seen? What had happened?*)
b) Her house was in a complete mess. The burglars . . . (*What had the burglars done? What had they stolen?*)
c) I saw Joe and Sarah at the party last night. They looked tanned and well, because . . . (*Where had they been? What had they been doing?*)
d) I couldn't believe my eyes when I read the letter. (*What had happened?*)

VOCABULARY

Make or do?

1   Read the following sentences carefully.
Last night I tried to do my homework. However, I kept making mistakes because the man upstairs was doing his exercises and making a noise.

Make usually means to create, bring into existence, or produce a result.
Do usually means to perform an action. However, there are exceptions to this 'rule', as you will see in Exercise 3.

2   Complete the following dialogues, using *make* or *do*.

a) 'That looks nice! What are you _____?'
    'I'm _____ a cake.'
b) 'What are you _____?' 'I'm phoning home.'

3   Read the dialogue below and work in pairs to put the correct form of *make* or *do* in the gaps. Some of the uses do not follow the pattern above – they are idiomatic uses and exceptions to the rule.

TINA: I've had enough, Sue. You __(1)__ such a mess in the flat but you never __(2)__ any housework. I have to __(3)__ it all.

SUE: How can you say that! I __(4)__ the washing up last night and __(5)__ the beds this morning. And I usually __(6)__ the shopping, too.

TINA: Usually? Once, you mean! Well, anyway, I'm fed up with you. You __(7)__ long-distance phone calls all the time and I'm sure you never pay for them.

SUE: Are you going to __(8)__ a fuss about that, too? You __(9)__ much more money than I do. I can't help it if I'm poor.

TINA: And while we're on the subject, is it really necessary to spend an hour in the bathroom every morning __(10)__ your hair? You needn't think I'm __(11)__ the cooking tonight, either. From now on, you can look after yourself.

SUE: You're very upset, Tina. Sit down and I'll get you a drink. It'll __(12)__ you good.

TINA: No, no. I've __(13)__ a decision. I want you to move out.

SUE: Oh, Tina, no! I promise I'll try to __(14)__ better.

4   What is the relationship between Tina and Sue?

5   In your vocabulary books write down in two separate columns the words or phrases that go with *make* and the words or phrases that go with *do*.

LISTENING

1   You are going to listen to a 'tale of the unexpected'. The items in the box are some of the words and expressions that come up in the story. Look up in the dictionary any new words you do not know, and predict:
– what the story is about.
– where the story takes place.

> come round   ward   beat   monitor
> operation   donor   surgeon   patient
> pass out

2 [18.1]   Listen to the first part of the story.

a) What are the noises you hear at the beginning of the recording?
b) Where is the narrator?
c) What has happened to him?
d) Who else is in the room apart from the hospital staff?
e) Why is this other person there?
f) What kind of person is Jim (the narrator), according to Mr Walton?

3 [18.2]   Listen to the second part of the story.

a) What does Jim want to know?
b) Why do you think Jim is becoming 'het up'?
c) What does he want to do?
d) Why do you think he is a VIP?

4 [18.3]   Listen to the last part of the story.

a) What is the problem with Jim at the moment?
b) What did Mr Walton want him to read in the newspaper?
c) What has upset Jim?
d) Why do you think the young man is smiling?
e) What do you think is going to happen?

SPEAKING

1   Read the first and last part of this horror story.

Rob wasn't sure what had woken him up. The first noise that he was fully aware of was a distant cry – a bit like a fox calling its mate. However, something about it made him think it wasn't a fox. He sat up in bed and then he heard something bang. It seemed to come from a room downstairs. He thought it must be the wind and went downstairs to close the window. Just as he realised that it was a perfectly still night with no sign of wind he heard a creak very near him and he turned round.

When he was found the next morning Rob was still alive, but he never spoke another coherent word as long as he lived.

2   In groups, decide on the following.

a) Who was Rob? (Describe his physical appearance and personality. What was his job? Give details about his family.)
b) Describe where he lived (the house and the town or village).
c) What did he see when he turned round?
d) What happened next?

3   Work out the story line. You may make notes but do not write out the story.

4   Rehearse your story. Try to use:
– a range of tenses (including Past Simple, Past Continuous, Past Perfect Simple and Continuous).
– a range of time conjunctions (*as soon as, when, after, before, until, by the time*).
– a wide variety of vocabulary, including the vocabulary of 'fear' from Unit 17.

5   Tell your story to the other groups. Which is the most original?

READING AND WRITING

Narrative

1 Read the story outline *A Ghost Waiter* and find information about:
– the characters.
– when and where the story takes place.

2 How is *Spooky Visitor at Pizza Parlour* different? What is the effect?

3 Find examples of the following features in the *Spooky Visitor . . .* story.

a) some introductory background information to the story
b) adjectives to describe feelings
c) adverbs to describe actions
d) a description of the place
e) idiomatic expressions
f) a wide range of vocabulary
g) a variety of verb forms
h) linking expressions
i) quotations from the characters
j) punctuation used for dramatic effect

4 Look back at the *Speaking* section and write up your story about Rob. Try to include some of the features listed in Exercise 3.

A Ghost Waiter

Barbara Posner and her husband didn't believe in ghosts at first. Last year there was a ghost waiter, number 25, in their restaurant in London. They knew he was a ghost because there was no waiter 25 and because lots of strange things started happening. Fridges stopped working and the electricity kept cutting out. In the end they asked a medium to find out what was happening. She said they were being haunted by a boy, Billy. He had been killed in a fight outside the restaurant and wanted to find his attacker. The medium told him to go away and things returned (more or less) to normal, except the Posners now believe in the paranormal.

SPOOKY VISITOR AT PIZZA PARLOUR

For more than six months waiter number 25 caused nothing but problems at a restaurant in London's West End, but the despairing owners couldn't sack him – because he didn't exist!

The strange employee had first made his presence felt at Pappagalli's Pizza House just before seven one morning when he carefully tapped his code number out on the electronic register and was given a card. The owners, Barbara and Mike Posner, couldn't understand how anyone had got in without a key and without setting off the alarms. And in any case, there WAS no waiter number 25!

Previously sceptical of the para-normal, Barbara readily admits she found the whole thing extremely spooky and scary.

For the following six months strange things started to happen – fridges were turned off without warning, the stereo system kept breaking down, the burglar alarm suddenly stopped working. Even light plugs and electrical things could not be relied on to work.

Eventually the Posners decided to ask a famous medium for help. As soon as she arrived she sensed the presence of a young man called Billy. Apparently he had been brutally killed in a fight outside the restaurant ten years earlier, and was looking for his attacker. However, the medium gently persuaded him to go away and she told the Posners that he had agreed.

> . . . she sensed the presence of a young man called Billy . . .

"After this, things calmed down, although occasionally something odd still happens," said Barbara. "We do wonder if Billy is still around, but hope that he's resting in peace."

The couple no longer take the paranormal with a pinch of salt and are considering re-naming their restaurant 'The Spooky Pizza Parlour'.

(from *Woman*)

Language reference

1 Past Perfect Simple

The Past Perfect Simple is used to talk about something in the past which happened before another action in the past. It shows which of the two past actions happened first and emphasises that the first action was finished before the other began.

*The burglars **had left** when the police **arrived**.*

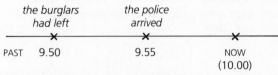

Two Past Simple tenses can be used when the sequence of actions is clear and when the second action follows as a result of the first.

*The burglars **left** when the police **arrived**.*

Sentences containing *until*, *as soon as*, *before*, and *after* can often have two Past Simple tenses because the time conjunctions make the sequence of actions clear without the use of the Past Perfect.

*As soon as I **heard** the news I **left** the house.*

However, the Past Perfect can still be used to emphasise the completion of one action before the other.

*As soon as they **had saved up** enough money they **got married**.*

FORM

Had + past participle.

AFFIRMATIVE
*I / She / You / We / They**'d** (**had**) **eaten** all the sandwiches.*

NEGATIVE
*He **hadn't drunk** anything.*

QUESTION
*What **had** they **left**?*

2 Past Perfect Continuous

The Past Perfect Continuous is like the Past Perfect Simple, except that it focuses on activities in progress (and therefore longer activities) up to or near the moment in the past we are talking about. See Review Unit 2 for verbs which do not normally have a continuous form.

*When she arrived I **had been waiting** for two hours.*

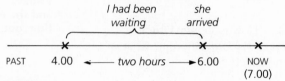

FORM

Had been + *-ing* form of the verb.

AFFIRMATIVE
*I / You / She / We / They**'d** (**had**) **been waiting** for two hours.*

NEGATIVE
*You **hadn't been waiting** for very long.*

QUESTION
*How long **had** he **been waiting**?*

So strong

SPEAKING 1

1   Work in pairs and discuss what you think is happening in this photograph.

2   The photograph is actually part of an advertisement and this is the caption which goes with it.

'ANOTHER EXAMPLE OF POLICE PREJUDICE? OR ANOTHER EXAMPLE OF YOURS?'

a) Does this give you any more idea of what the photograph is trying to say?

b) Look at page 160 and see if you were right.

3   The groups of people below are sometimes discriminated against. Think of examples of how they are discriminated against and, if possible, give reasons why they suffer in this way.
Example:
In Britain, old people are often discriminated against. They find it difficult to get jobs and some have to live in special homes. One reason for this is that their children don't have time to look after them.

a) old people
b) people of a different religion
c) women
d) the disabled
e) the poor
f) people with different political beliefs

Is the situation the same in other countries? Discuss.

LANGUAGE POINT

The passive

1   Underline all the verbs in this article.

2   Which of the verbs are active (e.g. *walked*) and which are passive (e.g. *was set upon*)?

3   Which of these are true of passive sentences?

a) We are more interested in the action than in who is responsible for the action.
b) The subject of the verb is the person doing the action.

A kicking . . . then one of the gang drew a knife

THE MAN in the grey overcoat walked quietly by himself. He threatened nobody, he spoke to nobody, he was abusive to nobody. But he was black.

And so he was set upon by a gang of hooligans, taunted, knocked to the ground, kicked as he lay there and menaced with a long-bladed knife. Now he is frightened it will happen again – so frightened that he will not allow his name to be published.

(from the *Evening Standard*)

PRACTICE

1   Match each of the sentences in group A with the contexts in group B.

A	B
a) Passengers are requested not to smoke.	1 a sign in a shop
b) Man killed in racist attack.	2 describing a process
c) English spoken here.	3 a mother telling off a child
d) You've been told a hundred times not to do that.	4 a newspaper headline
e) The biscuits are put into tins.	5 a shop assistant giving information
f) It's made of pure wool.	6 a sign on a train

Check with the *Language reference* for information on the use of the the passive. Choose at least three of the examples above and say why you think the passive is used in each case.

2   Match the words and expressions in column A with those in column B and then make sentences, using the verbs in the box in the correct form. Example:
*The ballpoint pen **was invented by** Mr Biro.*

A	B
a) ballpoint pen	Captain Cook
b) *White Christmas*	Mr Biro
c) *Mona Lisa*	Leonardo da Vinci
d) Australia	Brazil
e) *Sherlock Holmes*	Bing Crosby
f) World Cup (1994)	Arthur Conan Doyle

win	discover
invent	sing
write	paint

3   Complete these sentences using a passive construction. Only use *by* if it's natural to do so.

a) A bus nearly hit Keith while he was trying to cross the road. (*Keith . . .*)
b) Luckily, lightning doesn't strike many people. (*Luckily, . . . by lightning.*)
c) The incident shouldn't harm relations between the police and the community. (*Relations . . .*)
d) The snow is very heavy. British Rail has cancelled all trains to Scotland. (*All trains . . .*)
e) A police officer is interviewing her about the crime. (*She . . .*)
f) The burglars have stolen my stereo and television. (*My stereo . . .*)

See **Use your grammar,** page 152, for further practice of the passive.

VOCABULARY

Collocation

A collocation is a grouping of words which go together in a way that sounds natural to a native speaker.
The hooligans drew a knife. (We often say *draw a knife* to mean *pull out a knife*.)

Which of the words or phrases in the box go with the verbs *draw*, *have* and *get*? Some of the words or phrases might go with more than one of the verbs.

a bath	ready	a look
a baby	to a halt	lost
the curtains	a cold	
blood	angry	a party
a rest	a holiday	a cheque

PRONUNCIATION

Contrastive stress

1 [19.1]   Stressing individual words helps to convey the meaning of what we want to say (see Unit 13). Listen to this dialogue and underline the words that are stressed in each sentence.

PAT: Where do you live?
JULIE: On the second floor.
PAT: I thought you lived on the fifth floor.
JULIE: No, Colin lives on the fifth floor.
PAT: Surely Colin has an office on the fifth floor but he actually lives on the second floor?
JULIE: No, Colin has never lived on the second floor. He lives on the fifth floor and has an office on the ground floor. I live on the second floor.

2   In pairs, look at the words you have underlined for Julie and discuss why she stresses the words she does.

3   Circle the word you think carries most stress in each sentence in these dialogues. The first one has been done for you.

a) A: I like the (dog.)
  B: That dog?
  A: Yes, it seems a very friendly dog.
  B: You're kidding. It's the most vicious dog I've ever seen.
  A: Well, I like it.

b) A: Why are you running so fast?
  B: I'm not running. I'm jogging.
  A: Jogging? You're not!
  B: I am. I used to run twice as fast as this.

c) A: They serve wonderful fish there.
  B: Yes, but the meat's disgusting.
  A: Yes, you're right. And the wine's awful.

d) A: English is a really difficult language.
  B: Not as difficult as French.
  A: Well, the vocabulary's more difficult.
  B: Yes, but the grammar's hard in French.
  A: And the pronunciation is awful in both.

4 [19.2]   The first three dialogues in Exercise 3 have been recorded. Listen to the recording for one possible version of how words in the dialogues might be stressed.

5   Practise the dialogues in pairs. Decide for yourselves where the stresses come in the final dialogue.

LISTENING

1 [🔲 19.3] Listen to the first verse of a song about racial prejudice, and then discuss the images that came into your mind as you were listening.

2 [🔲 19.4] This time listen to the whole song and answer the following questions. You can read the words at the same time if you like.

a) What are the *barriers* that are being built? (line 1)
b) Who is the *you* in the song?
c) What are the *rights* that they are taking away, do you think? (line 3)
d) What is the *Something Inside So Strong*?
e) According to the Bible the walls of Jericho (line 16) were destroyed when the children of Israel shouted loudly. What is going to happen when the singer of this song sings loudly?
f) *When they insist we're just not good enough* (line 25) Who are 'they'? Who are 'we'? 'Good enough' for what?
g) *We're gonna do it anyway* (line 28) What are they going to do, do you think?

3 Do you think this is an optimistic or a pessimistic song? Give your reasons.

(Something Inside) So Strong

The higher you build your barriers
The taller I become
The farther you take my rights away
The faster I will run
5 *You can deny me*
You can decide to turn your face away
No matter 'cause there's . . .
Something Inside So Strong
I know that I can make it
10 *Though you're doin' me wrong, so wrong*
You thought that my pride was gone, oh no,
There's Something Inside So Strong
Something Inside So Strong

The more you refuse to hear my voice
15 *The louder I will sing*
You hide behind walls of Jericho
Your lies will come tumbling
Deny my place in time
You squander wealth that's mine
20 *My light will shine so brightly*
It will blind you
Because there's . . .
Something Inside So Strong . . .

Brothers and Sisters
25 *When they insist we're just not good enough*
Well we know better
Just look 'em in the eye and say
'We're gonna do it anyway'
'We're gonna do it anyway'
30 *There's Something Inside So Strong . . .*

(by Labi Siffre)

SPEAKING 2

1 Work in groups. Imagine you are going to produce a video for a song – either *(Something Inside) So Strong* or another song that you know. Start by taking a piece of paper and drawing an outline for a 'storyboard' like the example below.

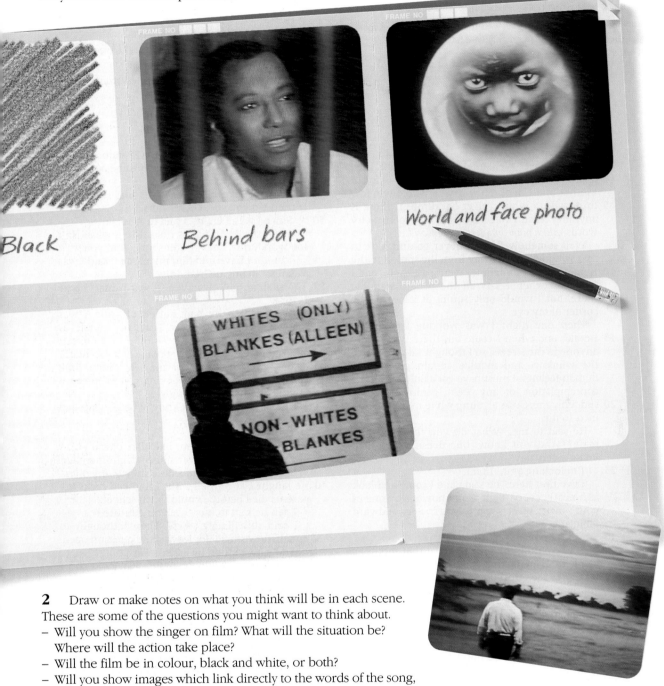

Black

Behind bars

World and face photo

WHITES (ONLY)
BLANKES (ALLEEN)

NON-WHITES
BLANKES

2 Draw or make notes on what you think will be in each scene. These are some of the questions you might want to think about.
– Will you show the singer on film? What will the situation be? Where will the action take place?
– Will the film be in colour, black and white, or both?
– Will you show images which link directly to the words of the song, such as the *barriers* (line 1) or someone growing taller (line 2) or something completely different?

3 Put your 'storyboard' on the wall and go round and look at those from the other groups.

READING

1 You are going to read an extract from a short story which takes place in Johannesburg in South Africa in 1960. Edward Simelane is a black South African who lives in Orlando, a part of Soweto, a black township outside Johannesburg. He has won a prize in the sculpture competition held to celebrate the Union of South Africa.

a) How do you think he felt when he won the prize?

b) Can you imagine the different reactions of whites and blacks?

2 These sentences describe what happens in the story. Can you guess the correct order?

a) He is offered a drink.

b) He is addressed by a white man he doesn't know.

c) He goes to look at his sculpture.

d) They go to where the white man lives.

3 Read the passage and check your answers.

You know the Alabaster Bookshop in von Brandis Street? Well, after the competition they asked me if they could exhibit my 'African Mother and Child'. They gave a whole window
5 to it, with a white velvet backdrop, if there is anything called white velvet, and complimentary words, *Black man conquers white world*.

Well somehow I could never go and look in that window. On my way from the station to the
10 Herald office, I sometimes went past there, and I felt good when I saw all the people standing there, but I would only squint at it out of the corner of my eye.

Then one night I was working late at the
15 Herald, and when I came out there was hardly anyone in the streets, so I thought I'd go and see the window, and indulge certain pleasurable human feelings. I must have got a little lost in the contemplation of my own genius, because
20 suddenly there was a young white man standing next to me.

He said to me, 'What do you think of that, mate?' And you know, one doesn't get called 'mate' every day.
25 'I'm looking at it,' I said.

'I live near here,' he said, 'and I come and look at it nearly every night. You know it's by one of your own boys, don't you? See, Edward Simelane.'
30 'Yes, I know.'

'It's beautiful,' he said. 'Look at that mother's head. She's loving that child, but she's somehow watching too. Do you see that? Like someone guarding. She knows it won't be an easy life.'
35 He cocked his head on one side, to see the thing better.

'He got a thousand pounds for it,' he said. 'That's a lot of money for one of your boys. But good luck to him. You don't get much luck, do
40 you?'

Then he said confidentially, 'Mate, would you like a drink?'

Well honestly I didn't feel like a drink at that time of night, with a white stranger and all, and
45 me still with a train to catch to Orlando.

'You know we black people must be out of the city by eleven,' I said.

'It won't take long. My flat's just round the corner. Do you speak Afrikaans?'
50 'Since I was a child,' I said in Afrikaans.

'We'll speak Afrikaans then. My English isn't too wonderful. I'm van Rensburg. And you?'

I couldn't have told him my name. I said I was Vakalisa, living in Orlando.
55 'Vakalisa, eh? I haven't heard that name before.'

By this time he had started off, and I was following, but not willingly. That's my trouble, as you'll soon see. I can't break off an encounter.
60 We didn't exactly walk abreast, but he didn't exactly walk in front of me. He didn't look constrained. He wasn't looking round to see if anyone might be watching.

He said to me, 'Do you know what I wanted to
65 do?'

'No,' I said.

'I wanted a bookshop, like that one there. I always wanted that, ever since I can remember. When I was small, I had a little shop of my own.'
70 He laughed at himself. 'But I had bad luck. My parents died before I could finish school.'

Then he said to me, 'Are you educated?'

I said unwillingly, 'Yes.' Then I thought to myself, how stupid, for leaving the question open.
75 And sure enough he asked, 'Far?'

And again unwillingly, I said, 'Far.'

He took a big leap and said, 'Degree?'

'Yes.'

'Literature?'
80 'Yes.'

He expelled his breath, and gave a long 'ah'. We had reached his building, Majorca Mansions, not one of those luxurious places. I was glad to see the entrance lobby was deserted. I wasn't at
85 my ease. I don't feel at my ease in such places, not unless I am protected by friends, and this man was a stranger. The lift was at ground level, marked 'Whites only. Slegs vir Blankes'.

(from *A Drink in the Passage* by Alan Paton)

4   Find the following words and phrases in the text. If you don't
know their meaning, try to work them out from the context without
looking at a dictionary. Tick the correct alternative.

a) *squint* (line 12)
   – look sideways with the eye half-shut
   – look steadily with the eye open
b) *the contemplation of* (line 19)
   – looking to see what I can do about
   – quiet thoughts about
c) *started off* (line 57)
   – started talking
   – began to move
d) *constrained* (line 62)
   – as though he were forced to move
   – unnaturally limited and uneasy in his action

e) *took a big leap* (line 77)
   – jumped across the street
   – took the conversation forward with another
     big guess
f) *expelled* (line 81)
   – forced out
   – held
g) *not unless I am* (line 86)
   – if I am not
   – if I am

5   Find an equivalent word or phrase in the text for each of the
following:

a) almost no one (lines 15, 16)
b) as though they were sharing a secret (line 41)
c) accidental meeting (line 59)
d) side by side (line 60)
e) not really pleased to do it (line 62)

6   Circle A, B or C for each phrase according to whether you think
it tells us more about Edward Simelane (A), van Rensberg (B) or
blacks in South Africa (C). You may circle more than one letter in
each case.

a) *I would only squint at it out of the corner of my eye.* (line 12)	A B C
b) *I must have got a little lost in the contemplation of my own genius* . . . (line 18)	A B C
c) . . . *one doesn't get called 'mate' every day.* (line 23)	A B C
d) *She knows it won't be an easy life.* (line 34)	A B C
e) *That's a lot of money for one of your boys. But good luck to him.* (line 38)	A B C
f) *You know we black people must be out of the city by eleven.* (line 46)	A B C
g) *I can't break off an encounter.* (line 59)	A B C
h) *He wasn't looking around to see if anyone might be watching.* (line 62)	A B C
i) *I said unwillingly, 'Yes'.* (line 73)	A B C
j) *I don't feel at my ease in such places, not unless I am protected by friends.* (line 85)	A B C

CREATIVE WRITING

1   What do you think happens to Simelane and van Rensburg?
Discuss how you think the story continues.

2   Write the next paragraph.

3   Show each other your paragraphs and decide on the best
continuation of the story.

Language reference

1 The passive

USE

The *passive* (see also Unit 10) is often used to focus on *what is done* rather than *who does it*. The passive can be used for the following reasons:

a) Because, at the time of speaking, the doer is not important or not known.
*The poor man **was killed** in a racist attack.*
(The fact that he was killed is more important than the identity of the killer. In fact, the killer's identity might not be known.)

b) To take personal responsibility away from the speaker.
*Your problem **will be looked into**.*
(The speaker is not saying 'I will look into it'. Politicians are very fond of using the passive for this reason!)
*Passengers **are requested** not to lean out of the window.*
(The railway company, for example, rather than a particular person, is addressing us. The notice sounds formal and impersonal.)

The passive can also be used to continue the theme of what is currently being talked about (new information is normally put at the end of the utterance).
*'Hamlet' is a marvellous play. It **was written** by Shakespeare.*
(The topic is 'Hamlet' – the new information is the author's name. In *Shakespeare wrote 'Hamlet'* the topic is *Shakespeare*.)

The passive is more often used in written language (particularly newspapers, reports, scientific writing, notices and announcements).
*Two Astronauts **Stranded** In Space.* (short for *have been stranded*)
*Nelson Mandela **was released** in 1990.*
*The experiment **was** first **conducted** by the Russians.*
*Martin Luther King **is gunned down** in Memphis.*
*The 14.00 flight to Paris **will** unfortunately **be delayed** by two hours.*
*The song **was sung** by Labi Siffre.*

FORM

Various tenses of *be* + past participle.

It	**is** **was** **has been** **had been** **may be** **is going to be** **will be**	**made** in Japan.
*They **are** / **were** / **will be** (etc.) made in Japan.*		
*The doors **haven't been painted**.* *When **will** the job **be completed**?*		

2 Comparing active and passive

The normal basic construction of an active English sentence is:

SUBJECT	VERB	OBJECT
The young woman	*wrote*	*the letter*

The subject of the verb (*The young woman*) is the person or thing doing the action (*wrote the letter*).

In passive sentences the action is done *to* the subject. So the person or thing who is not the doer can come first, in the position of the subject.

SUBJECT	VERB		AGENT
The letter	*was written*	*by*	*the young woman.*

If you want to say who the doer is, you add *by* followed by the agent.

Revision

LISTENING

1 [🔲 20.1]   You are going to listen to a traditional Australian story called *Wilar the Crocodile*. As you listen to the story, put the pictures in the correct order by numbering them 1 to 5. The first one has been done for you.

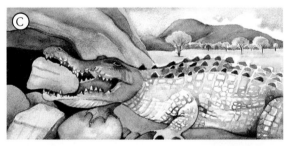

2   Discuss whether the following statements about the story are correct. Then listen again and correct them if necessary.

a) When Wilar saw the girls he decided he was going to capture Indra.
b) Jippi tried to save her sister.
c) Wilar took Indra to a cave.
d) He decided not to eat her because he wanted her to be his wife.
e) He blocked up the cave to stop Indra from running away.
f) He left her when he got bored with her.
g) Indra escaped by using her hair.
h) Her stomach was big because she had eaten too much fish.

3   Write a summary of the story using the notes below. Change the verbs into the appropriate tense, add any other words necessary and use the words in brackets to connect your sentences. If you want to, add any extra details you can remember.

a) Indra have rest near river / Wilar grab her (*while*)
b) He / take Indra to cave / not want to eat her yet / go to catch fish (*however, so*)
c) Indra frightened / very tired / fall asleep (*although, also, and*)
d) Wilar put mud and stones / entrance of cave / other crocodiles not come in (*so that*)
e) Tell Indra / she is his wife / stay with her (*and*)
f) Indra alone / try to escape (*as soon as*)
g) Stones heavy / use hair / move them (*so, to*)
h) Make hole big enough / escape / run away (*after, and*)
i) Jippi notice sister's big belly / think eat a lot of fish (*when*)
j) Men hit crocodile eggs / Indra produce (*that*)
k) Some of frogs / jump out of eggs / go to water / some to country / parents come from both places (*which, and, because*)

READING

1 The story you are going to read is about whales. Look at this dictionary extract and find out what a whale is. How do you pronounce *whale*?

> **whacking²** *n infml, esp. BrE* a beating
> **whale** /weɪl/ *n* **1** any of several types of very large animals which live in the sea, with a body like a fish's body but blood which does not change its temperature because they are MAMMALS. **2** a 'whale of a time *infml* a very enjoyable time: *We had a whale of a time at the party*.

2 Look at more vocabulary from the text in the box below. Ask other people in your class for the meanings of the words you don't know. Then look up the words in a dictionary. How do you pronounce the words? Which words have more than one meaning?

adolescent	a school (of whales)		the coast
to sizzle	to swallow	hot dogs	to splash
clumsy	rubbish		

3 Read the beginning and end of a story entitled *The Great Whale's Mistake*. In groups, invent a possible storyline.

> A mother whale and a father whale were swimming along the coast with their adolescent son whale when the mother saw a school of people on the beach.

> The young whale was so excited by this news that he spouted, and the people on the shore saw it and cried, 'Whales!' and somebody threw a beer bottle at them. The whales made for the deep distant water and later that night as they drifted off the Gulf Stream admiring the stars a large ship passed by and spilled oil over them, but they remained at peace with the world as it was, and afterwards dreamed of the unfortunate people far behind them making rubbish through the sweet summer night.

4 Read the whole story once quickly and try to summarise it in one sentence.

5 Look at the definitions below and match them to words from the last two paragraphs of the story.

a) *n* a measurement of weight equal in Britain to 2,240 pounds.

b) *n* **1** thick mud. **2** the product of waste (SEWAGE) treatment.

c) *v* to drop or unload (something) in a heap or carelessly.

d) *v* to throw or come out in a forceful stream.

6 Read the story more carefully and answer the following questions.

a) Why do you think the whales refer to a 'school' of people?
b) Why are people useless, according to the young whale?
c) Why do people exist, according to the young whale?
d) What do you think the 'Great Whale' is?
e) What is the mother's view of the world?
f) What do you think the 'metal box on wheels' is?

7 Discuss the following.

a) What is the 'Great Whale's Mistake'?
b) How does the writer make us feel sympathetic to the whales?
c) How would you respond to the whales' criticisms of the people?
d) Find any examples of humour in the text.

The Great Whale's Mistake

A mother whale and a father whale were swimming along the coast with their adolescent son whale when the mother saw a school of people on the beach.

'What's that?' asked the son whale, who had never seen a school of people before, or even a person on his own.

5 'People, son,' said the father whale. 'You see them all up and down this coast at this time of year. They cover themselves with oil and lie up there on the sand and boil themselves until they sizzle.'

'But they're such little things,' said the son whale. 'I'll bet I could swallow one whole and have him live in my stomach.'

10 His mother said she would not want her stomach filled with anything that had been boiled in oil and had sand all over it. As well as that, she said, it would be very unhealthy because they were filled with smoke and hot dogs.

'What do people do?' asked the young whale.

'They sit on the beach and stare at the ocean,' the father whale said. 'And they 15 eat hot dogs.'

The mother whale said that they also walked in the ocean now and again for a short time and splashed around in such a clumsy manner that the fish had to get out of their way.

'They seem to be useless,' said the son whale. 'Why did the Great Whale make 20 people anyway?'

'Son,' said the father whale, 'no creature in the Great Whale's universe exists without a purpose. If the Great Whale made people it was for a good reason.'

'Maybe people are the Great Whale's way of keeping down the hot dog population,' the young whale suggested.

25 'There are some things,' said the mother whale, 'that even whales can't understand. We must accept the world as it is and live at peace with it.'

The father whale drew their attention to a small group of people who had moved away from the school and were getting into a metal box on wheels. When they were all inside the metal box moved along the beach, throwing up a great 30 cloud of sand and destroying vegetation and birds' nests.

'What are they doing now?' asked the son whale.

'Making rubbish,' said the father whale. 'People make almost all the rubbish in the world and they use those little moving boxes to do it.'

He showed his son the dark gases which came out of the box.

35 'And inside the box,' he said, 'they are also preparing more rubbish.'

At that moment six beer cans came flying out of the box, followed by a bag containing a half-eaten hot dog, a mustard jar, some banana peel and an empty plastic body-oil container.

'Maybe that's the reason the Great Whale made people,' said the young whale. 40 'To make rubbish.'

'The world doesn't need rubbish,' growled the father whale.

'Now, now,' said the mother whale, who was always uneasy when religion was mentioned, 'we must accept the world as it is and learn to live at peace with it.'

'Sometimes,' said the father whale, 'I think the Great Whale doesn't know what 45 he's doing.'

'Your father has been very sensitive about rubbish,' the mother whale explained, 'ever since he dived into 800 tons of fresh sludge which had been dumped off the coast. He smelled disgusting for weeks.'

The young whale was so excited by this news that he spouted, and the people 50 on the shore saw it and cried, 'Whales!' and somebody threw a beer bottle at them. The whales made for the deep distant water and later that night as they drifted off the Gulf Stream admiring the stars a large ship passed by and spilled oil over them, but they remained at peace with the world as it was, and afterwards dreamed of the unfortunate people far behind them making rubbish through 55 the sweet summer night.

(*The Great Whale's Mistake* by Russell Baker)

GRAMMAR AND FUNCTIONS

Present and past

Put the verbs in the following text into the correct form. There
may be more than one possible answer. Some forms are in the
passive. You may also use the structure *used to* if appropriate.

The *thief* who comes to dinner

The first time Michael Dalton (1 *pay*) a visit to the Howell's family home, he (2 *not invite*). 'We (3 *sleep*) soundly upstairs when Michael (4 *break*) in,' Jean says. 'It was about six in the morning when my husband discovered we (5 *burgle*).'

It was fifteen months later that the Howells (6 *receive*) a letter saying the thief (7 *catch*). 'I immediately wanted to know what (8 *be*, his prison address). I (9 *feel*)

it was partly my responsibility to put his life back on the right tracks.' Not long afterwards, Jean and Michael started to write to each other and they (10 *be*) friends ever since. When his case came up in court Michael (11 *allow*) by the judge to go on an experimental probation scheme rather than go back to the kind of prison he (12 *send*) to many times before.

Now Michael (13 *try*) to go

straight and (14 *become*) a friend of the family. He (15 *call*) round nearly every day and (16 *play*) with the children. Recently, he (17 *even, go*) to church with them on Sundays. 'In the old days,' he says, 'I (18 *spend*) £200 a night going to clubs but the money (19 *all, steal*). In the last few years I (20 *make*) many new friends who care about me. I know I couldn't let Jean and her family down.'

(based on an article in *Bella*)

Future

Underline the correct form of the future in each of the dialogues
below.

a) 'Someone told me you *'ll leave / 're leaving* next Tuesday.'
   'Yes, I *'ll live / 'm going to live* abroad.'
b) 'I'm sorry my house is so cold.' 'Yes. When's the central heating *going to be mended / going to mend*?'
c) 'What colour shirt *will you buy / are you going to buy*?'
   'Light brown, I think. Do you think it *'ll look / 's going to look* OK?'
d) 'What can I get you to drink?' 'I'm *having / 'll have* an orange juice, please.'
e) 'Can you come for lunch on Tuesday?' 'Sorry. According to my diary I *'m meeting / 'll meet* Wendy at one o'clock.'

Making dialogues

Make dialogues using the cues in brackets. Do *not* use the words in *italics* in your dialogues. When asking questions, use either direct or less direct questions.

a) A is a shop assistant. B is a customer.
   A: (Greet. Offer to help.)
   B: (Politely ask for your money back for a necklace you bought. Give a reason.)
   A: (Refuse. Explain why not.)
   B: (Respond in any way you like.)

b) A and C are taking an English examination. B is a teacher.
   A: (Ask *permission* to use a dictionary. Give a reason.)
   B: (Say that using books is *prohibited* in this exam.)
   A: (Ask if it is *permitted* to go to the toilet.)
   B: (Give *permission*. Say that it is not *necessary* to ask.)

c) A is a customer in a restaurant. B is the waiter.
   A: (Attract the waiter's attention. Ask to see the manager.)
   B: (Agree. Ask politely what it's about.)
   A: (Say your fish isn't fresh.)
   B: (Make a polite excuse. Offer something else.)

d) A is renting a flat. B is the landlord.
   A: (Ask when it's *necessary* to pay the rent.)
   B: (Say strongly it's very *important* to pay weekly and in cash.)
   A: (Ask *permission* to keep a dog.)
   B: (Apologise, but say pets are *prohibited*.)

Conditionals; *wish*

Complete the sentences below. Example:
'You know it's really terrible. We never see each other much these days.'
'Yes, you're right. I wish *we saw (could see) each other* more often.'

a) 'My boss thinks I'm lazy.'
   'If I _____ you, I _____ another job.'
b) 'We can't go camping. It's too cold.'
   'I know. I wish we _____ enough money to stay in a hotel.'
c) 'I hate being alone.'
   'What _____ do, if you _____ on a desert island?'
d) 'Your handwriting is very bad.'
   'I know. I _____ type all my letters if I _____ a word processor.'

e) 'I'm going to Liverpool by car.'
   'If you _____ by train, you _____ in half the time.'
f) 'This country spends too much money on defence.'
   'You're right. I wish I _____ Prime Minister. I _____ more on education.'
g) 'Your feet are enormous!'
   'Yes, I wish they _____ a bit smaller.'

Spot the errors

Read and correct the following sentences.

a) 'How much cost the computer?' 'I'm sorry, I don't know how much did it cost.'
b) In 1907 the Norway became first country to give vote to the women.
c) I enjoyed the cake who we've just eaten.
d) The shops close early today, isn't it?
e) I must to hurry! I want getting there on time.
f) Unfortunately, the company now has a few clients.
g) Beverly said me she was very unhappy.
h) Jamie doesn't go to work since two days now.
i) This week's much colder as last week.
j) There's not many rice left. Go and get me any, please.
k) 'I can't remember the address.' 'No, so do I.'
l) Julia suggested to leave before it got dark.
m) I told her I wasn't hungry as I already ate lunch.
n) We were inviting to the party by the Managing Director.
o) Has Patricia told that her sister is ill? If not, please tell her as soon as possible.

VOCABULARY

Guessing vocabulary in context

Part A

Look at the sentences below. All the words in *italics* are nonsense words. Work out what those words mean from the context of the sentence. Example:

Tribbet must mean scarf, because it is something you put round your neck when it's cold.

a) It was a very cold day so I put a *tribbet* round my neck.
b) I was so *fliglive* that I drank a whole bottle of Coke.
c) I did three *tralets* yesterday but I failed them all because I hadn't studied enough.
d) I did the exam very *trodly* because I had a headache.
e) I *sarked* very late at work because I overslept.

Part B

In the sentences above decide whether the nonsense words are: adverbs; verbs (past tense); nouns; adjectives.
Example: *Tribbet must be a noun, because a comes before it.*

PRONUNCIATION

Sentence stress

[🔊 20.2]   Listen to the dialogue and mark the words which carry the most stress.

A: I don't really like the smell.
B: Well, I don't really like the taste.
A: Don't you? Why not?
B: I think it's awful.
A: It cost a fortune. We ought to eat it.

WRITING

Description

This is Aisha with her family outside her house. You have just met her for the first time. Write a letter to a friend about Aisha describing, for example, her appearance and personality, where she lives and what she does, her past life and her plans for the future.

Aisha and her family

Use your grammar

UNIT 16

Reported speech

a) Work with a partner. Look at the pictures and act out situations 1 and 2 below.

1

? HOSPITAL ← 600 YDS

friend / hospital

? on the phone

STUDENT A: You have just driven through a red traffic light. A police officer (Student B) has stopped you. What reason or excuse can you give?	STUDENT B: You are a police officer. You have just seen Student A drive through a red traffic light. Interview him / her. Take notes.

2

? see / burglar

? drop / key / drain

STUDENT B: Someone saw you climbing in through the window of a house which is not your home. A police officer (Student A) is interviewing you. What reason or excuse can you give?	STUDENT A: You are a police officer. Someone saw Student B climbing in through the window of a house which is not his / her home. Interview him / her. Take notes.

b) Work in groups.

1 STUDENTS A: You are now journalists. Interview each police officer about what his / her driver said.

2 STUDENTS B: You are now journalists. Interview each police officer about what his / her person said.

c) Write a group summary of what the people said. Example: *Juan told the police he had...*

UNIT 17

-ing or *to?*

Work in groups. You are friends at a dinner party. It is nearly the end of the year. Each person in the group should add a line to the conversation, using one of the verbs in the box below. Before you start, choose a secretary. He / She should listen for mistakes with the verb forms. If someone makes a mistake with the verb forms, he / she is out of the game. Use each verb only once. Example:

A: *I gave up smoking in November. It was very difficult.*
B: *Really! Well, next year I...*

give up	decide	feel like
try	learn	enjoy avoid
agree	promise	fancy
finish	want	hope arrange
begin	expect	plan
remember	can't afford	

UNIT 18

Past Perfect

Work in pairs.

STUDENT A
Look at page 156.

STUDENT B

a) You are a journalist. Student A is a film director. You saw this clip of his / her new film on television yesterday. Ask questions to find out what had happened and why. Then the film director will tell you the story.
Example:
Why were the family angry?

b) You are now a film director. Student A is a journalist. He / She is going to ask you some questions about your new film. The pictures below are scenes from the film. Decide on the order things happened and answer the journalist's questions. Then tell him / her the story beginning from the end. Say what the man had done and why. Use words like *when, before, after.* Example:
The woman was very angry because…

UNIT 19

The Passive

1 Work in pairs.

STUDENT A
Look at page 156.

STUDENT B

Carly   Chris   Anna   Phil   Diane

a) Answer your partner's questions about the people above who have had lucky and unlucky experiences. Example:
A: *Whose house has been destroyed?*
B: *Diane's has.*

Pam   Tony   Sue   Bill   Pete

b) Ask your partner questions to find out about the people above. Example:
B: *Whose wallet has been stolen?*
A: *Tony's has.*

1 Who / offer / a reward for catching a criminal / tomorrow?
2 Who / bite / by a dog last week?
3 Who / buy / jewellery every birthday?
4 Who / cure / of a serious illness / recently?

2 Find out if any of the students in your class have ever had any of the lucky or unlucky experiences in the pictures. If so, ask them to give you more information. Example:
Have you ever been given a prize? When? What for?

3 What other lucky or unlucky experiences have people had? Ask questions to find out. Example: *Have you ever been kidnapped?*

Additional material

UNIT 2

Present Continuous

STUDENT A
Look at your picture. Don't look at your partner's picture.
Describe what the six people are doing and wearing. Find eight
differences between your partner's picture and yours.

UNIT 3

Present and Past Simple: short answers

Quiz answers
1 False. Spiders have eight legs.
2 False. Tolstoy wrote *War and Peace*.
3 False. Ankara is the capital of Turkey.
4 True.
5 False. Tigers live in Asia.

6 True.
7 False. Bears sometimes eat meat.
8 False. Brazil won the 1994 World Cup.
9 False. He invented the telephone.

Past Simple and Past Continuous

STUDENTS A AND B
a) You were both at an airport yesterday when there was a
   robbery at the Duty Free Shop. A security guard (Student
   C) is going to ask you some questions. This was the scene
   at the airport just before the robbery. You are in the circle.
   Look at the picture for two minutes, then close your book.
   Make notes with your partner about what was happening.
   Example:
   I was having a drink ...
b) Answer the security guard's questions. Give as much
   information as you can.

UNIT 4

Present Perfect and Past Simple

STUDENT A
a) Read the first newspaper article on
   the right and then answer your
   partner's questions about it.
b) Now read the second newspaper article on the right and ask
   your partner questions to complete it. Use the Present Perfect
   or the Past Simple and the words in brackets to help you.
   Example:
   What has crashed in the United States?

A dangerous criminal has escaped from Pentonville
Prison. He made an underground tunnel in order to
get out. He has now kidnapped his baby son and
taken him to Mexico. He flew there last night. The
police have promised a reward for information
leading to Wilson's arrest.

An _____ (What?) has crashed in the
United States. But, by a miracle, no one
was seriously hurt. At the time the
weather _____ (What / like?), and
the pilot landed _____ (Where?).
Fortunately there was no traffic because
the crash happened _____ (When?). The
pilot _____ (What / do?) last night. Police
have just _____ (What / do?).

153

UNIT 6

Defining relative clauses

STUDENT A

a) You and the people in the pictures robbed a bank yesterday. You put the money in the bags. Student B is a police officer. He / She has arrested you and is going to ask you some questions. You have decided to tell the police about the robbery but you don't want to say where the money is. Look at the pictures and write some sentences about them. Use *who / that, which / that* or *where*. Example:
That's Trev, the man / drove the car.

b) Now answer the police officer's questions.

drove the car
(Trev)

blew up the safe
(Bill)

carried the gun
(Bert)

tied up the bank manager
(John)

the house

the car

the gun

UNIT 7

Describing people

STUDENT A

You are at this official reception. Look at the picture. The people you know are named. Answer your partner's questions about them. Then describe the people you don't know to your partner and find out their names. Example:

B: *Who's the woman at the back with long, blond hair?*

A: *That's Helena Acton.*

UNIT 10

Time conjunctions

> **STUDENT A**
> **a)** Your partner is going to invite you out to the cinema. Agree to meet there. Follow his / her directions from your house on the map.
> **b)** Now you are going to invite your partner out to a restaurant. Choose one of the restaurants on the map below but don't show your partner where it is. Invite him / her to the restaurant and agree to meet there. Give directions from his / her house using expressions like: *as soon as, after, before, until, when.*
> Example:
> *When you come out of your house, turn right.*

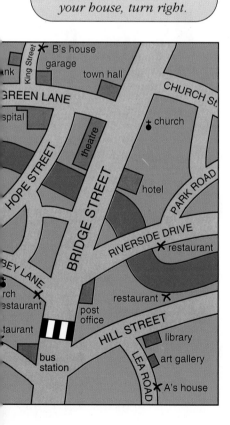

UNIT 11

Requests and offers, agreeing and refusing

water / plants

feed / snake

take me / airport

clean / house

> **STUDENT A**
> **a)** Your partner had to go to hospital yesterday. It was an emergency, and he/she will be there for two weeks. He / She asks you to do things for him / her. However, your washing machine is broken and you use your video all the time. Agree to the requests or refuse. If you refuse, make an excuse *(I'm sorry, but...)* and offer to do something else instead *(Shall I...? I'll...).*
> **b)** You are going on holiday for two weeks. You are telephoning your partner to ask him / her to do the things in the pictures for you. Remember to be very polite if you think it's a difficult request. Use expressions like *Can / Could / Will / Would you (mind)...?* or *I was wondering if...?*

UNIT 14

Obligation, prohibition, permission

> **STUDENT A**
> You have been at a residential summer school for a week. Your partner has only just arrived. He / She is going to ask you some questions. Use the list below to help you.
> Use expressions like *have to / don't have to; can / can't; are(n't) allowed to.* Example:
> B: *Can we use the phone in the Student Common Room?*
> A: *Yes, we can, but only for incoming calls. There's a payphone near the library.*

> **Summer school**
> * Phone in Student Common Room – incoming calls only. Payphone near library.
> * Computers available to students between 3 and 8 pm.
> * Photocopier only for teacher's use. Copies can be made in the town.
> * 80% of lessons must be attended.
> * Visitors allowed for meals on payment of £5.
> * Towels are provided by the school.
> * A bank service is provided on Tuesday and Thursday afternoons.

UNIT 18

Past Perfect

STUDENT A

a) You are a film director. Student B is a journalist. He / She is going to ask you some questions about your new film. The pictures above are scenes from the film. Decide on the order things happened and answer the journalist's questions. Then tell him / her the story beginning from the end. Say what the girl had done and why. Use words like *when, before, after.* Example: *When the family came home, they were angry because...*

b) You are now a journalist. Student B is a film director. You saw this clip of his / her new film on television yesterday. Ask questions to find out what had happened and why. Then the film director will tell you the story. Example: *Why was the woman angry?*

UNIT 19

The passive

STUDENT A

Carly   Chris   Anna   Phil   Diane

a) Ask your partner questions to find out about the people above. Example:
A: *Whose house has been destroyed?*
B: *Diane's has.*

1 Who / bite / by a snake yesterday?
2 Whose phone / just disconnect?
3 Who / often / kiss by famous film stars?
4 Who / give a prize / next week?

Pam   Tony   Sue   Bill   Pete

b) Answer your partner's questions about the people above who have had lucky and unlucky experiences.
Example:
B: *Whose wallet has been stolen?*
A: *Tony's has.*

UNIT 2

Present Continuous

STUDENT B

Look at your picture. Don't look at your partner's picture. Describe what the six people are doing and wearing. Find eight

differences between your partner's picture and yours.

Verb forms

Unit 1

Present Simple questions

Be and *have (got)*

AUXILIARY	PRONOUN		
Am	I		right?
Is	she / he / it		French?
Are	you / we / they		ready?
Have	I / you / we / they		(got) the keys?
Has	he / she		(got) any brothers?

(Note that speakers of American English as well as some British English speakers use *Do you have . . . ?* instead of *Have you got . . . ?*)

Do

AUXILIARY	PRONOUN	BASE FORM	
Do	I / you / we / they	need	more milk?
Does	she / he	like	chocolate?

Question words and phrases

QUESTION WORD	AUXILIARY	PRONOUN	
How	are	you?	
What	do	they	do?
How many	has	she	got?

Unit 2

Present Simple statements

AFFIRMATIVE
I / You / We / They **live** in England.
She / He **lives** in England.

NEGATIVE
I / You / We / They **don't live** in England.
She / He **doesn't live** in England.

Present Continuous

Be + *-ing* form of the verb.

AFFIRMATIVE	
I'**m (am)**	dan**cing**.
She'**s (is)**	
You / We / They'**re (are)**	

NEGATIVE	
I'**m not**	dan**cing**.
He **isn't**	
You / We / They **aren't**	

QUESTION		
What	**am** I	do**ing**?
	is she	
	are you	

Unit 3

Past Simple

Regular verbs: base form of the verb + (e)d
(e.g. *start* → start**ed**; *arrive* → arriv**ed**).
Irregular verbs: see list on page 159.

AFFIRMATIVE	
I	arriv**ed** late.
She	**went** out.
You	
We	
They	

NEGATIVE
He **didn't** arrive late.
You **didn't** go out.

QUESTION
When **did** you arrive / go?

Past Continuous

Past of *be* + *-ing* form of the verb.

AFFIRMATIVE
I / He **was** us**ing** it.
You / We / They **were** watch**ing** him.

NEGATIVE
He **wasn't** listen**ing**.
You **weren't** work**ing**.

QUESTION
What **was** it eat**ing**?
What **were** they do**ing**?

Used to

Used to is followed by the base form of the verb.
　　I **used to have** a car.
　　They **didn't use to have** a car.
　　Did she **use to have** a car?

Unit 5

Future with *going to*

Going to + base form of the verb.

AFFIRMATIVE	
I'**m (am)**	**going to visit** Paris.
He'**s (is)**	
You / We / They'**re (are)**	

NEGATIVE	
I'**m not**	**going to do** it.
She **isn't**	
We'**re not**	

QUESTION		
Where	**am** I	**going to live**?
	is she	
	are you	

SHORT ANSWER
'Are they going to meet you?' 'Yes, they **are**.' / 'No, they'**re not**.'

Language index

Irregular verbs

Note that some of these verbs have different Past Simple forms in American English.
For these variations see the *Longman Dictionary of Contemporary English*.

VERB	PAST SIMPLE	PAST PARTICIPLE	VERB	PAST SIMPLE	PAST PARTICIPLE
be	was	been	light	lit	lit
beat	beat	beaten	lose	lost	lost
become	became	become	make	made	made
begin	began	begun	mean	meant	meant
bend	bent	bent	meet	met	met
bite	bit	bitten	mistake	mistook	mistaken
bleed	bled	bled	pay	paid	paid
blow	blew	blown	prove	proved	proved, proven
break	broke	broken	put	put	put
bring	brought	brought	read	read	read
build	built	built	ride	rode	ridden
burn	burned, burnt	burned, burnt	ring	rang	rung
burst	burst	burst	rise	rose	risen
buy	bought	bought	run	ran	run
catch	caught	caught	say	said	said
choose	chose	chosen	see	saw	seen
come	came	come	sell	sold	sold
cost	cost	cost	send	sent	sent
cut	cut	cut	set	set	set
do	did	done	shake	shook	shaken
draw	drew	drawn	show	showed	shown, showed
dream	dreamed, dreamt	dreamed, dreamt	shut	shut	shut
drink	drank	drunk	sing	sang	sung
drive	drove	driven	sink	sank, sunk	sunk
eat	ate	eaten	sit	sat	sat
fall	fell	fallen	sleep	slept	slept
feed	fed	fed	slide	slid	slid
feel	felt	felt	speak	spoke	spoken
fight	fought	fought	spell	spelt	spelt
find	found	found	spend	spent	spent
fly	flew	flown	spill	spilt	spilt, spilled
forget	forgot	forgotten	spoil	spoiled, spoilt	spoiled, spoilt
forgive	forgave	forgiven	spread	spread	spread
freeze	froze	frozen	spring	sprang	sprung
get	got	got	stand	stood	stood
give	gave	given	steal	stole	stolen
go	went	gone, been	stick	stuck	stuck
grow	grew	grown	sting	stung	stung
hang	hung, hanged	hung, hanged	sweep	swept	swept
have	had	had	swell	swelled	swollen, swelled
hear	heard	heard	swim	swam	swum
hide	hid	hidden	swing	swung	swung
hit	hit	hit	take	took	taken
hold	held	held	teach	taught	taught
hurt	hurt	hurt	tear	tore	torn
keep	kept	kept	tell	told	told
kneel	knelt	knelt	think	thought	thought
know	knew	known	throw	threw	thrown
lay	laid	laid	understand	understood	understood
lead	led	led	wake	woke	woken
lean	leaned, leant	leaned, leant	wear	wore	worn
learn	learned, learnt	learned, learnt	weep	wept	wept
leave	left	left	wet	wet	wet
lend	lent	lent	win	won	won
let	let	let	wind	wound	wound
lie	lay	lain	write	wrote	written

Pronunciation

CONSONANTS			VOWELS			DIPHTHONGS		
	symbol	key word		symbol	key word		symbol	key word
1	/ p /	**p**en	1	/ i: /	sh**ee**p	1	/ eɪ /	m**a**ke
2	/ b /	**b**ack	2	/ ɪ /	sh**i**p	2	/ əʊ /	n**o**te
3	/ t /	**t**ea	3	/ e /	b**e**d	3	/ aɪ /	b**i**te
4	/ d /	**d**ay	4	/ æ /	b**a**d	4	/ aʊ /	n**ow**
5	/ k /	**k**ey	5	/ ɑ: /	c**al**m	5	/ ɔɪ /	b**oy**
6	/ g /	**g**et	6	/ ɒ /	p**o**t	6	/ ɪə /	**here**
7	/ tʃ /	**ch**eer	7	/ ɔ: /	s**aw**	7	/ eə /	**there**
8	/ dʒ /	**j**ump	8	/ ʊ /	p**u**t	8	/ ʊə /	**tour**
9	/ f /	**f**at	9	/ u: /	b**oo**t			
10	/ v /	**v**iew	10	/ ʌ /	c**u**t			
11	/ θ /	**th**ing	11	/ ɜ: /	b**ir**d			
12	/ ð /	**th**en	12	/ ə /	Chin**a**			
13	/ s /	**s**oon						
14	/ z /	**z**ero						
15	/ ʃ /	fi**sh**						
16	/ ʒ /	plea**s**ure						
17	/ h /	**h**ot						
18	/ m /	co**m**e						
19	/ n /	su**n**						
20	/ ŋ /	su**ng**						
21	/ l /	**l**ed						
22	/ r /	**r**ed						
23	/ j /	**y**et						
24	/ w /	**w**et						

Additional material

Unit 2 (page 14)

Unit 19 (page 137)

The policeman isn't chasing a criminal or harassing an innocent person. The photograph shows two police officers, one in uniform and one in plain clothes, chasing a third person.

Tapescripts

Unit 1

RECORDING 3

INTERVIEWER: I wonder if you'd mind answering one or two more personal questions. You have a husband who is a well-known actor and you also have a teenage daughter. How do you manage to balance your work life with your home life?

JUDI DENCH: With difficulty! This is, this is the shortest answer you're going to get! It's very, very difficult, especially that we have two houses – luckily that we have two houses – but, still, trying to do the shopping and the laundry and the washing and the ironing and think about what I need for the weekend, and think about petrol for the car, and think about somebody coming back into the house, you know, all those things, and Michael, of course, and Finty – I mean, they're – I couldn't do it without them 'cause they're just wonderful helps.

I: Have you got any pets?

J: Oh yes, we have three cats, one which won't come back to London – it stays in the country – and two which commute with us, and a dog and a rabbit and two donkeys. (Two donkeys?) They don't come back to London with us, either!

RECORDING 4

I: I wonder if you would mind telling me some of the things you like doing in your spare time? I mean, for example, sports, hobbies, holidays . . .

J: Well yes. I, I trained as a designer, a theatre designer, so I've never given up drawing, and I, I do draw and paint still quite a lot, 'specially on holiday. And we all have a go, 'cause Michael's wonderfully good at it, but he won't say he is, but he is – and Finty's very, very good at it indeed, and she draws all the time, so we do a lot of drawing and painting, and I like cooking, when I have the time to do it, though I don't like doing it under pressure.

I: What kind of things do you like cooking?

J: Well, Michael's a meat and two veg man, so he gets meat and two veg a lot, and that really. Bread and butter pudding – he loves bread and butter pudding, so we do that a lot, 'cause I have a secret recipe – and what else do I do? Michael loves gardening, he's very good at all that, and I've also got a passion for dolls' houses – I have a doll's house which takes up a great deal of my time. I, I love all that, but it's got to be absolutely perfect.

I: Do you like travelling abroad much?

J: Yes, I love it. We love it. (Where, in particular?) I was in Yugoslavia last year, with *Hamlet*, so the whole family – we all went – we had the most wonderful time with the company. We had a great, great time, swimming – we all swim like mad – and that was very good, that was lovely. So we might get back to Yugoslavia in August, I hope we will. We always take August off, 'cause it's Fint's holidays.

I: What, what kind of music do you like to listen to?

J: I like every kind of music but I do like classical music very, very much indeed. I was brought up on classical music. And so I love Bach and the Brandenburg. I love Mozart. I love opera. I love chamber music. And our daughter makes me go through the alphabet with pop groups. I don't know what they do or sing, but I, I am able to go through the pop, the alphabet of pop groups, though I'm not much up-to-date at the moment.

I: Judi, I'm very grateful. Many thanks.

J: Thank you – thank you very much indeed.

Unit 2

RECORDING 1

'. . . Hi! Yes, it's Clare. . . We're OK. . . Yes, of course we're watering the plants. . . Oh, they're fine. . . No, the house isn't a mess – one of us is cleaning it every day. . . Yes, I loved the dress. . . No, really! I'm wearing it at the moment, actually. Are you having a good time?. . . Oh, great! . . . David? Oh, I expect he's doing his homework in his room. . . Yes, the dog's fine, too. . . Of course we're not forgetting to feed him. What do you think we are?! . . . Yes, I know he's not allowed in the sitting room – we're keeping him in his basket in the hall. . . No, we're not eating junk food. Pauline is cooking at this very moment. . . Oh, I can't remember. Chicken, I think. OK, give Dad our love. See you soon. . . What? . . . Tomorrow! Well, why are you asking me all these questions then?!'

RECORDING 4

ANNIE: I like wearing the kind of clothes that I know my mother doesn't wear. I like, I like to look young and I like wearing bright colours and things that stand out in a crowd like, I like leather trousers and skirts, I like bright, bright colours, in my hair as well – like slides and things but also I dye my hair quite often. I don't see why I should look like everyone else in the street. It's fun. Clothes should be fun not something really serious. I could never spend, I don't know, £100 on a skirt for example. It's just such a waste of money.

SARA: I mean, I like dressing up sometimes, but most of the time I actually feel uncomfortable, especially for my job 'cause I, I teach and, you know, if I'm wearing a skirt or a blouse I go in and I feel as if I'm teaching really formally and stiffly just because of what I'm wearing, so I tend to like to wear, you know, I like wearing sort of stripey things and spotty things and, and bright bouncy things really, and I'm not really bothered about the fashion. So I just like to wear the sort of things, you know, that like I feel comfortable in.

LIZ: I like wearing quite smart clothes because I feel better that way. I like to feel that I'm presenting the right image because I come into work – I work in an office – and I feel that people need to have some respect for me. They're going to do that more if I'm dressed to look as if I have some control over my situation and everything else. I enjoy wearing these clothes and I therefore feel more comfortable in them, which is also an additional part of it. At the present moment I, I'm wearing a suit and, and a shirt and high heels, but that is not because I have to. It's because I actually feel better that way and that the image that I'm presenting will give people more confidence.

MIKE: Yes, well it's because I work in a bank really. I'm expected to wear formal clothes, pinstripe suit, tie, dark shoes, usually. Other times I do wear other, other sorts of clothes but I, I quite like wearing things like that. We're a bit of an old-fashioned firm and they, they insist that we do. . .

Unit 3

RECORDING 1

When I lived in Sri Lanka I lived in a town called Jaffna, in the north of the island, and I had two American friends who lived next door to me. And they were sitting at home one evening watching a video, and they were in their bedroom – and that was the only air-conditioned room in the house – and there was a knock at the door, and Stan went to answer the door and some boys came to the door, and they were asking for money for the rebuilding of the local library. And he didn't believe them, and he sent them away and he shut the door and went back into the bedroom. Just as he'd got back into the bedroom, suddenly there was a big noise, the door was broken down and four or five masked men rushed into the room carrying guns, and shouting at them. And they tied them up – they took hold of their hands and tied them behind their backs and pushed them around quite a lot. They put blindfolds on both of them and took them outside and pushed them into a van and drove them around for quite a long time, and took them off to some remote part of the island.

And all this happened while I was waiting for them in a hotel in Kandy because we had planned to send, to spend some time together – it was a holiday weekend. And, in fact, they'd been kidnapped by some extremists who were trying to, trying to get autonomy from other parts of the island. And they were kept for a week. They were kidnapped and kept for a week. And after that eventually they were released. They were very well treated overall but it wasn't a very pleasant experience. And after they were released they told us the story – they told us everything that happened to them. This was just before they were sent back to America.

And I saw them again about a year later, and they told me that even, even then – this was a year after it happened – they still were both very security-conscious, -conscious and they used to get up in the middle of the night and check all the doors and windows and they used to both suffer from terrible nightmares. And I think it still happens to them. A very difficult experience to get over.

Unit 4

RECORDING 3

Well, vocabulary for me is the most important thing. To be fluently, to be fluent you need vocabulary. I am always listen to music or watching TV or watching, listen to the radio and then when I hear some words I keep them in mind, and then one day after, or two, I still remember this word – I can't remember from where, but I still have it in my mind, then I start looking in the vocab-, in the dictionary or something like this. It's not just studying the vocabulary that the teacher give me in the class that I learn it. I learn it from, as I told you, from listen to music and television. Then to improve your English the most important thing is having new vocabulary because at the beginning you use always the same verbs and the same words.

I think if you are speaking with somebody – a friend or whatever, it's really important to be all the time trying to improve your English, not just to be fluent. I am always paying attention in my pronunciation. If I am talking to somebody, when I finish it I, I start thinking about what I said and trying to correct myself, even if I had made mistakes. I think it's very important to, to try to use correct words, correct verbs and pronunciation.

I really like to be corrected all the time, not just when I write but when I am speaking. If I am with someone chatting, I like when people corrected me.

Unit 5

RECORDING 1

Earlier on today, apparently, a woman rang the BBC and said she heard that there was a hurricane on the way. Well, if you're watching, don't worry, there isn't. But, having said that, actually the weather will become very windy, but most of the strong winds incidentally will be down over Spain and across into France.

RECORDING 2

The great cleaning-up operation is now underway in the wake of the hurricane-force winds which battered much of southern England in the small hours. At least thirteen people are known to have died and many were injured, hit by falling trees and masonry toppled in the gales. Power supplies have been disrupted and large sections of the rail network were left out of action. Our reporters have been assessing the scale of the chaos and the damage. We begin with the latest from the south coast.

RECORDING 3

This is David Smeeton in Southampton. In the southern region it's been a day of assessing the damage to hundreds of roofs, many of them torn completely off, while some homes are partially collapsed. Overnight scores of people were looked after in emergency centres.

And finally this is Andrew Roberts with a look at how the storms have affected the capital. Two people were killed as winds of 94 miles an hour – the highest ever recorded – gusted across London. In Croydon a motorist died when his car was crushed by a falling tree.

RECORDING 5

A: What do you think of this weather we're having, then?

B: Bit too hot for my liking. Can't breathe, it's so close. Brings on my cough something terrible. Give me a bit of cold any day!

A: I don't know what's happening to our climate.

B: What do you mean?

A: Hot one day, snowing the next. It was different in our day.

B: Can't be healthy, all this sun.

A: You're right. And it dries up the garden like nobody's business . . .

Unit 6

RECORDING 1

INTERVIEWER: This week's *Going green* interview comes from the home of Mrs Julia Moore. Mrs Moore, good morning.

MRS MOORE: Morning.

I: Mrs Moore, an article was written about you and your family recently, called 'Are these people criminals?' Do you feel it's just and fair for people to say that in your life-style you commit crimes against the environment?

MRS M: Well, no, I don't feel it's fair, because actually we do care about the environment, but the reality is I'm a working mum with two small children and I simply do not have the time to put all the principles that you could put into action in action. For example, if we take shopping to start with, you know, I do try to buy environmentally-friendly products if they are available, but quite often they are not on offer, so for example, you can't buy ozone-friendly flyspray. And for example with things like meat, me and my husband, Derek, avoid eating too much meat, but the children like sausages and they get them outside the home and so I do buy meat from time to time. With fruit, well, I try to buy loose unpackaged fruit but sometimes you just run out of time and that's what it's all about, you know: I just want to go into the shops, do my shopping once a week and then leave.

And then moving on to getting rid of the rubbish afterwards and the whole recycling issue. You know, OK, there are bottle banks around but they are difficult to find. They are often full. I don't like having glass bottles at home because if they get broken then they are obviously dangerous. And the same with newspapers. You end up with stacks and stacks of newspapers. If there was someone to take them away that would be fine, and I actually do believe it's the Government's responsibility. If dustbinmen took away sorted rubbish that would be fine, but as they don't, you know we just don't have the time and the energy to, to dispose of all this rubbish ourselves.

And then finally the whole sort of thing about transport. Well, we use lead-free petrol, but travelling on public transport with two small children really isn't an option, it's just not practical: it's dirty, it's unreliable, and it's expensive. I mean you can wait hours for buses and trains and they don't turn up.

You know if I try to put everything, all my principles, into action, can you imagine? I'd be hauling the children round on buses with bags full of heavy, broken, glass bottles – I really wouldn't have time to do anything else with my life.

Unit 7

RECORDING 1

Robin talking about Françoise

Well, I think it was her appearance initially that attracted me. She was in her early thirties, considerably younger than me, and she'd got these big, black eyes – you know, the kind that kind of catch the light, and – very appealing – and, I also liked her long, black, curly hair and this sort of dark Mediterranean type of skin, you know – she looks more Spanish than French. And then as soon as I got to know her it was, well, just her incredibly lively personality and sense of humour. And, yes, she was such an incredibly good listener and so understanding and supportive. I, I suppose that's, what's really kept the relationship going since then is her, her character and mine seem to be so compatible.

Françoise talking about Robin

Well, it was what you could call, actually, love at first sight. I really fancied him straight away when I saw him because, like he was tall, had blue eyes and he had a little bit of a double chin, sort of quite what we would say in French like 'well-wrapped', and he had a very charming smile as well, I remember that. Very nice voice as well, very sort of warm and, and going a little bald as well, but that. . . Altogether, I mean it's not features one by one that you can, you can say, you know, 'Yes, oh, the eyes are wonderful and the nose is wonderful and the lips are wonderful,' – you can't say things like that, but altogether it was, he had a type a bit like an American actor – like Paul Newman or Robert Redford or somebody like that. And physically sort of very teddy bear-like as well which is sort of very attractive, yes – very sexy.

And he was, he was a very, very funny sort of guy. Very sort of lively and contrasting to the other people around. He would always sort of crack a joke and, and be very, very open about his own life as well. He was very, straightaway very friendly with me as well, and very sort of, yes, like a good old friend that I would have known for quite a long time.

Simon talking about Emma

Well I think the thing that came over most strongly about her when I first met her was the fact that she's extremely caring and kind girl and somebody you can feel completely relaxed with when you're in her company and also a very good listener – any problems and she'll listen and make you feel a hundred per cent better. She's extremely attractive. A kind of oval face, short, fairish, wavy hair, big brown eyes, and gorgeous freckles, which appear when the sun is out. She's around twenty, medium height, and she's extremely bright. She's also independent, very mature. She's very energetic, likes to get up and go and do things. But she's a great girl. She's very kind, very caring. She's a lovely girl.

Emma talking about Simon

He's got a great sense of humour. He's very funny: he likes to tell jokes. He's very romantic: he likes to send me flowers, and we go out for meals and things and he's very kind and generous. He's very intelligent. He's young: he's in his mid-twenties. He's very slim and tall, and I like tall people. He's very patient, which he needs to be with me – very responsible – if you ask him to do something you know that he'll do it, and he's very reliable like that. He's got lovely blue eyes. He's got wavy hair. He's, he's well-dressed, although he does like to wear his jeans, he's quite casual in that manner, although he's very smart when we go out. And he's, I just find him very interesting and he's just a very kind person.

Unit 8

RECORDING 1

MELANIE: . . . and the living room overlooks a pond.

JULIE: Well, that sounds OK. What about the kitchen, though? What's that like?

M: It's not too bad as I remember. You go in the door and there's a window opposite with a fairly large sink underneath, and draining boards on each side. Oh, the cooker is next to the sink, on the right, in the corner.

J: Is there a washing machine?

M: Yes, under the stairs. The stairs lead up from the kitchen. And there's a freezer, too – a small one, on top of the fridge. Oh, the fridge is next to the washing machine, by the way.

J: Lots of space to put things?

M: Oh, enough, I think. Oh, there are shelves over the cooker. And I think there's a cupboard on the floor between the table and the cooker. Oh, and there's a round table in the middle of the room, with four chairs, to eat at, and another table opposite the window as you go in, on the right in the corner, that we can work at.

Unit 9

RECORDING 1

ANNOUNCER: Have you got an itch? If so, it could be that your body is trying to tell you something. In this morning's programme Peter Marsh asks the question: 'Is Our Future up to Scratch?'

PETER MARSH: According to the ancients, when a little bodily irritation occurs – suddenly and for no apparent reason – it can be a sign of something to come. For example, if you want to scratch your head, it's generally a good sign. If the itch is on the top of your head, you'll probably get promotion in your job. If it's on the right side, you will meet a female stranger – on the left, it will be a man. Itches to other parts of the body are signs too. If your right shoulder suddenly irritates you, you will receive a large sum of money. But if it is your left shoulder, unhappiness is sure to follow. As for the elbow, an itchy right elbow means you'll hear good news but if it's the left it means bad news. And watch out if you get a strong desire to scratch your knees. It means you'll soon be jealous of someone. But you will soon make a happy journey if it's the right knee and an unpleasant journey if it's the left. As for the lips. . .

RECORDING 3

PALM READER: Don't take anything that I say too personally. I'm just only telling you what I see. I mean I may be totally wrong but. . . it's a very straight mind line which shows a slight lack of imagination. You're pretty straightforward in your thinking and your emotions are pretty straightforward. Your fate line is slightly off in the early days. It looks as if you, your early family life wasn't too good. Almost, it just feels like there was a breaking away of the family, either that your parents were divorced or there was problem, there were problems in the family so you weren't terribly close to them. . . There was a very. . . well, it looks as if you've been married. . . from. . . quite early actually. . . twenty-five? . . . But there was also a relationship, it was very strong, with an older woman? . . .

You have two children? . . . And there was, or will be another one? . . . Well, I say 'was' because it's slightly doubtful. . . You. . . I don't know, I don't know what your job is, but I mean obviously you've been gardening today but. . . there's an artistic streak there somewhere. . . You didn't do, do you paint? Or you write? . . . Your very long little finger, so you're obviously. . . Yes, you write, or you do write, or. . . poetry or something. . . Something in that area. . . It's artistic anyway. . . You've got a good strong thumb. . . bit stubborn. . . You've got a bit of a nasty temper. . . little bit unsure of yourself in some areas. I mean, better, better now but as a child you were obviously very, very shy but I've got a feeling that was something to do with your family life, your family background. . . But you're a bit more sure of yourself now. . . But you have doubts about yourself. . . Very attracted to the opposite sex. . . Health line: again that's a break-up in your early days but that could have been emotional. . . Again I just get this feeling it was something to do with your family, but so. . . your health line was slightly broken up, got better as you got to late teens. . . Prone to headaches. . . And you'll be needing glasses I should imagine. . . Your eyesight's beginning to play you up a bit. . . And also chest infections. . . Sorry, you're not going to be a rich man. Oh, you'll be all right. You're not going to be a rich man because you quite like spending it. . . But in fact it looks as if you've gone through financial troubles for about four or five years, but they're getting better. Things will get better. In fact they're on the mend now.

Unit 10

RECORDING 1

Well, I think houses in the future will probably be quite small but I should think they'll be well-insulated so that you don't need so much heating and cooling as you do now, so perhaps very economical to run. Perhaps they will use solar heating, although I don't know, in this country, perhaps we won't be able to do that so much. Yes, I think they'll be full of electronic gadgets: things like very advanced televisions, videos, perhaps videos which take up, the screen takes up the whole wall. I should think. Yes, you'll have things like garage doors which open automatically when you drive up, perhaps electronic sensors which will recognise you when you, when you come to the front door even. Perhaps architects and designers will be a bit more imaginative about how houses are designed and perhaps with the shortage of space people will think of putting gardens on the roof and, and maybe rooms can be expanded and, and contracted depending on what you use them for, so perhaps there'll be a bit more flexibility about that.

Unit 11

RECORDING 1

HOTEL RECEPTIONIST: Mermaid, Luton. Can I help you?

GUEST: Yes, I'd like to book a room for the night of the 14th, please.

HR: Er, the 14th. . . Yes, that's OK. Single, twin or double?

G: Oh, double, please. With a bathroom. Could you tell me how much that'll cost?

HR: Er, yes madam. That'll be £95, including breakfast. Can you give me your name, please?

G: Yes, the name's Kate Andrews.

HR: And your daytime telephone number?

G: Yes, during the day . . . 0799 719377.

HR: . . . 377. Thank you.

G: Oh, another thing. Would it be possible to leave my car with you? I'm flying to Paris the next day and I'd like to leave it in your hotel car park.

HR: Yes, certainly. How long for?

G: A week. I'm coming back on the 21st.

HR: OK. I'll reserve you a place for eight days. Would you give me the number and make of your car, please?

G: Yes, it's a Golf and the registration number is H86 LYA. By the way, I don't suppose you could book me another room at the same time, could you? I want a double room for the night of the 21st.

HR: The night of the 21st . . . Yes, that's fine. What time will you be arriving on the 14th?

G: I should think around 10 – 10 o'clock in the evening.

HR: In the evening? Shall I order you a late dinner?

G: If you would, yes.

HR: OK. Well, if you could confirm this in writing, please.

G: Yes, I'll do that now. Thank you very much. Goodbye.

HR: Thank you madam. Goodbye.

RECORDING 4

1 'Sorry to bother you, Jim. It's Bob. I've got a problem. The car's broken down and I've got to get to London on Friday. I was wondering whether you could lend me yours for the day. Give me a ring and let me know, can you?'

2 'Oh, Gill. I'm sorry you're out. I don't like answerphones. It's Sally. I'm really thrilled about the news. Ray, Ray told me this morning. When is it? We are going to get an invite, aren't we? Listen, I'll, I'll phone you next week. All right? See you.'

3 'Hello, this is Mrs Wong from Cyberpic International. I know you're closed now but I wondered if you could get a message through to Mr Miller, the Managing Director, first thing in the morning. Could you tell him I was expecting someone to meet me at Sydney Airport and take me to my hotel? As I don't know where your offices are he'll have to contact me at the Hilton. Thank you.'

4 'Hi, Dave. This is your old pal, Frank. Remember? I heard your sister was ill. Mavis. I used to go out with her once. Lovely woman. You couldn't let me have her phone number, could you? I want to get in touch with her again. You know, to see if I could help. OK? Cheers.'

Unit 12

RECORDING 1

I work all night I work all day
To pay the bills I have to pay
Ain't it sad!
And still there never seems to be
A single penny left for me
That's too bad!
In my dreams I have a plan
If I got me a wealthy man
I wouldn't have to work at all
I'd fool around and have a ball

Money, money, money
Must be funny
In the rich man's world
Money, money, money
Always sunny
In the rich man's world
Aha, aha, all the things I could do
If I had a little money
It's a rich man's world . . .

RECORDING 2

If I were a rich man
Diddle deedle diddle digga digga deedle diddle dum
All day long I'd iddy biddy bum
If I were a wealthy man
Wouldn't have to work hard
Diddle deedle diddle digga digga deedle diddle dum
If I were an iddy biddy rich
Iddle diddle diddle deedle man

I'd build a big tall house
With rooms by the dozen
Right in the middle of the town
A fine tin roof with real wooden floors below
There could be one long staircase just going up
And one even longer coming down
And one more leading nowhere just for show

RECORDING 3

KEITH: Well, actually I think probably the first thing I'd do because I've got a bit of a weakness for nice cars – I love Mercedes Benz cars – there's something about really nice. . . I think I'd waste a bit of money on a nice car. . .

SUE: I think, I think I would want to perhaps do something completely different with my life. I think I might actually give up my job and go back to college and perhaps study medicine and try to become a doctor.

BEN: If I had all the money I wanted and was going to spend it on myself then I would travel in great comfort. I think that would be one of the main things. I, I love travelling. Nowadays it is expensive to travel in comfort. I read travel magazines. I read about all sorts of luxurious hotels in other parts of the world and I think, well, I would like to go and spend two weeks in the Bel-Air hotel in Los Angeles and that's what I'd spend my money on if it was for me.

NORMA: I would set my husband up in business back in Liverpool. He's a carpenter. And to go home, that's, that's all I want. But it's not possible now because there's no chance that he would get any work there. That would be lovely, wouldn't it?

Unit 13

RECORDING 3

Programme 1

BEVERLY ROBERTS: At one o'clock. Inflation is at its highest level for eight years. Prince Charles comes out of hospital, the operation on his arm a success. His nurses say: 'He was an absolute sweetie.' And Status Quo tell us their plans for a major comeback. Beverly Roberts reporting.

Trouble again for the Government. Prices have increased by over 10% for the first time since 1982. The new official statistics from the Government are a shock. They were expecting a rise in prices but not one of a full percentage point to 10.6%. Geoffrey Daniels has the details.

GEOFFREY DANIELS: There's no doubt that this is a disaster for the Government. I think everyone was saying that inflation would pass 10% but the worst forecast I heard in the City was 10.3%, so for it to leap up to 10.6% is very serious, and some would say shows the failure of the Government's present policies.

BR: Have you seen any Government ministers looking sheepish?

GD: I haven't seen any yet, but. . .

Programme 2

ALAN TAYLOR: *The World Today*. Thirty minutes of news and comment. This is Alan Taylor. The headlines. The United Nations act together to secure world peace. We speak to the Secretary General about the Security Council's latest peace plan for Europe and we'll be seeking the views of the American Ambassador who explains why his country has its doubts. The Manchester Rail Disaster. We hear from British Rail and from those families fighting for compensation. And inflation is in double figures for the first time for eight years. In the twelve months to August, the Retail Price Index rose to 10.6%, much higher than expected. The Chancellor of the Exchequer tells *The World Today* that the figure will not change Government policy. The news now from Katherine Shepherd.

KATHERINE SHEPHERD: The Secretary General of the United Nations, Mr José Ricardo, has confirmed that the Security Council has agreed on a peace plan for Europe which it hopes. . .

Unit 14

RECORDING 1

MIKE: It's a very expensive hobby. It's going to cost about three and a half thousand, but you don't have to pay all at once. You know, you can pay each lesson as, as you go along. There's quite a lot of studying to do. In fact you're not allowed to go solo until you've got your air law exam and. . . But I enjoy the studying – that's one of the things that's, you know, been very, very exciting. And you have to do a lot of exams. Of course, you can't fly unless you're, you're fairly fit and you have to have a, a medical exam. In fact you can't go solo either until you've got your medical certificate.

JULIE: They're fascinating creatures and it's one of the hobbies that, once you get involved in you want to know more about, and however long you study bees and bee-, bee-keeping you'll never know everything about the insects. They have a, quite a unique lifestyle. And of course there's always the benefits of taking the honey off at the end of the honey season, which makes a little profit, although it's quite an expensive hobby. You need quite a lot of equipment. The hives themselves are quite expensive, unless you're a good woodworker and can make them yourselves, and the extractors and things. But it keeps you occupied throughout the whole year because, while you're harvesting the honey in the summer, you're making up the hives and the frames in the winter, ready for the following season.

BRUCE: Well it's, it's something that anybody can participate in, from the keenest person like myself, who travels all over the world to see the birds, unto somebody looking out of the window in their kitchen, and there's so much involved in it. It gets you to places where you wouldn't normally go – i.e. some wild places, very remote places, because birds are attracted to the quieter, remoter places, usually – for example, up in, up into mountains and on river estuaries where not many people go, and also you meet such smashing people. Generally, well almost entirely, I think people interested in birds are nice sort of people.

RECORDING 2

One of the things I liked most about going to university was living away from home, and the, and the freedom it gave me. So I could stay out as late as I wanted – I didn't have to explain to anyone where I'd been, and although we obviously had to do some work in order to get through the exams, well we didn't need to go to all the lectures if we didn't want to. Oh, it was incredibly relaxed; we were allowed to do whatever we wanted, within reason.

Unit 15

RECORDING 1

ANDREW: What sort of things do I buy? Well, I buy lots of meat because it makes me feel full of energy . . . and it's nice. I buy very little other fresh food, though. I prefer my meals out of the freezer. But I do like fruit, so on Thursdays I go to the market and get some apples, bananas, melons . . . things like that. I know I don't eat many vegetables. The trouble is there aren't any vegetables I really like. Anyway, I, I have hardly any time for cooking these days.

BRIGITTE: Well, I can't eat food with additives – none at all – so when I'm in a supermarket I have to spend a lot of time looking at labels. Actually, I, I don't eat much tinned food. Or, or even frozen food. I prefer everything fresh. And as for sweet things, they're not very good for you so I never have any chocolates or things like that in the house – although sometimes I, I do buy a few home-made biscuits from a friend. What else? Oh, I like dairy products, particularly milk and yoghurt. And, oh yes, every Saturday I buy a little cheese as a treat. I try not to eat too many eggs, though. I don't want a heart attack!

Unit 16

RECORDING 1

ANNOUNCER: It's 11.47 and now *Pet Subjects*. Fergus Keeling explores the special relationship between people and their pets. For the first programme in the series he visits Ann Webb at her home in Hertfordshire.

INTERVIEWER: I've come to see Ann's collection of spiders. Tarantulas mostly, Ann, are they?

ANN WEBB: They're all tarantulas, yes. They're all the big hairy spiders.

I: How many do you have?

AW: There's about 80 at the moment.

I: When did you buy the first one?

AW: About 1982 we bought the first one.

I: And I know, your, your husband Frank is also quite passionate about spiders.

AW: Oh, absolutely, yeah. He's passionate about all animals, not just spiders.

I: Are, are these animals pets?

AW: They are to me, yes. They're, they're all part of my family. So therefore they're pets. They're not to everyone, of course. I mean, some, some people study spiders for scientific research and various other reasons, I suppose, and a lot of people don't have, accept them as pets, but I do, and most of mine have got names.

I: What do they feed on, Ann?

AW: Well they feed on live insects which is perhaps a thing that would put off a lot of people from keeping them, but mine feed mostly on house crickets because they're easy enough to breed. But they'll eat locusts and they'll eat cockroaches and anything obnoxious really.

I: So when, when is feeding time?

AW: We feed ours once a week, because that's all they need. I mean, in the wild they'll sometimes go six months, a year, without feeding, because they don't stray from their burrows – they sit there and wait for the food to come to them. Of course it doesn't always come.

RECORDING 2

I: Is it possible for you to take one out?

AW: Yeah, we'll get Cleo out for you.

I: What do you actually get from a moment like this when you're sitting holding Cleo?

AW: Probably sounds silly, but I'm almost in awe of my spiders. To me they are so beautiful and so graceful. I actually get lost for words when I'm holding a spider.

I: You're sitting here quite calmly and and, and this tarantula's covering both your hands. Now some people listening will be shuddering at the very idea, of course.

AW: Of course they will. Of course they will. Most people will. I should think 90 per cent of the population would be absolutely terrified.

I: Is that terror justified?

AW: No, these spiders have got a very, very bad press. James Bond films, *Raiders of the Lost Ark*, etc. made it worse, and newspapers do their best to make it even worse still because they believe that these spiders are deadly and they're not. There is not a tarantula in the world that will kill a human being. Their bite – if they do bite, which they don't, they don't – they're not naturally aggressive towards anything so they don't bite just because they want, they feel like it, but if they do, then it's the equivalent of a bee sting, and that is all. This is

another Mexican red-knee. This is Arabella, and she's quite a sweetie. Hello darling, aren't you – you're very sweet.

I: You're obviously completely passionate about spiders, aren't you, Ann. (Oh yeah.) Why?

AW: Don't know. That's an awful answer, isn't it, but it's true. I'm often asked that – 'Why do you like them?' I don't really know, I just do. I like their beauty, and their grace and their individuality – their peaceful lifestyle. I just love them.

RECORDING 3

REPORTER: Mrs Kirkwood, what did your aunt leave to you in her will?

MRS KIRKWOOD: Er, £350 and a photo album! But then even her cats haven't got anything. She obviously wanted to leave it all to dear old Fred, who got £26,000.

R: What was your reaction when you heard the news?

MRS K: Well, the thing is you've got to understand that Dolly was very eccentric and so the family aren't a bit surprised. Mind you, it's ironic that we will have to go on living off my £100 a week pension, while Fred will be able to have a life of luxury.

R: And what do you think Fred will do with the money?

MRS K: Unfortunately, the only things he can spend it on are his favourite lettuce, tomatoes and courgettes! But we're not bitter – I'll look after Fred as well as I can – although probably not quite as well as she did!

Unit 18

RECORDING 1

Heart to Heart, by MD Stevenson

'He seems to be doing well, doesn't he, Sister? He should be coming round pretty soon.'

I've got news for you, Nursie, he's come round already, even if he hasn't got his eyes open. I suppose I did have a vague impression of being wheeled out of the recovery room, but now – now I know I'm safely back in my special private ward. Yes, and with some other poor devil's heart beating inside me, doing very nicely too, thank you. Oh yes, the full treatment going now and two nurses on duty – one of them's a looker, anyway. There's a young lad over in the corner, too. I wonder what he's doing. Scruffy looking little blighter, even in a mask and white coat. Oh well, I suppose he's monitoring something or other. I can't really believe it yet. I made it! Mind you, the consultant always said I would. Nice old boy, Mr Walton.

'You're tough, Jim,' he told me. 'I wouldn't attempt this operation if you were one of these nervous imaginative types, but you'll come through it all right.'

By God, he was right. That young lad doesn't take his eyes off me. I made it.

RECORDING 2

The consultant was chuffed when he saw me this afternoon. 'A wonderful job, Jim.'

I couldn't resist asking him, even though I knew I wouldn't get much of an answer. 'What was he like, this donor bloke? An accident, was it?'

Mr Walton put on that superior surgeon look that he doesn't wear very often. 'You could say that, I suppose. Don't you worry, Jim. You'll make better use of it than he would have done.'

Well, at least I know it was a man's heart.

The nurses are bustling about again. They don't take a lot of notice of that young lad – almost brush him aside, you could say. God I'm tired again.

Mr Walton was a bit less enthusiastic today. Something about not getting all het up. I'm not getting het up, dammit. I'm not awake long enough to get het up. I'm bored though. 'What about the telly?', I asked him. 'Or at least a look at a newspaper?'

'We'll see, Jim,' he promised. You see, nothing too good for the VIP patient. I forgot to tell him about the young lad, though. Pity. He's still over there, glowering. Miserable little devil.

RECORDING 3

They're working like mad on me. All of them, and I can't do anything but lie here, helpless. I can't even tell them . . . I . . .

It was the paper that did it. Mr Walton brought it in himself.

'Here you are, Jim. Read all about yourself!'

It was there, too. On the front page. 'Mr James Wetherall was given the heart of a twenty-year-old youth, killed in an accident.' First time I'd ever managed to get my name in the papers. It was when I turned over the page I saw it.

'Killer Dies in Police Chase

A youth of twenty died after the car he had stolen left the road during a police chase. Previously he had been involved in a fight in which a twenty-eight-year-old man was stabbed to death.'

And that was as far as I got, because there was a picture, too. It was him – the lad in the white coat in the corner. Like the consultant said, I'm not an imaginative type, but I'd swear the picture is of that youth who's been there day and night, not taking his eyes off me.

I must have passed out when I realised it. And when I came to, there was this lot round me. And me, I can't move and I can't speak. I can only look, across to the corner where that youth is still lounging, looking back at me. And he's smiling now, damn him. He's smiling.

Unit 20

RECORDING 1

This is a story about Wilar the crocodile. One day, a long time ago when the world was very young, there were two sisters. One was called Indra and her younger sister, Jippi. They had been walking for a long time and they sat down to have a rest near a river. Wilar, the crocodile man, was in the river and he saw them. And he said to himself, 'I'm going to have one of those girls.' He swam through the river, and the girls didn't see him coming. And when he got close enough, he grabbed Indra. Jippi was very frightened and ran away screaming for help.

Wilar took Indra back to his cave. He didn't want to eat her yet, so he left her in the cave and he went back to the water where he caught himself lots of fish to fill up his belly.

When he came back to the cave, Indra was asleep: she was very tired and frightened. Wilar didn't want to touch her yet, so first he put a lot of mud and stones in the entrance to the cave so that other crocodiles couldn't come in and disturb him. Then he said to Indra, 'You are my wife now, and I am going to stay with you.'

Wilar didn't leave the cave for several days, but then when his belly was empty and he got hungry again, he had to go out and look for food. Before he left the cave he blocked it up again with mud and stones to keep the girl safe, but also to stop her running away.

When Indra found herself alone, she decided she'd try and break through the entrance, but the stones in the entrance were so heavy and it was hard to shift them. She couldn't do it with her hands, so she tied her hair around the stones and began to pull the stones away from the mud.

When she'd made a hole in the entrance she tried to squeeze her way through. She got her head and her chest through, but her belly was so big, she couldn't get out. She had to come back inside the cave and make the hole bigger. Finally she managed to push her way out and run away.

Of course many people were looking for Indra and with them was her sister Jippi. Jippi saw Indra running from the cave and she shouted to the others. She said, 'Look, my sister is coming back.' When Indra reached them, Jippi noticed she had such a big belly. She said, 'Sister, why are you so fat? You must have eaten a lot of fish.' But Indra didn't answer her. Instead she squatted down near the ground and out of her belly came a big pile of crocodile eggs.

Well, the men hit the eggs with their clubs, and every time they broke an egg a frog came out and jumped away. Some of the frogs went to the water, and some of the frogs went to the country. That was the first time frogs came into the world, and they can live in both places because their father came from the water and their mother came from the land. The frog doesn't have any hair because Indra lost all her hair when she pulled the stones away from the entrance to the cave.

The elements are the be all and end all of everything. They provide the answers to many of life's burning questions: What are we made of? What keeps us alive? They also help us to understand such things as how to reduce our carbon footprint, and how to make a car run with the only emission being water.

The quest for answers about the world, the universe and everything in it, began a long time ago, and still there is so much to know. Out of the dark mystery of the gold-seeking alchemists emerged something pure – knowledge of the elements.

Inventors know and understand the elements and how we use the elements changes all the time – as new properties are found or harnessed, suddenly a humble lightbulb turns into an energy-efficient, automatic downlighter.

As a doctor, I have certainly been very glad to know about the elements. But it is also nice to know what I am slipping on as I ski down a mountain, what makes a television work, and that the blood of spiders, octopus, and snails is blue because it's full of copper!

All this and more is the subject of this fun and fascinating book. The study of the elements has unravelled the mysteries of the Universe, and provided some brilliant stories along the way. So let's go ele-MENTAL!

ROBERT WINSTON

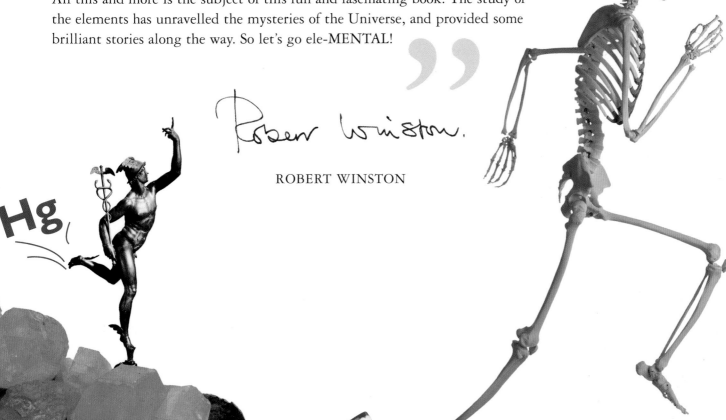

Hg

In the BEGINNING

· ·

We are STARDUST

· ·

What's in a NAME?

· ·